THE ECONOMIC
PURSUIT OF
QUALITY

THE ECONOMIC
PURSUIT OF
QUALITY

THOMAS MICHAEL POWER

M. E. Sharpe, Inc.
ARMONK, NEW YORK
LONDON, ENGLAND

Available in the United Kingdom and Europe from M. E. Sharpe,
Publishers, 3 Henrietta Street, London WC2E 8LU.

Library of Congress Cataloging-in-Publication Data

Power, Thomas M.
    The economic pursuit of quality.

    1. Economics. I. Title.
HB171.P697   1988   330   87-12128
ISBN 0-87332-436-6
ISBN 0-87332-449-8 (pbk.)

Printed in the United States of America

To the woman who has brought the quality into my life, to my wife, Pamela Shore, this book is gratefully dedicated.

Contents

Preface

This book attempts to change the popular understanding of what economics and the economy are all about. It seeks to undermine the popular association of economics with commercial activity, necessity, quantitative dollar flows, and the production and sale of goods. It seeks to document the fact that it is actually the pursuit of discretionary qualities—subjective, disputable, aesthetic qualities—that both motivate economic activity and are its primary inputs.

Changing this popular perception of economics is important because, increasingly, the determinants of our economic well-being are not produced by commercial businesses and automatically evaluated by the commercial market. Instead they flow from diverse, noncommercial sources. If we are going to protect and improve our economic well-being, at the very least we need to know where we should focus our attention. Current popular economic perceptions mislead us.

This book is aimed at the informed noneconomist. Economic jargon and mathematical formulations have been avoided in favor of plain English, and professional economists will find little that is new or original except the emphasis. This might surprise noneconomists, but the fact of the matter is that there are two quite different types of economics in use in policy discussions. There is professional, academically based economic analysis. And then there is a popular "folk economics." Only a very small part of the population has much regular experience with professional economic analysis. Economists keep it that way by speaking in a private language and hiding behind nearly incomprehensible models. The "folk economics," on the other hand, is closely tied to the world of business and to peoples' experiences in the commercial world, and is regularly reinforced by the business community, local political and civic leaders, and the mass media.

The misconceptions of this "folk economics" are the target of this book.

Those widely held beliefs seriously distort economic policy, especially local economic-development policy. The book seeks to correct that by drawing on the more critical professional economic analysis. This is not to suggest that professional economic analysis is without its own faults. It too can distort and mislead, and this book also tries to underline its limitations in guiding our pursuit of improved well-being. Professional economists will wonder about what they will see as an unnecessary, repetitive emphasis on the guiding role of subjective preferences and cultural values in economic activities. I can only say in defense that my twenty years in the classroom, lecturing around the nation, and testifying in legal proceedings have taught me that certain misconceptions about economics are so deeply ingrained that this repetition of some basic points is necessary.

Professional economists must bear some of the blame for the widespread misunderstanding of some of the most basic of economic principles. Urban and regional economics have been around for half a century, yet the economic models and policies used to guide almost all local economic-development efforts are in gross conflict with current urban and regional economic knowledge. Environmental and resource economics has been around for a quarter of a century, yet environmental debates are rarely informed by what we have learned from this research.

This is not entirely the result of oversight or academic isolation. Economists show great deference to the business community. Business leaders are the entrepreneurial heroes in economists' models of how an ideal, competitive, free enterprise economy will lead to the best of all possible societies. We economists tend to let business leaders, especially at the local level, speak for the whole of the economy. Given our century-old obsession with showing the hidden social logic of the commercial economy in the face of Christian and socialist attacks on it or its results, this commercial bias in economics is not surprising. But it is dangerous to general economic welfare and destructive of good economic policy.

This book, then, seeks to bring our ''folk economic'' knowledge up to date. If this is achieved, such knowledge will be able to play a critical and creative social role instead of serving, as it does now, only to obscure reality and protect the status quo.

Acknowledgments

This book has developed through a variety of classes taught at the University of Montana. I wish to thank my students for pressing me on various issues and "keeping me honest." I wish to especially thank the faculty and students of the Wilderness and Civilization Program of the School of Forestry. The University of Montana has provided continuous support for this project through grants and release time despite an ongoing fiscal crisis.

I wish to thank my colleague, Professor Richard Barrett, for suffering with me through this project despite his doubts and misgivings about the emphasis of the book. His critical review has helped me eliminate some of the confusion and error. He would want to be absolved, however, of any responsibility for the final product.

Becky Moser suffered patiently through the preparations of the many drafts of this book and kept the production rolling. The staff at Typing/Word Processing Services at the university helped considerably with the final editing (when I would let them) and with the production of the final manuscript.

THE ECONOMIC
PURSUIT OF
QUALITY

CHAPTER ONE

The Power and Mystique of Economics: Sharing the Power, Eliminating the Magic

1. The Misdefinition of Economics

When economics or the economy is mentioned, most people immediately think of commercial business activity, dollar flows of income, jobs, and markets. They also think in terms of quantities: numbers of jobs, dollars of income, and prices. Economics, in ordinary thinking, is the quantitative weighing of dollar costs and commercial values.

The common perception is that qualitative concerns about the noncommercial or nonbusiness aspects of our lives are "*non*economic." Thus, concern about the preservation of natural areas or wildlife, about the quality of the air or water, or with the character of our communities are thought of as noneconomic, aesthetic or moral or political concerns.

This book will attempt to show that nothing could be further from the truth. Economics, even market-oriented economics, is mainly about the provision or protection of *qualities*. Individuals' and groups' subjective judgments about quality dominate all economic activity. Ultimately, economics is not primarily about business, money, and markets. Its focus is far broader than that. In fact, a narrow, quantitative, market definition of economics so grossly distorts economic analysis that it ceases to be a safe or reliable guide to public economic policy. Only if economics is forced beyond these conventional limits is it actually useful.

This chapter outlines the general problems with which this book will attempt to deal, namely the destructive impact of that narrow, market-oriented, quantitative definition of economics. It will then outline the approach we will take to demonstrate the dominant role quality and noncommercial resources play in determining economic welfare. Finally, this broader approach will be applied to the analysis of the local economy and the determinants of local economic well-being.

2. The Power of Economics

There is power in the language and concepts of economics, a power that intimidates and manipulates. Corporate executives and vulgar Marxists alike insist that only economics really matters, that economic forces are the dominant social forces to which we must conform our behavior, institutions, and even our thoughts and culture. Most of us cower, even if resentfully, in the face of these assertions of economics' natural predominance, or else we retreat to the high (but "soft") ground of moral objection and cultural critique. "Not by bread alone. . ." we mutter at the barbarians, our economists, who have seized the centers of public-policy analysis.

At a purely literal level, the source of the power of economic concepts is straightforward enough. Economists deal with the stuff of survival: scarce resources, jobs, and income. The implicit assertion is that we must first survive by "providing ourselves with a living." That is the overwhelming social project that must consume a major part of our effort and imagination, lest we fail individually and collectively. Because it is the prerequisite for all other activity, we have to mold all other institutions, including our politics and culture, so that at the very least they are consistent with it. If we are not only to survive but to prosper, our noneconomic institutions must be more than just consistent with the economy; they must directly support it. And since most of our adult life is spent making a living and most of our childhood is spent in play and education aimed at preparing us for adult work, the economy also dictates, directly or indirectly, our personalities, behavior, and values.

We all feel that power, in debates over public policy as well as in individual and household decisions. It is debilitating at both the personal and social levels; many people, even most, are paralyzed by economic arguments or concepts in exactly the same way that "math anxiety" strikes a significant part of the population. The syndromes are similar and both are cultural in origin, but "economics anxiety" has far more important consequences because mathematicians in general do not rule us or claim some natural dominance for their concepts and vision. Economists do. To many laymen, economic analysis is simply mind-strangling. The complex and confusing formulations of issues and policies are a maze of interwoven riddles that no amount of concentration and effort can solve. Painfully contorted faces greet most economic discussions. Math anxiety has a role in all this, because economics makes heavy use of quantitative measures and mathematical tools: To the contorted faces is added the nervous sweat that grade-school mathematical "word problems" have always elicited.

Finally, economics produces a certain amount of embarrassment in many people. Most of us are not rich. Most of us struggle each month to make sure the bills get paid, the house gets painted, and the children get off to school. We do not feel we have been particularly successful in managing the household economy. Standing amidst the muddle or shambles of our personal fortunes, we do not have much confidence that we can comprehend the infinitely more complex larger economy, local, regional, or national.

This helplessness would be simply a curious cultural and psychological problem were it not for the fact that the language and concepts that trigger it are said to represent the social forces to which we must bow. And not everyone is intimidated by economics. A clearly identifiable group in our society not only does not shrink from economic argument, it wraps itself in the language of economics and thereby appropriates to itself the imputed power of economics.

3. The Distribution of the Power of Economics

It is mainly the business community that has captured the language and power of economics. This capture has been so successful that to the vast majority of people, "economics" means business and finance.

This gives this particular group considerable cultural and political power: If economics represents inevitably dominant social forces and the business community is the social group that manages our economy, then clearly the business community should dominate all other groups. That the power of economics becomes very unequally distributed can be seen in almost any public-policy debate, contemporary or historical; economics almost always seems to identify rationality with the protection of the financial interests of the business community.

Consider environmental protection. We are regularly reminded that it costs something substantial (in terms of jobs, productivity, incomes, and consumer prices) to protect or repair a damaged environment. The "economic" message is that if we try to hold business firms responsible for environmental damage, it is we who will lose. Better to leave businesses alone than burden them with increased costs. The same is said about health and safety regulations in the workplace. Economic justification is lacking, we are told, for most such regulation. The public-policy conclusion is that, to ensure prosperity, we must "get the government off businesses' backs."

Labor unions fare no better than health and safety regulations. Unions, economics seems to tell us, are anti-economic while the business firms they confront are quintessentially economic. Unions saddle the economy with rigidities in the form of work rules and job-security arrangements, which lower labor productivity and management flexibility. In addition, unions use coercive monopoly power to raise wages faster than productivity. This, we are told, causes inflation, makes American goods noncompetitive, and eliminates jobs. Obviously this is an anti-economic result. Better to leave businesses free to conduct their own affairs, unhindered by unions.

Similarly, economics seems to protect businesses from charges of discrimination or exploitation. Women and blacks are paid substantially less than white males, not because of any implicit sexism or racism but because women and blacks have inferior work habits and histories. Or the supply of blacks and women in the job markets in which they apply exceeds the demand. It is the rational economic forces of supply and demand that lower their wages, and attempts to override those forces will be counterproductive: Minimum-wage and equal-pay rules will raise the cost of hiring women and blacks, and businesses will not be able to hire as many. The net result will be *zero* pay for some of them instead of low pay. Better to let businesses continue to hire them at very low wages. At least that maintains job opportunities.

It would be easy to go on in the same vein. Economic analysis almost always seems to give the same answer: Any public policy that imposes a financial burden on business is anti-economic and socially irrational. The financial interest of the business community is the same as the economic interest of the larger community.

For workers, minorities, women, environmentalists, and poor people, economics almost always seems to give the "wrong" answers. It explains why things have to be the way they are. It explains the rationality of the status quo. For business firms, economics gives the "right" answers. It elevates this small sector of our society to a preeminence. It is the sector that organizes and manages the stuff of survival, and it would be the essence of social irrationality to burden or harm it in any way. Social rationality, as expressed in economics, demands that we strongly support, not hinder, our business minority.

4. The Historical Origins of the Power of Economics

The equating of "economics" with business, finance, and market-oriented activity is not simply the result of sloppy thinking, sloppy language, or general intellectual laziness or cowardice on the part of those of us who are not part of the business community.

Economics developed as a distinct field of study specifically seeking to prove the social logic of an unfettered market. That is, its initial intellectual project was to demonstrate how it was that a free market, unhindered by government and medieval guild restrictions, could transform private, profit-seeking business interests into the social interest. As a fledgling social science, economics consciously and specifically sought to champion the profit-seeking behavior of the business community.

Economics did this not because a dominant social group sought intellectual justification for its apparently anti-social behavior or because economists were the "hired guns" of a dominant group. Quite the opposite: The first economists denounced the status quo. Early texts, such as those of Adam Smith, Thomas Malthus, and David Ricardo, were anything but dispassionate and scholarly. They were polemics against the wisdom and public policy of the time.

Under attack were the medieval economic institutions that had been retained by the emerging nation-states of Europe. The medieval centuries had left behind a strong distrust of individual pursuit of private financial gain; such activity was seen as divisive and potentially anti-social. Economic actors were expected to regulate themselves through guild restrictions and to be regulated by those who spoke for the larger society, namely the state as represented by crown and/or parliament. Wage levels, the price of basic goods, the level of exports and imports, the movement of workers, the number of firms producing particular goods, interest rates, advertising and marketing, investments in major industries—these and more were subject to state control (or attempted control).

The dominant social class was not the business community. Rather, it was a shifting mix of landed gentry, royalty, military leaders, and church officials. Successful merchants could marry or buy their way into ruling circles, but they were looked on with suspicion. Those who produced goods or developed resources were treated with the disdain accorded everyone else (such as peasants or urban workers) who got their hands dirty.

But the medieval economic institutions were breaking down. Worldwide trade was becoming increasingly important. The operations of the state and military were becoming increasingly dependent on markets that neither could control. Merchants and manufacturers were rising in importance despite the resistance of the traditional ruling classes. Early economists championed the cause of this emerging business class against the landed gentry and other forces of tradition. Early economic writings attacked the traditional constraints on market-oriented economic activity and urged that the pent-up productive forces of the new business class be let loose.

The arguments of early economists intentionally collided with contemporary notions of moral behavior. Adam Smith was a moral philosopher and theologian who set out to prove the counterintuitive and socially subversive notion that unhindered private pursuit of personal gain would result in far more *social* gain than would regulation of individual economic activity. This was an attack not only on existing economic policy, but on the long-held Christian suspicion of and disdain for worldly accumulation. Christ had had few good things to say about merchants and rich people. The medieval church's preaching had been almost entirely "otherworldy" and anti-materialist, despite its leaders' penchant for comfort.

The early economists thus had a very difficult intellectual, moral, and political challenge. In a very real sense, they were intellectual revolutionaries, supporting the "bourgeois revolution" and laying the base for the industrial and corporate revolutions that followed.

The important point for our discussion is that economists, from their first days as practitioners of a separate social science, were not intent simply on helping a particular class gain economic and political power. In understanding and demonstrating the social logic of private market activities, they began as critics, not apologists. Their task was to challenge the received corporatist vision that blended medieval institutions with the bureacratic apparatus of the nation-state. To do that, economists had to explore the "invisible hand" of a free-market, private-enterprise economy. For most of the last 200 years, they have worked diligently on this project. But with the passage of time and the emergence of business leaders as the dominant class, "business economics" has to a large extent abandoned its critical mission for a largely apologetic defense of the new capitalist system. The result has been the close association of economics with commercial markets, businesses, dollar income, and profits.

5. Rejecting the Equation of Economics with Markets and Business

From an historical point of view it is easy to understand why economics, even as a critical social science, originally emphasized market phenomena and business. From a political point of view it is even clearer why the business community appropriated to itself the language and concepts of economics. But accidents of history and self-serving posturing certainly cannot be trusted to guide a social science or policy.

Clearly, economics is not only, or even primarily, about business and commercial markets. If it were, it would suggest that in "primitive" societies, where commercial markets and businesses did not exist, there were no economic problems and individuals engaged in no economic activities. Similarly, in socialist countries where the commercial market and private enterprise have been severely limited or eliminated, such a definition of economics would suggest that economic problems had vanished. If only it were so easy!

Economics is the study of the way societies develop and use the scarce resources at their disposal to pursue their diverse goals. It could be safely equated with the study of markets and businesses only if two conditions were met. First, all societies would have to depend primarily on markets and businesses to allocate resources and distribute goods and services. Second, *all* valuable goods and services, *all* things of value to any society, would have to be bought and sold on commercial markets. The first condition has never been met. The second cannot be met, even conceptually. The fact of the matter is that in all societies there are some important goods, services, and resources that people *do not want* handled by commercial markets. And in every society there are valuable goods, services and resources that *cannot* be handled very well by a commercial market.

The first group of valuable things that in our own society we do not want provided through a commercial market includes basic education, roads, human lives (consider slavery or the selling of children), parks, political offices or positions, votes, sex, and the like. Basic food, housing, energy, and medical care are increasingly provided outside the market as well, through social assistance programs. We doubt the basic fairness of a market allocation in such cases, or believe that markets would degrade the value of the goods at issue.

In the second group—valuable things it would be hard to imagine commercial markets handling well—are things like defense against external and internal aggression (just visualize competing private armies and police forces), clean air, scenic natural wonders, species threatened with extinction, and stable, secure communities. It is hard to see how anyone could be excluded from enjoying them once they were provided at all; one could hardly expect to make people pay for them in a commercial market setting or expect someone to try to produce and sell them for a profit.

If the economy and commercial business completely overlapped, there would be no need for economics or economists in our society. We would leave everything to business firms and their advisors. It is because there is at least the possibility that there are resources, goods and services that we want, and that cannot always be well provided for by commercial markets and businesses, that we have economics: a field that looks critically at how well all of our resources are actually used in satisfying our objectives. The potential or real failure of the commercial market and business to use resources well, or to provide all the valuable things we seek, is the main focus of economic analysis in a market economy like our own.

6. An Accurate and Adequate Definition of Economics

Economics is the analysis of the rational development and use of a society's scarce resources. Rationality is judged by reference to that society's individual and/or collective values or objectives. If we would prefer situation A, yet resources are overwhelmingly committed to bringing about situation B, there is something irrational or inefficient about the way we are using our scarce resources.

This definition may seem impossibly vague. But some reflection will show that it encompasses what most people think of as "economic" or "the economy," and, as will be seen, allows us to escape from the parochial "business" vision of the economy that ordinary language forces upon us.

In business, the objective is simple and specific: to maximize profits. The manager's job is to use the available resources as best he or she can to attain this objective. In the household, the objective is more general and complex. Given the limited income available and the diverse set of needs and wants of family members, how can the household squeeze the greatest amount of satisfaction out of limited resources? For the larger market economy, we judge the efficiency of various economic arrangements by asking whether, if we reorganized production in some way, we could satisfy all the needs we meet now plus some additional ones. If we could, we know we are not using our resources efficiently. This sort of analysis leads us to conclude that unregulated monopoly, price-fixing, special-privilege legislation, etc. are "uneconomic" in the sense that they reduce our ability to satisfy our needs and desires from the resources at our disposal.

All societies have to make economic decisions of this sort. The definition above does not apply only to the market-oriented institutions on which Americans have chosen to rely. Nor does it tie economics to the historical peculiarities that surrounded its emergence.

Note the breadth of the definition. Economics deals with *all* scarce resources. Rationality is judged with respect to *all* values or objectives people may have. If a scarce resource with alternative uses is required to satisfy a particular objective, we have an economic problem no matter what the resource or what the objective.

Many vitally important resources in our economy are nonmaterial and are supplied largely outside the context of the market economy. The resources that determine the productivity of our labor force are among these. In 1980, 83 percent of all family income came as a reward for labor effort. Clearly, this is our dominant economic resource. But what is it? It is not just the number of workers, the number of warm bodies collected in a business. Nor is it simply the number of hours put in on the job. Neither of these quantitative measures get at what it is that is valuable about labor effort. If mere numbers of people or hours were the productive resources, the most overpopulated nations would be the most prosperous.

The economic resource we call labor is primarily a set of qualities and attitudes that are then meshed with nonhuman resources through another nonmaterial input, called technology or organization, to produce goods and services. "Labor" is really "labor effort" and consists of a set of subjective attitudes toward work we have come to call the work ethic: responsibility, pride in one's work, the desire to be productive, willingness to work cooperatively. It includes the education, experience, and knowledge of the work force.

Likewise, it is a subjective set of values and attitudes that weaves labor effort into a productive force in our private-enterprise economy. It has come to be labeled the entrepreneurial spirit—the drive to achieve—or, simply, as enterprise (as in "private enterprise" or "free enterprise"). This, too, is not a quantitative or material input. It is subjective and cultural.

The third crucial input in the productivity of our work force is technology. This is often translated to mean the material instruments of production: electric motors, computers, industrial robots, and the rest. But that is not primarily what technology is. Technology is a mix of accumulated knowledge and experience and organization. The assembly line did not make use of new machines, it simply organized machines, workers, and managers differently. The computer is not just an assemblage of metal and ceramics. It represents the slow accumulation of basic knowledge from fields as diverse as physics, mathematics, linguistics, electrical engineering, and graphics, organized in a particularly productive way. Without the ideas embodied in software to organize and use the computers' abilities, the computer would be merely a scientific curiosity.

The resources on which the productivity of our economy depends are for the most part fundamentally qualitative and cultural, not quantitative and material.

Just as important, they are not produced primarily for sale on the market. The work ethic, education, entrepreneurial spirit, and basic knowledge are "produced" or developed in a nonmarket setting: in our homes, in our public schools, in our nonprofit research institutions, and in our culture generally. Despite this, surely no one would argue they are noneconomic. Obviously, they are the fundamental economic building blocks. And labor productivity and technology are hardly unique in economics as basically qualitative inputs, not produced primarily by or for profit-oriented market situations. They are typical.

7. The Role of Quality and Subjective Judgment in Economics

Consider the terms in which environmental protection or the maintenance of a neighborhood's character are usually debated. "Economics" is pitted against the largely "social" or "aesthetic" concerns of those who would pursue their vague notions about the "quality of life."

The suggestion is that subjective judgments about quality are somehow noneconomic. A little reflection will show that this is simply not the case. Economic activity is now and always has been centered on the pursuit of the qualities that we judge to be attractive and, therefore, important.

Food will serve as an example. The popular language of economics clearly suggests that the pursuit of sufficient food for survival is a major economic activity. The primary worker in a family is the "breadwinner" and "brings home the bacon." Basic economic issues are "bread-and-butter" issues, and qualitative concerns are dismissed by noting that "You can't eat the scenery!"

Embedded in this popular economics is a narrow vision of what economics is all about: coping with necessity. It would imply that what we pursue when we purchase our food are the calories, vitamins, and minerals that allow good health. But is that true?

If it were, economics would predict that we would all be eating a regular diet of only soybeans and leafy greens. This would be the least-cost way of obtaining the nutrients we need. How many of us have adopted such a diet? Almost no one, because what we seek in food is not primarily health or survival. We primarily pursue taste, texture, visual attractiveness, variety, and a set of cultural values associated with food. We seek both aesthetic and sensual pleasure in our eating, and simultaneously express ourselves and our cultural values. That is why we shop in supermarkets that cover acres of land. That is why we peruse long aisles that may be devoted to dozens or even hundreds of varieties of a single type of food.

We do not seek food for the calories it contains. If anything, we seek to strip the food of those calories so that we can enjoy more eating without harmful consequences. We do not consume unusually large amounts of meat and dairy products for their nutritional value: The medical profession is emphatic that the heavy consumption of these items is killing us prematurely. Our preference for meat and dairy products is cultural and aesthetic, not biological.

Alternatively, consider our clothing. Is it the least-cost solution to the need to protect our bodies from the elements? Hardly. We do not wear standardized clothes made from low-cost, durable materials and requiring minimum tailoring. Our expenditures on clothing reflect the dominance of style, self-expression, and variety. Texture, color, and cut play a far more important role than durability and minimum cost. We even pay extra in order to display a particular designer's name or logo!

Again, aesthetic and cultural judgments dominate. In fact, they dominate most economic activity. A list of some major household expenditures will bear out the point.

• Housing: Architects, interior decorators, landscape architects, etc. labor to produce a "pleasing environment."

• Household energy use: We choose fuels and energy-using appliances on the basis of comfort and convenience.

• Dining out: In choosing restaurants, we focus on the "atmosphere" or "environment" the establishment provides as well as the quality of the food and wine; we also care about the quality of the service.

• Entertainment: In choosing our entertainment in the home, we have to judge the visual and sound qualities of stereo systems, televisions and VCRs; in addition, we have to choose from innumerable records, tapes, videos, and TV shows. Outside the home, we have to choose from a broad variety of performing artists and styles. Only our subjective tastes and preferences, as informed by our larger culture and limited by our budgets, can guide us in this.

• Transportation: Our choice of cars, use of buses, trains, airlines, etc. are guided by our judgments of comfort, convenience, and fun. We rarely have to travel long distances to survive. The most superficial analysis of advertisements indicates the important role of style and cultural values in the production and sale of private cars, vans, and trucks.

The pursuit of quality, as guided by our individual aesthetic judgments and the larger society's cultural values, clearly dominates the commercial economy. Such qualitative considerations may also be expected to dominate nonmarket decisions about resource use. Chapters Two and Three develop from both a conceptual and an empirical point of view the details of this "economics of quality." They will show that, conceptually, the things we purchase from businesses or pursue through noncommercial activities are really "bundles of qualities," which different individuals evaluate in different ways. This, however, has never represented one impossibly complex problem. It is a problem we overcome daily as individuals, business firms, and public decision-makers. Empirically, it will be shown that satisfying our "survival needs" represents only a small fraction of economic activity; the pursuit of qualitative values consumes almost 90 percent of our economic effort. This emphasis on quality, not survival, is not a characteristic of recent affluent societies alone. As far back as our historians and anthropologists have been able to carry us, humans have pursued aesthetic and cultural values even when their survival was threatened. Quality has never been a trivial or low-priority objective.

8. When is Quality Economic?
Market and Nonmarket Pursuits of Quality

Two points should be clear from this discussion. First, the pursuit of quality is an important, even the dominant, type of economic activity. Second, although peoples' judgments about quality differ and even conflict, systematic resource decisions can be rationally guided by these judgments.

One of the most frequent assertions in public discussions of environmental quality or the quality of life is that decisions on these matters are mainly noneconomic, moral, or social, because everyone's judgment on such matters is unique. Some people think mountainsides stripped of vegetation are ugly; others see them as a sign of a well-managed forest. Some people like grizzly bears and wolves in natural areas; others are terrified of them. Some people like developed campsites, others prefer primitive wilderness camping. Some people are disgusted by gaudy commercial strips, others see them as an exciting and dynamic aspect of community development. Because of such disagreements, we are told that such decisions clearly lie outside the scope of economics.

If this were true, clothing, motion pictures, music, radio, television, publishing, cosmetics, architecture, interior decorating, food, and so on would also be "noneconomic" and not subject to rigorous economic analysis. Clearly, producers and consumers in all of these fields must make subjective, aesthetic judgments. Equally clearly, there is substantial dispute over those judgments: new wave, punk, and disco music did not receive unanimous support from critics. Commercial TV and radio are regularly panned by some critics as a wasteland, and defended by others as giving people what they want. Styles in clothing offend some while inspiring others.

Subjective, aesthetic judgments are made daily by producers in almost every industry and by their customers. There is no need for unanimity in those judgments. Wide differences in opinions about the value of the goods and services produced not only do not paralyze the decision-making process, they enrich our culture with variety and innovation. Those differences are at the heart of the marketing of goods and services, and businesses and consumers deal very adequately with these differences every day.

If there is a problem, it is not the dominance of aesthetic considerations, nor is it the existence of conflicting judgments. The "problem" is that some sought-after qualities are adequately provided for in a commercial market setting and some are not. Most people would agree that popular music, with its many styles, is adequately handled by the market economy. Some may feel that popular music has negative impacts outside the market: There are periodic attacks on rock and roll for its implicit or explicit sexuality and allegedly maniacal influence on the young. But in general we are willing to trust the market to serve our widely divergent tastes in music.

But when it comes to the music of a songbird or the nonmusic of a landing jet plane, markets may not serve us very well. That is not because of complex aesthetic problems, but because it is hard to imagine how wild songbirds could be produced for a profit or how a peaceful and quiet neighborhood can be privately purchased in the presence of a regional airport.

The economic problem with these environmental qualities is not that they are qualitative or aesthetic, but that adequate and acceptable property rights and commercial markets do not exist to help us assure an appropriate level of their "production" and "consumption." This may be true simply because of the character of the environmental services at issue or because we have consciously chosen to remove some services from a commercial setting.

But the absence of a commercial market for these environmental services and qualities does not make them any less important or any less scarce or any less "economic." All it does is make it harder to determine socially the appropriate level of "production" or protection of these nonmarketed but valuable goods and services.

The fact of the matter is that some scarce and valuable goods and services are marketed, and some are not. In both cases, economics seeks to evaluate the social rationality of the way in which the society uses scarce resources to provide valuable goods and services. Economics cannot use the market as a sole reference point. If it did, it could not evaluate how well markets themselves are working. If economics were not perfectly capable of developing nonmarket standards by which to judge the social rationality of resource use, it could never have undertaken its two-century-old ideological mission of explaining and defending the social logic of a market economy.

The primary job of economics is to develop tools for judging the rationality of all resource uses, whether or not private property and commercial market institutions are involved. It would be a gross violation of this mission to dismiss as "noneconomic" the analysis of how we pursue environmental and social qualities simply because we do so largely outside the market. In fact, *because* we do not have commercial markets to assist us in these pursuits, this is an area of priority concern for economists. Since we know markets and private businesses will be of little use in the providing or protecting these important resources, we need to develop alternative ways of making sure we are doing the socially rational thing.

Note the reversal here of the conventional wisdom. Rather than concerns with environmental quality being noneconomic because they are subjective and noncommercial, they are important economic concerns precisely because there is no operating market to provide even an approximately rational level of protection or an approximately optimal supply. In the absence of such a market, economists must find new ways to obtain information on relative importance or value.

Over the last several decades economists have developed a variety of tools to estimate the relative importance of nonmarketed qualities of life. Chapters Four and Five discuss these tools, and Chapter Six goes on to show the economic values revealed by the empirical valuation of nonmarket environmental resources. A large part of our economic well-being is determined by the quality of these nonmarketed resources.

Economics, then, when done competently, focuses not just or primarily on resources, goods, services, jobs, and income provided through private businesses and commercial markets. It also analyzes the contribution to our well-being from the natural, social, and public environments. Some of this consists of "gifts of nature." Some is provided by public agencies or not-for-profit private organizations outside of a commercial setting. All of these contributions must be taken into account in analyzing our economic well-being.

9. How We Look at the Local Economy: The "Economic Base" as a Distracting Vision

The economics profession and the business community have given us a variety of ways of thinking about our local economies—those of our towns, cities, and states. Some are very formal, complete with imposing mathematical equations, while others are very informal, built around the commonsense folk economics that has developed over decades as communities have contemplated their economic difficulties and debated ways out of them.

All of these conventional views of the local economy have a common feature. They seek to understand the local economy by focusing on the "key" economic activities, the activities that trigger or cause most others. We look for the "heart" of the economy, or its "base." If we can find that, perhaps we can cut through the complexity and confusion of economic activities that surround us.

The concept of an economic base divides the local economy into two parts, one causally related to the other: Changes in the base are assumed to cause changes in the rest of the economy. Thus, this general approach allows us to distinguish basic as opposed to secondary or tertiary sectors of the economy.

The economic base is usually identified with what an area specializes in producing. That specialization leads to production for "export" to surrounding areas. Those "exports" bring a return flow of income that is spent and respent, putting more people to work and generating more income. As a result of export activities injecting money into the local economy, there is a multiple expansion of economic activity. Income and employment multipliers are regularly calculated for various basic industries. The rise and fall of these industries is then seen as determining the changes in the overall economy.

Chapter Seven develops this common model of the local economy and analyzes the vision it provides. The conclusion is not primarily that the economic-base approach is wrong (although empirically it may well be), but that it offers only a partial vision of the local economy. For that reason, it is misleading. It distracts us from some very important determinants of how well our local economy operates, and diverts us toward frustrating, self-defeating economic policies. It suggests that local economic well-being is tied to the dollar volume of exports—that an area's wealth is enhanced by scraping and clawing at the earth to obtain valuable resources, which are then fashioned into some usable form with the sweat of the local population and sent away for others to enjoy. A community improves itself by sending away the valuable things it has or can make! This is clearly a gross distortion. The opposite is closer to the truth: A community is made better off by the things it can provide for itself and by its ability to obtain from others those things it cannot easily produce. Local production and imports, not exports, determine how well off a community can be.

The only function of exports is to obtain the income that allows an area to import what it cannot easily produce. The more self-sufficient an area is, the less important externally produced goods and services are, the more "developed" its economy is and the less its economic well-being is tied to exports. This certainly is a different view of exports than that offered by the economic-base theory.

Dependence on export-oriented activity for jobs and income also brings volatility. Export industries link the local economy to the national and international economies, allowing fluctuations in outside conditions to affect the local economy. The export industries "import" and amplify national recessions and depressions. It is through them that booms and busts are transmitted. Thus, with access to national and international markets goes a loss of control over and possible destabilization of the local economy. This important aspect of the economic base is rarely discussed. A more developed and less export-oriented economy is more stable because of its diversity and self-sufficiency.

The theory behind the economic-base model is very primitive and incomplete, even from a conventional economic point of view. It assumes that people move to where jobs are. New industry is seen as creating jobs that then draw people to an area where they earn income and spend it. In spending it, even more jobs are created. Further population growth is possible, and the cycles of growth roll on and on.

In economic jargon, it is the industrial demand for workers that brings the population to a particular area and allows it to survive. But the most elementary of economic propositions is that the interaction of supply and demand determines economic outcomes. We have no more reason to believe that workers move to where there is a demand for workers than to believe that the supply of workers in a particular area is what attracts industry to that area. Economic causality surely runs both ways. That is why many in the nation's traditional manufacturing areas worry about firms and industries moving to areas of cheaper labor and other resources, in the Sunbelt or overseas. The single-direction causal assumption of the economic-base model has to be rejected on both theoretical and empirical grounds.

10. A Broader Vision of the Economic Base: Local Quality

From the "supply side," an area's economic base consists of all those character-istics that make it an attractive place to live, work, or do business.

The character, quality, and cost of the available work force is certainly part of this. A skilled, well-educated, and disciplined work force willing to accept average or somewhat below-average wages would be a key attraction to most businesses. The character of the local school system, the vocational-technical training programs, and the institutions of higher education and research influence this. So do community attitudes. They not only help determine the quality of the work force, they also determine the educational and cultural opportunities available to the relocating executives, their families and employees.

The character and quality of other public services is also important: the water, sewer, road, and highway systems, the adequacy of police and fire protection, and the like. They are the infrastructure that enables economic activity to proceed smoothly.

All of these services are provided through public agencies and are largely financed through taxes. If taxes are kept low by underfunding these basic ser-vices, businesses are unlikely to find the lower taxes, on net, an attractive feature of the area, for they pay in the form of lower-quality public services.

To these bread-and-butter characteristics have to be added the less easily defined and measured characteristics that give an area its definition and personal-ity. These include the richness and depth of its culture and community; more broadly, they include the entire "climate" and "environment," natural and human-made—the qualities of life in that area. As argued earlier and as discussed in detail in Chapters Four and Six, these are very important in determining peoples' well-being. They count for a great deal in individual economic decision-making.

This broader definition of an area's economic base has distinct advantages over the export-oriented vision. The latter concentrates on businesses that serve national and international markets. Those businesses and their markets are large-ly beyond the control of any local agency. In that sense, the conventional model focuses our attention on those aspects of the economy over which we can exercise little or no control. That certainly is distracting and dysfunctional from a public-policy perspective. In fact, it is worse than that. By establishing the large export-oriented corporations as "primary" or "basic" in the local economy, the con-ventional model increases the economic and political power of those corporations. It suggests that we need to give them everything they ask for, or we will suffer serious economic consequences. This reduces even further the range of policy options that seem available to protect local economic well-being.

The alternative vision of the economic base focuses on those things that local policy *can* influence: the character of the schools, the quality of the infrastructure, the attractiveness of the community and its surroundings. This provides multiple handles for public policy aimed at improving both the local quality of life and the economic base. Instead of frustration or despair in local economic policy, the alternative definition offers a hopeful, "can't-lose" vision for public policy. We can improve our communities and build our economic base simultaneously.

11. Does It Matter Anyway?
The Policy Implications of This Alternative Vision

Once we abandon a narrow, export-oriented vision of the economic base, we can consider local economic policy in quite a different light. (Chapters Eight and Nine analyze the limits of traditional economic boosterism, local governments' efforts to boost the profitability of local businesses and "chase after smokestacks.") In evaluating alternative development strategies, one must look closely at the source of new jobs in the United States during the last decade and a half. It most certainly has not been in relocated smokestack industries. It has been in the expansion of small, local firms. Increasingly, these firms manufacture nothing for export; they serve local markets. Despite the insistence that economic growth is not possible in this way, we will see that this is just the sort of productive specialization and division of labor upon which all economic development is based. This shift in economic activity toward locally produced services follows important shifts in the way we live and judgments we have made about what it is that determines our well-being. Local economic policy cannot ignore these shifts and still be effective or functional.

Traditional economic boosterism has concentrated on attracting new businesses, which has dragged almost every city and state in the nation into an intense competition for factories. In that competition, communities are encouraged to sacrifice the very things that make them attractive places to live and work. Business taxes are lowered, and public services and schools are starved for funds. Environmental standards are relaxed, and the natural environment deteriorates. Yet since very few new jobs are provided by migrating, footloose firms, almost no communities get significant new jobs and incomes in exchange for their sacrifices. This type of competition leaves almost all areas worse off. We give away an important part of our economic base and receive little or nothing in return.

To avoid this type of destructive competition, local economic policy's traditional emphasis on quantitatively defined economic *growth* (in number of jobs and dollars of income) has to be replaced by a broader, qualitative focus on economic *development*. It is the development of a thriving, vital economy that we seek, not growth. And that development includes significant nonmarket elements, including public services, the natural environment, educational and cultural endeavors, and the character of our communities. Chapter Nine outlines this type of development strategy.

Chapter Eight explains why quantitatively focused economic policies are likely to fail. It puts growth-oriented local economic policies into the market context in which they attempt to operate. In the national market context, where population and capital move freely among cities and states, most of what local policy attempts simply cannot be achieved.

Consider efforts to boost per-capita income by getting more high-wage industries to locate in a particular area. The conventional view of the local economy assumes that people move to where jobs are; the broader the range of job possibilities and the higher the wages in an area, the greater will be the number of people moving there. When more high-wage jobs open up, either some people who were about to move out of the region for lack of work will stay, or people from outside the region will move in because of the new jobs, or both. In the end, there will be more people in the region than would otherwise live there. When the new employees spend their wages, that money will circulate through the local economy, creating additional jobs in the lower-wage, derivative, or secondary sector of the economy. The multiplier tells us how much income in the low-wage sector will be generated or how many low-wage secondary jobs will be produced.

The net effect could be more people working in high-wage jobs *and* more people working in low-wage jobs *and* a bigger total population. What will the impact be on per-capita income? There is no reason to believe it will rise. The proportion of high- and low-paying jobs may not change at all. Per-capita income is total income divided by total population, and both of them, the numerator and the denominator, have risen. Per-capita income could fall, remain the same, or rise. If population follows jobs and income and more people come seeking work than there are jobs, per-capita income will fall, not rise, while unemployment rises instead of falling.

Or consider the attempt to get the economy to grow in order to provide jobs for young people as they seek to enter the work force.

Traditional policy for economic growth assumes that if local economic conditions are booming, young people will take jobs close to home. But the data available do not verify this. Local economic conditions have little impact on gross out-migration. The main determinants of out-migration are the age, education, and family migration history of the potential migrants. Young, well-educated people from families that themselves have migrated tend to move away from home no matter what the local economic conditions. Local conditions determine where they move, but not whether they move. This means that boosting local economic growth will not provide jobs for the area's young people. Rather, it will provide jobs for the young people of other areas. That is unlikely to be a policy objective with high priority.

Finally, consider attempts to reduce taxes by expanding the tax base through economic growth. The general idea is that if the economy expands, there will be more taxable property over which to spread the local government's current revenue needs. This assumes, of course, that local government services and expenditures will not have to grow with the economy or at least will not have to grow proportionately. But the evidence is all to the contrary: As cities and towns grow, expenditures grow *more than* proportionately, and taxes rise. Local governments provide very definite services to the population and business community. If these are not expanded when the city expands, the quality and availability deteriorate or diminish. This represents a real loss to existing residents and, often, an unacceptable level of services to the new residents. Because of this and other forces, local government's expenditures and tax rates rise with economic growth, not fall.

Chapter Eight develops these examples and others in more detail. The major conclusion is that, in a market economy with free-moving population and capital, one region cannot be significantly better or worse off than another. If it is, people will move and that movement will eliminate the difference. Thus, if money incomes and the benefits from the social and natural environments in particular areas are, taken together, significantly superior to those found in other areas, several things will happen. First, people will migrate to the area and fewer people will leave it. This will increase the competition for jobs and drive money wages down. The increased population will also degrade the social and natural environments somewhat. The net effect will be a decline in the level of well-being. Simultaneously, the out-migration from areas of lower well-being will cause labor shortages, and wages will rise. Reduced congestion in these areas will reduce the pressure on their social and natural environments. Firms will be discouraged from locating or expanding in the higher-wage area; the low-wage areas will look more attractive. This too will push wages down in the high-wage areas while moving environmental quality in the opposite direction.

People, businesses, and investment capital will shift whenever there are significant differences in economic well-being between areas. These shifts will tend to eliminate the differences. As a result, no area is likely to remain significantly better or worse off than any other.

This does not mean that local economic policy can achieve nothing. It can seek to protect those aspects of local economic well-being that are most important to the local population. To the extent that people have remained in an area or moved into it because it has social, cultural, and natural qualities they found attractive, the degradation of these qualities can make that part of the population worse off. Quantitative growth at the expense of those economic qualities can both eliminate something of value to the existing population and increase wage competition, which lowers money income. This would clearly leave existing residents worse off. In addition, even if money incomes rise as the social and natural environment deteriorates, existing residents may well not be compensated for their losses. The existing population may be hurt by the economic growth.

What, then, is the point of pursuing quantitative economic growth? It cannot make one area better off than another for any significant period, but it can damage some of the more important determinants of the existing residents' economic well-being.

Chapter Nine outlines an alternative approach to local economic development. It begins by discussing the goals of local economic policy. In place of vaguely defined growth it focuses on the actual "use values" people want from the local economy: good work, biological and social necessities, a stable community, and the qualities that make life stimulating and satisfying. A "thriving," "vital" economy is the objective, not merely a growing one.

The intended beneficiaries of such local policy are also emphasized: the existing local residents. Local policy does not aim at solving national employment and poverty problems by trying to generate jobs and income for the unemployed, underemployed, or disadvantaged wherever they are. As basic as this is, it has important implications for local policy that are often ignored.

The proposed development strategy focuses on improving the much more broadly defined local "business climate." It does so by both supporting the local "spirit of enterprise" and by improving the quality of the community.

A thriving local economy is built around the creativity, innovation, and risk-taking of resident entrepreneurs. The community's social and cultural environment must respect, support, and reward these residents, but this does not mean abandoning the taxes that support basic services and educational institutions. Nor does it mean abandoning regulations that protect the local quality of life. To improve the vitality of the commercial sector, the policy would support the founding, survival, and expansion of local small businesses. It is these businesses that have been the source of most jobs. To the extent that they allow a community to replace imported goods with locally produced goods, this can have the same type of stimulating effect as new export-oriented firms. The greater self-sufficiency would also have a stabilizing effect on the local economy.

Supporting local enterprise does not mean subsidizing or financing local small businesses. It does mean seeking to improve technical business skills through a small-business "extension program." Improving such skills reduces the firms' risk of failure and increases their access to normal commercial finance.

The second goal of a local economic-development program should be protecting and improving the quality of public resources and services. These include the local school system, the institutions of higher education, and the research institutions that determine the quality of the local labor force and the rate of innovation. Another factor under this heading is the quality of the local infrastructure, especially the transportation links with other areas. Other "public goods" such as clean air and water, security from crime, absence of blight and congestion, and the like have significant effects on local economic well-being and ought to be considered as part of any economic-development program. Natural beauty, recreational potential, and cultural atmosphere are playing increasingly important roles in local economies as well.

These two approaches to local economic development—helping small businesses survive and expand and improving the quality of a broad range of public resources and services—can be seen as part of a ''can't-lose'' strategy. Even if they fail to attract new firms and people, they directly benefit the existing residents. This is not something that can be said for the give-aways required from local areas if they are going to join the industrial-recruiting sweepstakes.

The book ends on a somber but hopeful note. Chapter Ten surveys the factors that determine individual economic well-being in a market capitalist economy such as ours. Despite its astounding material productivity and the free rein it gives to most economic actors, this type of economy also imposes serious burdens on both individuals and communities, burdens that hamper the pursuit of well-being in a way local development strategies can do little about. These limits of capitalism are not offered to demoralize or paralyze local economic improvement efforts, but simply to help all participants understand the context in which they are operating.

Despite these constraints, the local economic-development strategies put forward in this book contain the seeds of an alternative vision: what our economy could be like if some of those structural flaws were removed. The book ends with a discussion of that grander vision.

CHAPTER TWO

The Dominance of Quality in Economic Pursuits: Survival Needs, Food, and Health Care

1. Introduction: Necessity and Quality in Economics

The power of economics, its claim to priority over other social concerns, is tied to the widely held perception that economics deals with the material basis of human survival. The economy not only produces these basic goods (food, clothing, shelter, and medical care), but it also provides individuals with the jobs and income which, in a market economy, are prerequisites for obtaining them.

It is not that economics assumes that we are only or primarily interested in survival or material goods. Economists quite purposely insist on talking in terms of wants, not needs. It is noneconomists who seem to assert that because we have to survive before we can pursue other, "higher" objectives, economics must focus on material goods and necessity. If that is what economics does, the assertion of its priority seems intuitive and obvious.

This perception or assumption about economics is what leads to the dismissal of concerns about the quality of an experience as being largely noneconomic and of second or lower priority. Quality is seen as subjective and disputable, not easily evaluated and even more difficult to measure. In contrast, economics is seen as concentrating on things so "real" that they are easily measured, quantified, and valued in money terms. This type of comparison easily leads to the conclusion that there is something dispensable about quality, that "it's nice to have, but you can't feed your family with it." The well-off can concern themselves with frills, but workaday people and their economy cannot.

This dismissal of quality as largely peripheral to our lives and our economy is the basis for much of the criticism of environmentalism as elitist and anti-economic. The same judgment is used to attack educational programs that do not teach the "basics" or job skills. It is behind the criticism of measures to protect the character of neighborhoods and communities. Government spending that goes beyond the provision of "essential services" is also vulnerable to this type of attack.

Thus, parks and natural areas are labeled playgrounds for the rich. Zoning and development restrictions are accused of creating high-rent districts. Language, art, music, and even physical-education programs at our schools are gutted so that resources can be focused on English, math, computer, and business-skills courses. Government support of the arts and humanities is seen as either an illegitimate invasion of the private sphere or a subsidy for the upper class.

This chapter and the next will explore the factual basis for these common attitudes about economics and our economy. They will seek to show that it is the pursuit of quality that dominates our economic activity. It is quality on which our economic production focuses. It is quality that we pursue in the marketplace as we spend our incomes. Human quality is the major reason that our economy works so productively.

This dominance of quality in modern economic activity is not new, tied to the emergence of an affluent post-industrial society. As far back in time as our information goes, we find human beings not only or even primarily engaged in a struggle to survive. Rather, what we know of earlier cultures and societies, no matter how primitive they seem to us, indicates their overriding concern not with merely staying alive, but with living in a particular style. That is what human culture is all about.

We begin this exploration of the pursuit of quality with an impressionistic overview of what the American economy is actually focusing on these days. We then proceed to analyze in some detail in this and the next chapter just how important in the American economy the production of food, clothing, shelter, and medical care for survival actually are. From this we draw some conclusions about what fraction of the American economy deals primarily with necessities and survival. Before drawing general conclusions about the crucial role of qualitative pursuits in economic activity, we also look back over previous, "primitive" societies.

2. The Economic Pursuit of Quality: An Impressionistic Overview

Any casual review of just how we experience our economy from day to day will challenge the assumption that the pursuit of subjective qualities is somehow peripheral to economic activity or even noneconomic.

The "survival" or "necessity" view of our economy is certainly at odds with the most visible intrusion of that economy into our personal experience: advertising. It is difficult in the United States to go anywhere, do anything, without being confronted with a corporate message about how we should be spending our money.

Those messages do not usually suggest how to survive at least cost. They assert that we are fun- and excitement-seekers, not austere homesteaders scrambling to survive. We are urged to spend our money on almost everything *but* survival: style, challenge, beauty, pleasure, status. The list is long but rarely includes necessity.

It does not even have to be *our* money we spend. Credit cards companies urge us to lavish borrowed money on extravagances. People who are going hungry or sleeping outside in the cold are never allowed to obtain credit cards. Rather, the advertisements tell us to plunge into sensual and aesthetic experiences "so worldly, so welcome!" Our daily experience interacting with our economy's rich variety of products provides a similar message.

Recall your last trip to the supermarket—a modern American invention that typically presents a maze of aisles stocked with thousands of products. What is startling is not the fact that we use so many items in our homes, but the variety in each category.

The laundry-products aisle, for instance, contains dozens of soaps, detergents, and other items. Each is advertised as unique, designed to affect the color, feel, and odor of our clothes in its own distinct way. Other products promise to do the same for our floors, carpets, and bathrooms. What are being marketed are subtle differences in their effects on the subjective, sensual qualities of our belongings. The fact that our preferences for these attributes vary widely does not prevent firms from producing these products at a profit, nor does it prevent us from choosing among them. The subjective, "aesthetic" nature of the services promised does not force us to stand in the aisle, baffled, debating the qualitative merits of each product. We spend almost no time or effort making our choices. We grab our preferred product, put it in the cart, and move on quickly to make other equally qualitative and subjective decisions in the next aisle.

That may be the frozen-food aisle, where we not only face the need to choose from among a dozen or more vegetables, but also from different brand names and different cuts or qualities—not to mention the vegetables already variously seasoned or sauced. (Or do we want them fresh, from the produce aisle?) Then there is the meat aisle with various types of red meat, poultry, and seafood. Beyond the basic choice among different animal sources, there may be many cuts to choose from for each type of meat. The cheese counter, especially if the supermarket has a deli section, will confront the customer with dozens of cheeses and cold cuts. The wine, beer, soft-drink, cigarette, candy, and cookie sections will raise the same need to make subjective choices about what qualities the shopper wishes to purchase. The very range of choices demonstrates the lack of unanimity or even consensus in our preferences. Yet we, the store, and the producers have no unusual difficulty adjusting our economic choices to these diverse, subjective preferences.

Alternatively, reflect on your last visit to a shopping mall. This is an even more recent American marketing invention, a re-creation of the traditional bazaar, market, or fair. In this reincarnation there may be dozens—even hundreds—of small specialty stores as well as several large department stores. The variety and choice are again dazzling. One finds, for instance, not just shoe stores, but shoe stores just for runners or just for dancers or just for backpackers or just for urban cowboys. Each has dozens or hundreds of types of shoes. Subjective preference, social role, and qualitative judgment again guide our choices.

We could continue with a tour of book stores, clothing stores, record stores, stereo and electronics stores, sporting-goods stores, jewelry stores, liquor stores, toy stores . . . The range of choices makes it difficult even to imagine a complete list.

Instead of shopping, we could stay at home and listen to the radio or watch television or read a magazine. But first we would have to choose from the dozens of alternatives available. Our subjective tastes and preferences would have to guide us. But in the process of exercising that choice we would again be bombarded with advertising for many different products.

Consider those advertisements. As pointed out above, they are not often devoted to telling us how we can survive and satisfy our basic needs in a least-cost way. They deal instead with style, convenience, and quality. Advertisers seek to attach complex cultural images to their products, and trumpet subtle or imagined qualitative differences between their products and those of their competitors. The emphasis is entirely on the subjective and the qualitative. The products marketed are really not products at all but "bundles" of qualities and qualitative services (Lancaster, 1971).

Table 2.1 lists some of the many goods and services consumers purchase but which we probably can all agree are in no sense essential to our survival. We spend hundreds of billions of dollars on these goods.

Look over the items in the table and consider the role that diverse aesthetic judgments play in their production, marketing, and purchase. We judge restaurants by the taste of their food, the atmosphere they provide, the quality of the service. We use alcohol to modify our mood. In choosing the type we will imbibe, we can consider dozens of beers, hundreds of wines, many basic liquors, and a nearly infinite variety of mixed drinks.

Thousand-dollar stereo and video systems are quite common. We stand in showrooms surrounded by dozens of sound systems, listening to the subtle differences in the music each system produces. Record and tape stores offer us thousands of collections of music. We must choose the style, the artist, the particular album.

No one is likely to dispute that the provision of any of the goods and services in Table 2.1 involves economic activity or that obtaining them involves economic choices. Yet disputable, subjective, qualitative judgments are at the heart of the production and consumption of all of them. And survival and necessity have nothing to do with them. Why, then, are these economic but a golden eagle or

Table 2.1

Personal Consumption Expenditures on "Luxury" Goods, 1979*

Goods or service purchased	Consumer expenditure (in billions of dollars)
Meals and drinks at restaurants	$119
Alcoholic beverages	56
Recreational goods and services:	143
Radio, TV, stereo, records, musical instruments, etc.	29
Recreational vehicles	23
Toys and sports supplies	18
Admission to amusement events	9
Flowers and potted plants	6
Books	9
Foreign travel, nonbusiness	18
Intercity travel, nonbusiness	14
Tobacco products	28
Toilet articles and preparations	20
Barber shops, beauty parlors	11
Jewelry and watches	14
Stationery	7
Telephone, nonbusiness	36
Domestic services	9

*Dollar values expressed in 1984 dollars using the consumer-price index.
Source: National Income and Product Accounts, 1976–1979, Special Supplement, Survey of Current Business, Bureau of Economic Analysis, U.S. Department of Commerce, July 1981

scenic vista or a secure neighborhood non-economic?

In reflecting in this way on our daily experience with the market economy, what is startling is the general absence or invisibility of real necessities. One has to hunt for the generic section of the supermarket to come close to it, or perhaps go to a military-surplus store. And even here the choice is broad.

The fact is that, rather than the provision of necessities being at the heart of our economy, we have largely removed the pursuit of necessities from the operation of our market economy. Basic food, clothing, shelter, and medical care are now assured to almost all citizens by public and private agencies. We do not consciously let fellow citizens starve or go without clothing, housing, or medical care. We have welfare programs, food stamps, soup kitchens, public housing, emergency shelters, church missions, Medicaid, and more. Hospitals receiving public funds are forbidden to turn people away simply because they cannot pay.

This is not to say that no one is poor, hungry, homeless, ill-clothed, or medically neglected. Many are. But consider the shock and concern we feel when we discover that the public and private programs we have in place to keep people from going without the basics are not working. Even the most conservative among us are committed to maintaining a safety net so that no citizen will go without the means of survival. In fact, our major concern with poverty is not that it threatens the survival of the poor. Rather, the concern is that poverty destroys the dignity of the individual and blocks his or her participation in the larger society. This broader social and cultural concern underlines the fact that economic activity and well-being are not mainly about obtaining biological necessities. Social and cultural values are far more dominant.

We no longer trust our market economy to see that everyone gains access to the necessities. Social policy, not economic policy, sees to survival; our economy is then allowed to focus on the quality of life beyond survival and necessity. This is vitally important, for it reverses the common perception of what economic activity is all about. What we leave to our market economy is not the means of survival but the pursuit of the quality of living.

3. Food as a Necessity in our Economy

When survival needs are discussed, food usually leads the list: food, clothing, shelter, medical care. What could be more necessary?

Food has become a symbol of the basic needs the economy is assumed to serve. For that reason,we will begin our look at the quantitative importance of survival needs in our economy with an investigation of just what we get for the money we spend on food.

It should be pointed out at the start, though, that however basic food may be to survival, expenditures on food are a relatively small part of American household spending. Judged by its importance in the "market basket" of goods around which the consumer-price index is built, only about one out of ten consumer dollars (11.3 percent) is spent on food consumed in the home. This "survival need" certainly does not dominate the expenditure patterns in our economy.

Periodically, the U.S. Department of Agriculture conducts a detailed survey of how Americans spend their food dollars. A scientific sample of households is asked to record every food purchase for a week. These expenditures are then combined to provide a picture of American food habits (U.S. Department of Agriculture, 1982). An analysis of this information can tell us a lot about the role biological necessity plays in our food expenditures and the part of our economy that produces, processes, and delivers that "survival" food.

One-third of our food dollars is spent in restaurants. Although this money obviously provides calories, protein, and other nutrients, what is purchased in a restaurant is not only (or primarily) nutrition. Only a tiny fraction of the population eats away from home out of necessity. Restaurants provide convenience, service, an atmosphere, variety, and tastes not readily available at home. These subjective, qualitative attributes are primarily what is being purchased. We can start, then, by treating these food expenditures as not tied to survival or necessity.

The remaining two-thirds of our food expenditures cover an incredible variety of products. Some of these products are clearly unneeded from a nutritional point of view, and many may actually damage our health. Even if we treat alcoholic beverages as something other than food, over 3 percent of our home food dollar goes for nonnutritional beverages: soft drinks, tea, coffee, etc. Five and a half times this amount (over $60 billion) is spent on alcoholic beverages. Eight percent goes for snacks, desserts, flavorings, toppings, etc. Included in these are bakery products (other than bread), sugar, sweets, snacks, potato chips, french fries, ice cream, nuts, condiments, salad dressing, gravies, and sauces.

The largest category of home food spending is meat: One-quarter of the home food dollar goes for red meats, poultry, and fish. Another 10 percent is spent on eggs and milk products. Thirty-five percent of Americans' food expenditures, then, are for such high-protein animal products.

To most Americans these expenditures on meat, cheese, and eggs are the core of their basic diet. These are the foods around which meals are built. They are, in a fundamental way, seen as necessary for a nutritious meal. But a closer look at the meat category shows that it is not only "basic," low-cost meat that is being purchased. One need not eat steaks or pork chops or roast beef or ham to survive, yet only slightly over a quarter of the home expenditures on beef—only 12 percent of total home meat expenditures—are on ground beef. Much more money goes toward steak. The pursuit of survival is not driving this choice.

What's more, meat and other animal products are not the only source of protein. A mix of grains and beans with a minimal supplement of milk solids could provide a perfectly adequate and far cheaper source of protein for Americans (Register and Sonnenberg, 1973; Lappe, 1982). Ironically, that is exactly what we feed livestock: wheat, corn, and other grains, soybeans, and protein supplements that are perfectly nutritious and palatable to human beings. The cost of turning grain and vegetable protein into meat is very high. In beef production, sixteen pounds of grain and soy protein, which we could eat directly, produce one pound of meat. That feed contains eight times as much protein and twenty-one times as many calories as a pound of hamburger (Lappe, 1982, p. 69). It would be far more efficient for us to obtain nutrients directly from the grain. For other animals this transformation of one type of human food into another is not as inefficient, but in all cases considerable food value is lost.

If all we were trying to do was survive and be healthy, we would eat the grains and protein supplements instead of feeding them to animals first. We do not do this because our eating patterns have little or nothing to do with our survival. For cultural and aesthetic reasons we prefer red meats to soy protein and grains, even though the latter are much cheaper and, because of their lower fat and cholesterol content, represent less of a threat to our health. We spend much more than is necessary to obtain our protein because of some very particular and highly subjective preferences. Nothing in our biology explains these preferences. They are simply tastes we have developed.

To estimate how much of our food expenditures is required to obtain adequate nutrition, we could formulate a basic survival diet and estimate its cost. The U.S. Department of Agriculture (USDA) regularly does exactly that. In order to determine what the food-stamp allocation to each type of low-income family should be to assure adequate nutrition, the USDA estimates a "thrifty" food budget. That budget is intended to show the lowest expenditure that will maintain human energy and health using conventional, readily available foods.

At the beginning of 1983, the average cost of food per person under this budget was $62.27 per month (USDA, 1983, p. 28). For the same period, Americans' actual food expenditures averaged $145.27 per month (U.S. Department of Commerce, 1983, Table 2.2). That is, Americans spent two and a third times as much on food as was necessary, according to USDA calculations, for nutrition. Almost 60 cents out of each food dollar is spent not on basic nutrition but in pursuit of more subjective and qualitative objectives like taste, texture, and variety.

But even this exaggerates the role of nutrition in our food economy. The USDA's "thrifty" budget assumes that all Americans buy the same types of foods in supermarkets. Existing American food preferences and cultural values determine what foods are included as much as nutritional requirements and cost do. If, instead, we simply determined the least expensive way for an American to obtain adequate nutrition, the cost would be much lower.

Human beings can get adequate protein and calories from a variety of readily available grains and legumes (such as beans) as long as the nutritional inadequacies of one are made up by another. Wheat, corn, and rice contain considerable protein, as do many vegetables. Beans are especially rich sources. Other required nutrients absent from these grains and beans can be obtained cheaply from greens such as spinach or sprouted and "greened" grains and beans. Small quantities of nonfat milk solids or vitamin supplements could complete a survival diet. Table 2.2 shows one such diet and its cost. It provides for all nutritional needs using foods readily available to all Americans. A diet with much greater variety could be constructed for about the same cost; Table 2.2 simply presents one of the simplest examples.

The monthly cost per person under this survival diet would be $20.17—less than one-third the figure under the USDA budget. Since actual food expenditures are $145.25 per person per month, this indicates that only 13.8 percent of food expenditures, only about $1 of every $8, has to do with nutrition. A more technical and thorough analysis of the cost-minimizing nutritious diet would produce similar results. If 117 foods are considered and sixteen nutritional needs are taken into account, a linear programming calculation indicates that adequate nutrition would only cost 84 cents per day, or $27.50 per month (Bassi, 1976, p. 37, in 1984 dollars). If economics is primarily about necessity and survival, the

Table 2.2

A Survival Diet

Food	Amount	Calories (Kcal)	Protein (grams)	Calcium (Mg)	Vitamin A (IO)	Thiamine (Mg)	Riboflavin (Mg)	Niacin (Mg)	Vitamin C (Mg)	Price (1984) ($/lb)	Cost per month ($/mo)
Soy beans[1]	1.75 c. cooked	403	34.0	226	80	1.1	0.31	2.7	0	0.34	2.28
Spinach[2]	3.5 ounces	26	3.2	93	8,100	0.1	0.20	0.6	51	0.60	4.03
Dry milk[3]	1 ounce	121	12.0	436	10	0.12	0.60	0.3	0.23	1.63	3.61
Wheat[4]	10.6 ounces	990	42.0	108	0	1.71	0.36	12.9	0	0.18	3.63
Cornmeal[4]	3.5 ounces	355	9.2	20	510	0.38	0.11	2.0	0	0.32	2.15
Rice[4]	3.5 ounces	360	7.5	32	0	0.34	0.05	4.7	0	0.33	4.43
Vitamin C supplement	1 60-mg pill per week										
Total		2,255	107.9	915	8,700	3.75	1.63	22.7	59.8		20.17
Recommended Daily Allowance		2,300	56	800	5,000	1.00		13	60		
Useful protein at 60% utilization			64.8								

Notes:

1. Unprocessed soy beans are the cheapest source of vegetable protein at 1984 market prices. They are also the hardest bean to prepare in a way palatable to human beings. The Chinese mastered this centuries ago. Americans, until the recent development of a variety of textured soy protein products, did not find soy beans an acceptable food source. In a survival setting, however, it is assumed the Americans would be as innovative as the Chinese. Other beans, more familiar to Americans, could be substituted for soy beans.

2. Other greens (turnips, mustard, chard, etc.) or sprouted beans and grains could be used, too.

3. Dried egg solids could also be used as a cheap food supplement.

4. Any mixture of grains including those not listed here (barley, buckwheat, rye, sorghum, oats, etc.) could be included.

vast majority of our food production and consumption is clearly extra-economic or noneconomic. This would be a silly conclusion; a more appropriate one would be that the pursuit of subjective, aesthetic and cultural values in food, as in other areas, is clearly economic.

4. Subjective Preferences and the Pursuit of Quality in Medical Care

While it may be easy, on reflection, to see the dominant role of subjective, qualitative preferences in food expenditures, spending on medical care may appear to be an example of economic activity driven solely by necessity.

Medical expenditures are a rapidly growing part of our economy. Each year the share of our economic activity committed to providing medical care increases. In 1950, it was 4.4 percent. By 1982, fully 10.5 percent of all of our economic production as judged by the GNP was committed to providing medical care. The economic importance of medical expenditures is expected to grow further, especially as the population ages and the percentage of senior citizens grows.

But even in this area, where survival is often at stake, questions of quality, of the quality of life, surface and even dominate.

Everyday language hints at this. We seek to eliminate "disease," to feel at ease with ourselves again. We provide "care." The root of the word health is "hale," as in "hale and hearty," sound and vigorous. Clearly, what we pursue with our medical expenditures is so subjective that we have difficulty naming or defining it. The World Health Organization has provided one definition: "Health is a state of complete physical, mental, and social well-being and not merely the absence of disease or infirmity." This brings us back to all the subjective and qualitative aspects of well-being.

We will discuss several aspects of our medical expenditures to try to discover what part of them is clearly survival-oriented and what role the pursuit of subjective preferences plays. First, we explore the increasingly important role of cosmetic and mood medicine. We also discuss the pursuit of comfort and convenience in the treatment of non-life-threatening illnesses. Then we turn to medical problems brought on by production and consumption activities that are themselves nonessential and that are guided by our pursuit of qualitative objectives, such as good-tasting food. Finally, we consider medical expenditures on life maintenance and find that concerns with the quality of life cannot be ignored even here.

a. Cosmetic Medicine

One rapidly growing area of medical treatment pursues aesthetic objectives almost exclusively. Cosmetic medicine seeks to improve the appearance of the body so as to bring it into conformance with some subjective standard of beauty.

It is not just movie stars any more who seek nose jobs, face lifts, belly tucks, hair implants, hair removal, fat removal, and breast enhancements. Increasingly, middle-class Americans turn to medicine to sculpt and mold themselves. Plastic surgery has developed to a point where those who wish to spend the money have considerable choice in their appearance.

But cosmetic medicine does not end with these rather dramatic surgical interventions. Families increasingly invest thousands of dollars to give their children straight teeth. Although the dental community can provide a health rationale for this common, costly treatment (aligning teeth for better chewing and digestion and reduced wear), the primary motivation is cosmetic. We are pursuing an attractive smile and face for our kids. At a less costly level, we turn to medicine to clean and polish our teeth, to fight skin blemishes such as acne, to lose or to gain weight, and to stop hair loss.

We spend billions correcting weakened vision. Some substantial part of this is simply so that we do not miss a full visual experience. We do not need 20/20 vision to survive and function, but the richness of our experience would be reduced without it. What is lost is quality.

The cost of correcting our vision has increased dramatically as more emphasis has been placed on style and convenience. We are increasingly turning to contact lenses instead of glasses. Contact lenses protect our appearance; they can also enhance it, by changing eye color. The more one spends on contact lenses, the more comfortable and convenient they are. Early, rigid lenses were uncomfortable and had to be removed and washed daily. Some of the more recent soft lenses can be left in for weeks without discomfort.

Those who do not invest in contact lenses may invest in different styles of eyeglass frames, colors, and materials. The range of options is almost as wide as that for clothing, and style is just as dominant. There is almost no limit to what one can pay in the pursuit of that style, as witnessed by the designer frames that have at times been the rage.

b. Mood Medicine

Well-being is subjective: it consists of what we feel. To most of us it does not matter whether the source of trouble is physical damage to our body or emotional stress. Our ordinary language labels both "hurt" and "pain."

For that reason we turn to medical doctors for relief from both. Psychiatrists are, by definition and training, medical doctors. Insurance policies regularly define "qualified physician" to include licensed psychologists. Care for our "mental health" is an important, and growing, part of our overall medical expenditures.

Almost by definition, mental health and emotional suffering are subjective phenomena. This is not to suggest that they are of secondary importance. When it comes to health, the inadequacy of the simplistic physical model becomes clear. Not only can we not define the experience of pain and suffering in physical terms, but we cannot treat it in that way either. Mind and body interact in a complex and dynamic way. Our frame of mind often determines whether we get ill and even whether we die. It also affects what we experience when we are ill. Similarly, changes in or failures of the body influence our emotions.

What we are underlining here is simply that our medical expenditures also focus on subjective experiences as badly defined (but very important) as moods or feelings. We increasingly seek medical help to deal with our depression, our tension, our loneliness, our alienation, our agitation. These matters go to the core of a life worth living. The medical profession may treat these problems with mood-altering drugs, relaxation therapies, or recommended changes in lifestyle.

Chemical therapy for some emotional conditions has become somewhat of a scandal, with physicians dispensing mood-altering drugs that are then used for recreational purposes or overused to the point of addiction. In any case, many of us do not wait for a physician to prescribe a drug to assist us in handling emotional stress. We turn to readily available legal drugs such as alcohol and a wide range of illegal drugs. When these drugs in turn cause problems, we turn to the medical community to help us break our dependence.

c. The Medical Pursuit of Comfort and Convenience

The human organism, at least in a reasonably stable, familiar environment, is remarkably resistant and resilient. Most diseases do not threaten life or seriously incapacitate us. The most common, say the cold and the flu, cause considerable discomfort but are not usually life-threatening. Many injuries are of a similar nature. We turn to medicine in the face of these not to save our lives, but to reduce the level of discomfort and speed the recovery so that the disruption to the regular pace of our lives is minimized.

Most over-the-counter drugs are designed to help us function in the face of minor illnesses: colds, coughs, diarrhea, hemorrhoids, upset stomachs, headaches, constipation, and the rest. Bandages, sunburn treatments, anti-inflammatory and anti-itch creams, and antiseptic lotions also help minimize the inconvenience and discomfort of minor medical problems. We spend billions of dollars on such self-help. Few would argue that we do so in pursuit of survival. The comfort and convenience we seek from these expenditures are, in a way, difficult to distinguish from the satisfaction of fine food, the comfort of familiar food, or the convenience of fast food. Most medical treatment in non-life-threatening situations attempts to protect or improve various qualities of our lives.

d. Medical Expenditures as a Cost
of Consumption

Other organisms—microbes and the like—are not the only—or even primary threat to our health. More often, our own patterns of consumption and our style of life are the problem. This is important in evaluating the survival function of medical expenditures because those expenditures may simply be part of the cost of habits that are anything but necessary. Cigarette smoking is hardly necessary for survival; it provides pleasure or relaxation or some cultural benefit. If it causes lung cancer, heart disease, or respiratory problems that require medical treatment, it is not clear that one should term that treatment a "necessary" expense. It would be more accurate to say that the medical expenditures were part of the costs associated with the pursuit of the subjective preference through smoking.

We have argued above that the American diet is built around the pursuit of attractive tastes and convenience, not nutrition. That diet is linked to six of the ten leading causes of death in American adults. If alcohol and cigarettes are included, eight of the ten leading causes of death are tied to our taste preferences. These include heart disease, cancer, strokes, lung cancer, diabetes, liver disease, hardening of the arteries, and accidents (Lappe, 1982, p. 118). We consume enormous amounts of sugar, salt, and fat in our candy bars, soft drinks, potato chips, and other convenience foods. We alter our moods and perceptions with alcohol, nicotine, and other drugs. One of the costs of pursuing those tastes and feelings is a significant portion of our medical expenditures, including spending intended to avert premature death.

This point can be extended to the production process. If, to produce stylish clothes or attractive household furnishings, we damage workers' health on the job and pollute the air and water, the resulting health expenditures are part of the cost of the pursuit of style and beauty. If the business system that makes possible our incredible array of consumer goods, most of which are in no sense necessary, creates tensions and pressures that ultimately damage the participants' health, this damage too is part of our pursuit of affluence, not a confrontation with necessity.

e. Medical Expenditures and Health

Many consider medical expenditures the ultimate necessity because they often occur in a crisis as we struggle to keep someone from dying. There is nothing subjective about death; staying alive is not a luxury. But if, in an aggregate sense, that crisis intervention does little to extend our lives or reduce the impact of disease, questions can be raised about how "necessary" those expenditures are.

If we analyze what measures have led to the steady increase in life expectancy over the last century or two, medical treatment in life-threatening situations will not be on the list. Statistically, the contribution of the dominant form of medical care in this country is very, very small.

The most important health measures were not medical at all in the conventional sense. They included improved hygiene in the handling of water, food and sewage; piped disinfected water, the pasteurization of milk, and the collection and treatment of sewage. They also included a more reliable and larger variety of food so that malnutrition declined (McKeown, 1976). Other preventive public-health measures (as opposed to private, crisis medicine) were also important: inoculations and public education about the role of personal hygiene in the control of infectious diseases.

Despite this dominant role of public-health activities in protecting and enhancing our health, only 2.7 percent of our health expenditures in 1982 were in this category; 97.3 percent of the third of a trillion dollars we spent protecting our health were for private treatment (U.S. Department of Commerce, 1984, Table 146).

Overall health is *not* determined by private medical expenditures. The essential factors are behavior, diet, and the natural and social environments (McKeown, 1976, p. 167). This is seen most directly in the relationship between diet, alcohol, and smoking habits and ill health and early deaths. It also is seen in the clear medical evidence on the impact of pollutants in our workplaces, air, and water. Finally it is seen in the effects on our mental and physical well-being of the pressures and strains of modern urban industrial life in a competitive society. There is little we can do to improve our aggregate health if we wait until these conditions have almost killed us and then seek salvation in expensive high-tech life support.

f. Life, Death, and the Quality of Life

It is exactly on the frontiers of modern medical life support where quality of life considerations emerge. Increasingly, medical technology allows us to keep a body alive almost indefinitely. Heart and lung machines can sustain a brain-dead person for a long period, or keep alive those who are still quite conscious but totally incapacitated.

As technology continues to improve, even more will be possible. We all could be put on artificial life-support systems as our natural lives draw to a close. Or our bodies could be frozen and carefully preserved for that future day when we might be cured. We could pursue organ transplants or artificial organs as our vital organs deteriorate. Ultimately, there seems to be no limit to the amount of money we can spend to stave off death.

But already, individually and socially, we are limiting our expenditures. Many doctors and patients do not see biological survival as the ultimate goal of medicine. Rather, they believe some minimal quality of life is needed to justify survival; patients, families and medical professionals often support disconnecting the life support and accepting death in cases where the brain-dead or incapacitated are being sustained by machines.

In life-or-death crises, people are choosing quality over survival itself. This underlines the elemental fact that the pursuit of quality, the pursuit of particular, attractive ways of living, has always been the objective. We will return to this point in the next chapter, when we examine qualitative pursuits in primitive, nonaffluent societies.

CHAPTER THREE

The Dominance of Quality in Economic Pursuits, Continued: Clothing, Housing, and Stone Age Economics

1. Protection from the Elements:
Clothing Expenditures and the Pursuit of Necessity

a. Introduction

The survival function of clothes is to protect the body from the elements, and the only truly necessary tailoring is that required to allow a person to engage in other survival activities while wearing the clothing. Choice of materials would be based on a trade-off between durability and the resource cost of making the clothes. In many places and seasons, little or no clothing is needed for protection.

Functional considerations are far removed from our production and purchase of clothing. Cultural convention, style, appearance, cut, color, and texture dominate, not protection from the elements and durability. There are few areas of "basic" production and expenditure where the pursuit of shifting styles plays such an explicit role. These aesthetic standards not only render clothes obsolete before they are worn out, but they add considerably to their initial cost. In addition, convention requires that we have multiple sets of clothes, each appropriate to particular places and occasions.

b. Necessary Clothing Expenditures

One way of estimating what truly functional clothing would cost would be to look at what it costs the United States military to clothe a soldier in the field. Field clothing, as opposed to the dress uniform, is intended to be functional, cheap and durable.

Data are available on both the "standard issue" of clothing to new soldiers and

Table 3.1

Functional Clothing Items in Military Standard Issue

2	belts	2	glove liners
1	buckle	8	pair socks
2	pair of combat boots	2	towels
2	caps, combat	4	trousers, combat
4	coats, combat	6	undershirts
2	coats, cold weather (field jacket)	1	coat, all weather
1	glove shell	6	pair underwear

Source: USDOD, 1984

the cost of maintaining and replacing this clothing over a long period. In 1984, the standard issue of clothing to new enlistees cost about $450 (U.S. Department of Defense, 1984). But this includes a tailored dress uniform with three pairs of dress trousers and five dress shirts, two dress hats, dress shoes, dress gloves and necktie, insignia, brass buckles, etc. At least one third of the cost of the standard issue is accounted for by these "luxury" items. This would put the initial cost of the remaining clothes at $300. Table 3.1 lists these items.

After the first six months, the Army provides an allowance of $6.80 per month for two and a half years to maintain and replace this clothing. For soldiers who continue in the service after that, $13 per month is provided. Some of this is meant to maintain and replace the dress-uniform items. If we again assume that this takes one-third of the clothing allowance, $8.66 per month is intended to maintain and replace the functional clothes over an extended period. Over five years, the combination of the initial cost and clothing allowance would come to $128 per year. This compares with the $664 per person (including small children) Americans spent on clothing in 1983. We spent over five times what the military calculates is necessary to clothe people against the elements.

Alternatively, we could make up a list of the minimal clothing a person would need for protection from the elements and cost it out at prices based on style-free mass production. Table 3.2 does that for both northern and southern U.S. climates. Specialized work clothes are not included. The cost of these would be part of the cost of producing particular products and could be treated as "necessary" only insofar as the product itself was necessary.

If a third of our population is assumed to be living in the warmer southern climates, the average cost of "necessary" clothing is about $143 per person per year—roughly one-fifth the actual 1983 figure.

Table 3.2

Civilian "Survival" Clothing

Item	Quantity	Unit cost	Total cost northern climate	Total cost southern climate
Pants, heavy cotton	2 pair	$10	$20	$10
Pants, heavy wool or synthetic*	1 pair	15	15	0
Shorts, light	3 pair	3	0	9
Shirts, light, short sleeve	7	2	14	14
Underwear	7	2	14	14
Socks	7	1	7	7
Coat, heavy*	1	25	25	0
Jacket, light, rain*	1	15	15	15
Shoes, light	1	10	10	10
Boots, heavy*	1	25	25	0
Hat, stocking	1	5	5	0
Mittens	1	5	5	0
Gloves	1	5	5	0
Sweater or heavy shirt*	1	10	10	10
Total			$170	$89

*These items will last longer than one year. Thus the total cost of the item is the cost listed here times its life expectancy. For a heavy coat that will last, say, three years, the cost is $75, not the $25 listed here as an annual cost.

c. The Aesthetic Function of Clothing

Our clothing purchases, then, are not driven primarily by the pursuit of protection or function. The cut or style, the texture of the material, and the color or pattern of colors are all very important. We wrap our bodies in particular ways to make them more attractive or beautiful, to express ourselves and our moods, or simply to conform to convention.

The extent to which we cover our bodies varies, especially for women. The infamous hemline rises and falls from year to year. So does the appropriate length of sleeves and height of the collar. For men, the acceptability of shorts and their length (Bermuda, sports, briefs) is a matter of transient styles; a similar thing is true of short sleeve shirts.

We choose among various materials on the basis of texture and the social meaning of that texture. Wool, cotton, linen and silk and their synthetic imitations give quite different impressions. A silk dress conveys quite a different meaning than a wool suit. Cotton denim pants are not a substitute for worsted wool ones. A cotton flannel or wool shirt has a social function quite different from that of a starched cotton or silk shirt.

Difference in textures allows a wide range of contrasts and impressions: dull or shiny, rough or flat, coarse or fine, bulky or gossamer, crisp or limp, stiff or pliable, hard or soft, rigid or spongy, elastic or stretchy, warm or cool, bristly or downy, etc. (Horn, 1968, p. 245). To texture is added the tailoring or line or cut: curved, rounded, and flowing or angled, square, and cornered. Each of these conveys a distinct mood or feeling whose appropriateness by age and sex shifts with the styles (Sahlins, 1976, pp. 182–183). Color adds a third source of complex variation. Dark, subdued solid colors, subtle, light pastel patterns, and bright contrasting colors—all convey their own messages appropriate to different occasions, age, and stations in life.

We weave these three elements of clothing design into an almost infinitely complex set of patterns. Cultural and aesthetic expression is the primary social function of our clothing expenditures, not protection from the elements.

d. Clothes as Social Vestments

We do not simply choose a single style of clothes that best suits our individual preferences. We purchase multiple sets of clothing, each in a different style, a different mix of cut, texture, and color.

We have clothes for work—usually, a variety of sets of clothes for work. Clothing will vary depending on the type of job. For bureaucratic or white-collar jobs, more expensive and stylish clothes will be worn; on agricultural or industrial jobs, a different style. In retail trade and services, still a third style will be worn.

Off the job, our clothes are even more complex (Sahlins, 1976, pp. 140–141). We have "house clothes" in which we lounge, and clothes for work about the home. If we are outside the home in a public setting, quite different clothes will be worn depending on what we are doing. At a sporting event, we will wear one type of clothes if we are spectators but a quite different kind if we are participants. If it is a "special occasion" we are attending, the clothes we will wear will depend upon whether the occasion is sacred or secular. If it is a secular special occasion, what we wear will depend on whether it is a formal occasion such as a formal dinner party, or a "gala" event, or an informal one such as a cocktail party, or a night at the theater. We even have sets of clothes to sleep in: pajamas, nightgowns, bathrobes.

We fill our closets and dressers with a volume and variety of clothes that cannot possibly be explained by the need to protect our bodies. When people complain that "they have nothing to wear," they mean they do not have currently stylish clothes, attractive to them, that suit the occasion. Aesthetics and style clearly dominate our clothing expenditures.

2. Necessary Housing Expenditures

a. Introduction

Protection from the elements requires more than clothing. The functional requirements of housing include a cost-effective degree of thermal integrity, space to prepare meals and engage in other household production, space to sleep and sanitary facilities.

The amount of space required is hard to specify. It has varied considerably depending on wealth and position in many societies: castles, palaces, and mansions for the elite, very small quarters for the common worker. As income has risen, so have the size and quality of housing people purchase. Space, and the quality of that space, seem to be luxury goods.

Recently, however, a psychological literature has developed that is interpreted by some as suggesting that mental health requires a certain amount of space per person; crowding we are told, elicits serious mental and physical problems. This literature may tell us something about various animals' responses to living closely with others of the same species, or the social problems of very large congested cities. But human families have a long history of living in very close quarters. Most primitive shelters were single rooms, and quite small at that. Housing in the early industrial revolution consisted of a room, or two at the most, for working-class families. Often, more than one family would share the space.

There is no evidence that mental-health problems were greater in these societies than in our own with the more generous space provided by modern housing. The evidence on mental health seems to go the other way. Our housing and community patterns do not appear to promote mental health as well as other societies did despite the more meager living space they offered the typical family.

b. An "Adequate" American Home

Consider the home that most Americans would consider "standard," even if a significant percentage of our population cannot now afford it. That home would contain a bedroom for each child, a larger master bedroom for the parents, at least two bathrooms, and a largely automated kitchen with dishwasher, garbage disposal, microwave and conventional ovens, large refrigerator/freezer, etc. There would be an eating area and a separate living room. A den or study would double as an extra bedroom. The basement would contain a large finished recreation room as well as a small shop and laundry, complete with a clothes washer and dryer. An attached double-car garage would provide additional storage and work space. The heating and cooling system would be designed to handle any extremes in outside temperature and still maintain the inhabitants in the preferred comfort range. Each room would be decorated to suit the household's individual or collective tastes including attractive wallpaper or paint, furniture, rugs, carpets, cabinets, drapes, curtains, paintings, etc.

All of this costs a lot. Almost 30 percent of American consumption expenditures go toward housing, household furniture and equipment, and household operation. In 1983 that came to $2,650 per person or almost $11,000 per year for a family of four (U.S. Department of Commerce, 1984).

c. The "Survival" Component in Housing Expenditures

Few would argue that, to be shielded from the elements, a family of four has to spend eleven thousand dollars a year on housing. Some substantial part of this is spent in the pursuit of an attractive living environment. That is what we pay architects, landscape architects, interior decorators, and homebuilders for. Our furniture is not primarily functional. We want it to be stylish and attractive. Our kitchens contain all the equipment and utensils that they do, not because we would starve or suffer from malnutrition without them, but because it makes food preparation more convenient and the food more appealing. We heat and cool our homes in the ways we do not to avoid the health effects of exposure to the weather but because we want to be comfortable in a convenient way at all times. The large amount of inside space we buy, furnish, and maintain is not required for our physical or mental health. Sprawling suburban ranch-style homes on spacious individual lots and the communities they make up have not been associated with improved mental health, but the opposite. We purchase all that space so that all family members can more conveniently express themselves. A spacious interior is simply aesthetically attractive and allows a broader range of nonconflicting household activities.

If we strip away the expenditures for a more attractive interior environment, comfort, and convenience, we are left with only a small residue.

Consider the following: In 1982 the median purchase price of a house in America was $82,500. The average size of a housing unit was 1700 square feet. Americans were paying $48.50 for each square foot of living space (U.S. Statistical Abstract, 1984). Purely functional shelter—a heavily insulated building on an insulated concrete slab, like a warehouse, garage, or metal building—can be built for about $15 per square foot (King, 1984, pp. 26–194). If we draw on past American experiences and those of other societies, a family can live reasonably comfortably with 100 square feet per person. It would be very crowded by conventional standards, and space would have to serve dual functions, but the family certainly could survive and function. Millions of families do so today and hundreds of millions did in the past.

Four hundred square feet of functional shelter at $15 per square foot would cost $6,000 to construct. That is only about 7 percent of what the median house, new or used, now costs. Heating, cooling and other maintenance costs are proportional to the area being maintained and would be similarly reduced, especially with a totally functional, nonaesthetic approach. Given that much of the heating and cooling is for comfort and convenience, not survival, this is especially true. We could bundle up or strip down inside; it is just not as comfortable and convenient, however, as maintaining a constant inside temperature.

Furnishing costs would fall proportionately, too, because of the smaller area. If only basic, functional household equipment were included (sanitary facilities, heater, refrigerator, stove, cooking and eating utensils, etc.) without regard to convenience or style, the cost would also be a small fraction of what we now spend.

It seems clear that if we ignored the quality of the environment we were creating and the comfort and convenience of using that space, focusing only on shelter from climatic extremes and space for survival functions (cooking, eating, sleeping, and sanitation), we could cut our housing expenditures by 90 percent or more. The question this book raises is why the pursuit of private interior environmental quality is considered ''economic'' by almost everyone while the pursuit of outside, publicly available environmental quality is largely seen as extra-economic, noneconomic, or anti-economic.

3. Necessary Survival Expenditures:
A Summary

If we take food, clothing, shelter, and medical care to be the biological necessities, we can attempt to estimate part of our expenditures that are committed to the pursuit of necessity.

National data on personal consumption expenditures are reported in general categories, which include these particular categories or at least something quite close to them. Food expenditures are reported but they include tobacco products, alcoholic beverages, and restaurant meals. ''Clothing'' expenditures are reported but they include ''accessories, jewelry and watches.'' ''Housing,'' ''household maintenance'' and ''furniture and household equipment'' expenditures are reported, but those categories include almost anything home-related on which you might spend money. ''Medical care'' lumps together cosmetic surgery, public health, and cancer treatment, among many other items.

Simply adding together the reported expenditures on ''food,'' ''clothing,'' ''shelter,'' and ''medical care'' would account for over two thirds of all personal consumption expenditures. This would suggest that the most economic activity is in fact committed to the pursuit of necessity.

But as this discussion indicates, these categories include far more than necessities. The point of the exercise that has taken up most of this and the previous chapter was to pare down these expenditure categories to what is truly bare necessity. The conclusion was that about 15 percent of food expenditures is on food necessary for nutrition and caloric energy. About 20 percent of clothing expenditures is needed for protection from the elements. Only 10 percent of housing and household expenditures is necessary to provide protection from the elements. We did not attempt to estimate what part of medical expenditures is truly necessary, simply noting that many of those expenditures go for beauty, convenience, or comfort, not survival. In addition, because of the neglect of public health and the emphasis on crisis medicine, most of the expenditures are actually wasted. Our subjective and conservative judgment is that, at most, only one-third to one-half of expenditures on health care expenditures are necessary for survival.

If this estimate is applied to personal consumption expenditures, we find that necessity drives only 11 to 12 percent of such spending. Almost 90 percent of our expenditures pursue something more than biological survival and relief from necessity. Table 3.3 shows these percentages by category.

4. Survival and Necessity in More Primitive Societies

Few are likely to have been surprised by the factual material presented above demonstrating the minor role the production of necessities plays in our economy. The reaction is likely to be that, in a society as technologically advanced and as rich as ours, biological necessity is naturally no longer the driving economic force. However, it is likely to be asserted that in the not too distant past, it certainly was, and that in most less developed societies today, it still is.

The implied fairly recent development from scarcity to affluence offers an intuitive explanation of why economics still conjures up a struggle for survival.

In some earlier period, maybe only a generation or two away, the economy's job was to assure survival; and it is upon survival that most of the world still has to focus. Or so folk history would suggest.

This approach admits that in our own economy, the pursuit of quality dominates, not the pursuit of necessity. For the purposes of this book, that may be sufficient. But lurking in this intuitive history is the suggestion that necessity could easily return to dominance; that because we must struggle to maintain affluence, it may be valuable to continue to give priority to economic concerns as if they dealt mainly with survival.

This section will explore the accuracy of the belief that we only recently emerged from the struggle for survival, a struggle in which most of humanity is still engaged. The anthropological record will be reviewed briefly to see if the contemporary focus on the pursuit of quality is in fact new in human history.

Table 3.3

Percentage of Personal Consumption Committed to "Necessities"

Personal consumption category	Percent of personal income, 1979[1]	Percent necessary for survival[2]	Percent of personal consumption that is necessary[3]
Food	21.9	13.8	3.0
Clothing	7.7	20.0	1.5
Housing	29.7	10.0	3.0
Medical Care	9.5	33.0–50.0	3.2–4.8
Total necessary	68.8		10.7–12.3

[1]*Survey of Current Business,* Special Supplement, Bureau of Economic Analysis, U.S. Department of Commerce, July, 1981.
[2]See text above.
[3]Column 2 × Column 3.

We begin by exploring the assumption that except in societies relatively rich in material goods, the struggle to simply survive dominates. The picture this as-Persumption suggests for primitive societies is one of constant struggle to obtain food and provide shelter, of a life that is short, brutish, and plagued by hunger and disease.

In examining this picture of primitive societies, it is important not to focus on the underdeveloped Third World of the present. What we find in most of the underdeveloped countries today is a struggle to build a social and cultural order to replace the one that dissolved under Western European colonization. These are societies struggling amidst almost complete cultural breakdown. Their traditional patterns of production, consumption, and social organization have been destroyed. Their poverty, desperation, and disease are due to this unraveling of one culture and failure, thus far, to create a viable new one. These situations cannot be taken as typical of what life was like before the emergence in this century of our affluent society. In fact, it is easy to show that the interaction of these contemporary underdeveloped societies with our own economy is heavily responsible for the disintegration of their culture and the destitution they now experience.

We wish to go beyond these contemporary disrupted societies and focus on primitive societies in a state of equilibrium. In those societies, what role did necessity and survival play?

It does not necessarily tell us anything to respond to this question with the assertion that survival had to be a dominant concern or the society would cease to exist. All biological and social organisms must meet certain requirements imposed by the natural environment or cease to exist. But this tells us nothing about how these requirements will be met and how much of the time and human energy available will be devoted to the task. A rich person in our society has to eat, obtain shelter, and resist disease just as any member of a more primitive society would have to. But just as knowledge of this biological fact tells us little about the rich person's life-style, it also is not very informative about the character of primitive societies. Specific, detailed observations of patterns of life and livelihood are needed.

Our current anthropological knowledge supports the following general conclusions about stable primitive cultures:

• Population levels were controlled in a variety of ways so that the human population did not press heavily on the biological carrying capacity of the physical environment (Wilkinson, 1973; Sahlins, 1972, chapters 2 and 3).

• Shortages of food and materials for protection against the elements were not typical. Rather, materials for meeting physical necessities were relatively plentiful in the natural environment (Wilkinson, 1973; Sahlins, 1972; Herskovits, 1965; Johnson, 1978).

• Disease and debilitation were no more widespread than in our own society. Stable cultures allowed biological adaptation to the other organisms in their environment (Dubus, 1968, pp. 69–72).

• Life did not consist of a continuous struggle to survive. Leisure time was plentiful (Sahlins, 1972, chapters 1 and 2; Johnson, 1978).

• A broad range of choice was open to these societies as to how to use the available human and natural resources. Relatively rich cultures developed to guide these choices (Douglas, 1982).

• Style and quality were dominant aspects of even the most primitive of these cultures; Survival was assured with some confidence (Douglas, 1979; Taylor, 1973; Dalton, 1971).

Economic anthropologist Marshall Sahlins, after a detailed quantitative analysis of the available empirical evidence on many different primitive peoples, went so far as to label primitive hunter-gatherers the "original affluent societies." The basis for this was their extensive leisure time. Only two to five hours a day had to be devoted to obtaining necessities and preparing them for consumption (Sahlins, 1972, chapters 1 and 2). The remaining time was available for socializing, ritual, storytelling, arts, crafts, celebrations, adult play, and resting or sleeping. Allen Johnson has carried this further, directly comparing the free time available to members of a primitive Amazon society with that enjoyed by modern French families. He found that contemporary French families had considerably less free time because they spent more time engaged in both production and consumption activities (1978, pp. 55–58).

Not only did adults in hunter-gatherer groups not work continuously and intensively to obtain and prepare food, but these societies developed a variety of cultural patterns that limited the numbers of people engaged in such work. Young, ablebodied people, presumably the strongest part of the population, often engaged in no production activity at all until as late as their mid-twenties. Our modern habit of largely excluding our young people from the work force until after college had a precedent in Stone Age societies (Sahlins, 1972, p. 54). This is hardly the use of labor power that one would expect of people hovering just above starvation.

Many other anthropologists have noted the way culture specifically eases the struggle to survive. A society whose dominant concern is to survive is in peril and in fact, unlikely to continue. Primitive societies, however, adapted to their physical environments in ways that kept life-threatening scarcity at a considerable distance. One way of doing this was to limit the population relative to the environment's carrying capacity. Sahlins (1972, chapter 2) summarizes the results of a dozen studies of the degree to which slash-and-burn agriculture, for instance, exploited the habitat's biological potential to produce food. Those studies indicate that people used only 20–65 percent of that potential. Wilkinson (1973) and Herskovits (1965) have made the same point.

This broad margin beyond subsistence is indicated not only by the limited demands survival-oriented work made on time and labor but in the cultural choice that primitive societies exercised. Not all of the potential food sources were tapped. Readily available foods, used eagerly by some societies, were ignored or proscribed by others. What were delicacies to some were revolting to others.

This can still be seen today. To the Hindus of India, the killing and eating of cattle is both sacrilegious and repulsive, but to the nomadic tribes of East Africa, cattle are a staple food. In Papua New Guinea, pigs are a dominant source of meat; to Jews and Moslems, pigs are religiously proscribed. Americans treat corn as a vegetable and consider corn-on-the-cob a treat. The French treat corn as a feed grain, appropriate for animals but not for humans. Organ meats or the food found in the digestive tract of the slaughtered animal are prized by some peoples; others forbid them or consider them poisonous. Insects and insect larvae are a readily available food source in most places, but only certain peoples take advantage of them. Most others would be astounded or disgusted at the thought of eating such things.

Primitive societies chose some available foods and rejected others. Tastes for particular foods dominated, not an unrestricted, hunger-driven search for nutrition. The broad exercise of subjective preference and waste observed in our own society is visible even in these supposedly subsistence societies (Herskovits, 1965, pp. 271–272).

From a modern perspective, some of the cultural adaptations that limited the demands on the natural environment to well within what it could tolerate may seem harsh. One of the central adaptations, population control, included infanticide and dangerous abortions as well as other crude forms of birth control. The point is not to romanticize these primitive societies but to note that scarcity was not their overriding concern. From the very beginning of society, to be human was to live in a way not directly driven simply by the need to survive. One cannot turn to some imagined past to explain our association of economic activity with necessity.

5. The Dominance of the Subjective and the Qualitative in Determining Economic Productivity

Many common definitions of the economy include some statement to the effect that it focuses on satisfying our material needs. In common language, an economy works if it "provides the goods." Our preoccupation with economic activity is variously attacked for its "materialism" and applauded for the flood of goods it produces. Some social scientists have insisted that only a materialist approach to social analysis can be scientific. Folk wisdom, along with some professional analysis, emphasizes the need to maintain contact with the "real world" of material necessity, which dictates how we have to behave if we are to be productive as individuals and as a society.

Economic theory and professional economists, however, do not support the materialism in the common conceptions of our economy and economic activities. Economists long ago gave up talking in terms of human needs. "Need," they insist, is a value-loaded term that cannot be objectively defined. Instead, economists speak in terms of "wants." "Necessity" vanishes, at least from the analysis of consumer demand. Individuals' "material needs" play almost no role in economics. Given the discussion above about the dominant role of the pursuit of quality in individual economic activities, it is not surprising that the economist's tools emphasize taste and preference.

One might expect, however, that in the production of goods, material reality will reassert its dominance. After all, we have to make our goods out of something and if we ignore the laws governing the physical world we are not likely to be very productive.

It is easy to picture the production process in physical terms and see the material relationships that must be developed and respected. The integrated steel mill with its furnaces, chemical treatments, rolling mills, forges, and stamping machines is a symbol of this. Chemistry and engineering dominate in providing examples of a useful product drawn from the otherwise useless raw material.

But we will not get very far if we try to explain the overall level of productivity in our economy using only the total amount of material inputs (tons of steel, quads of BTUs of energy, number of workers or hours of labor, etc.). One cannot explain differences in the economic productivity or in the growth of productivity among societies by referring to the amounts of material fed into the economic process.

Economists for many decades now have described the economy almost entirely in terms of the use of capital and labor. Raw materials such as iron ore or coal or agricultural products have not been seen as central in determining how productive an economy was. They certainly were fundamental, but they were not the source of growth, the engine that drove the economy. Most societies have access to raw materials, but only a few have been able to harness them in the way we have. Economists have sought to explain that difference in productivity.

Central to that explanation are labor and capital but not just the number of warm bodies and the accumulated wealth. Many societies that in the aggregate are very poor have large numbers of warm bodies available to work—maybe too many—and no lack of wealth accumulated in the hands of the elite. Yet their economies stagnate.

To explain our productivity one has to talk in terms of the technology embodied in our capital and the attitudes, behavior, and knowledge embodied in our work force, including our managers and entrepreneurs.

This moves us into a realm far less palpable than the material universe our ordinary language assumes is the domain of economics. Technology, after all, is ideas put to work. But ideas do not, of their own volition, "go to work." They can be the playthings of intellectuals, objects of curiosity, or common toys, or they can be given practical use: consider Chinese fireworks compared to our cannons and explosives, static electricity compared to modern electronics, video games compared to computer-controlled robotics, or the theory of relativity before the development of nuclear weapons and power.

What puts ideas to work in an economic sense is a set of attitudes or values, one that constantly seeks to improve the way we produce things and does not hesitate because of the change that is involved.

In the case of our society this set of attitudes and values included a secular and religious acceptance of acquisitive behavior and the rewarding of enterprise. The combination of these in the entrepreneur drove and still drives, capitalism.

The entrepreneurial spirit did not emerge easily. A millenia and a half of Christian teaching had attacked acquisitive behavior, the taking of interest on loans, and the life of wealth and comfort. The New Testament is loaded with condemnations of the rich and of attachments to the things of this world. Medieval society was collectivist by nature. Even the trading centers, the towns, set strict legal limits on merchants' practices in the production and sale of their goods. Enterprise was not regularly rewarded. All this had to be overcome for a free-wheeling capitalist economy to emerge.

Thus, one of the most fundamental resources of our economy is a set of attitudes and values. Without it, our extensive natural resources would not have been translated into the affluence that we now take for granted and that much of the rest of the world covets.

The crucial economic attitudes and values, though, are not only or primarily those of our business leaders. Equally important are the attitudes and values of the workforce. Labor is not simply a certain number of calories expended or a particular number of hours spent on the job. The attitude, knowledge, experience, and responsibility of the work force is far more important. Careless work can sabotage any technology. A work force that will not discipline itself is unlikely to be disciplined by a boss into a productive force. Slave societies are not very productive. A work force with limited financial ambitions will be difficult to motivate with wage incentives. Our work force had to develop a set of values complementary to those of the entrepreneur, including a work ethic, respect for the boss's authority, and an open-ended acquisitiveness.

As improvements in the productivity have slowed or stagnated over the last decade, increasing attention has been focused on the American worker's frame of mind, the mental state that controls that workers' productivity. This has increasingly meant concern with the quality of the work situation and how it affects worker morale. The ''quality of work'' has come to be recognized as an important determinant of overall worker productivity. Sophisticated technology that ignores the work force and the demands placed on that work force is likely to fail.

Any personnel manager knows that more is needed than a certain number of workers or workers with particular physical skills. An important part of the hiring process is screening people for the appropriate set of attitudes and values. Simply because this involves qualitative judgments about subjective frames of mind does not make it either noneconomic or impossibly complex.

The basic point is that in the production of goods just as in their purchase and consumption, subjective attitudes, values and preferences play a dominant role. Those subjective values are the force that has driven our economy to the levels of productivity that have historically been its most distinctive feature.

6. Our Perceptions of Economic Necessity and Survival

It should be clear that necessity and survival are not the focus of our collective economic activity. The pursuit of something quite different, namely quality, is the driving force. But we cannot just drop as misleading or incorrect the implications of our ordinary language and shared intuition that economics is mainly about necessity and survival. Such a strong and persistent suggestion has to be tied to something in our experience. It cannot simply be a mistake.

There are two primary sources for this contradiction between our individual and collective perceptions of the dominance of economic necessity, on the one hand, and the reality of affluence and the dominance of quality on the other.

One source lies in the insecurity on which our economic system is built. Most of us produce little or nothing of what we consume. What we do produce requires using the tools, equipment, and property of others. With our own resources, we produce almost nothing. We depend on others to hire us and put us to work. This is the reason for our heavy emphasis on creating new jobs. Even after we have succeeded in the job market, our job tenure depends on shifting spending patterns in the local, national, and international markets. We, and even our employers, can control little or none of this. Fluctuations in the international prices of automobiles, steel, computers, or food can cost thousands of us our jobs. No one can easily intervene. Quite intentionally, no one is in control. And once out of a job, we are deprived of the tools, equipment, and capital to produce anything. We are cut off from productive activity, forced into idleness.

Most of us know that we are vulnerable to this. Our efforts cannot block it. The potential is real. The insecurity is always there.

We face an off/on, hot/cold, all-or-nothing set of economic circumstances. Either we are employed and pursuing the broad range of qualities our economy flaunts before us, or we are unemployed and threatened with almost complete exclusion from the social world built around the pursuit of those qualities. We may not need those qualities in any biological sense, but we most certainly need to pursue them if we are going to participate fully in our community's social life.

It is that possibility of exclusion that terrorizes us: our exclusion from productive work and the exclusion of our families from normal social activities. Our inability to control our job tenure or the availability of other jobs assures that economic insecurity will haunt us no matter how affluent our life-style, no matter how distant an issue survival actually is in our economic activities.

What is scarce is secure employment, not the necessities of life. This is not a "natural" scarcity imposed by the physical world. It is a social construct. We could assure everyone of a job at average wages, but we choose not to because of our fears about the impact this would have on work incentives. In fact, in a capitalist market economy this very vulnerability and economic insecurity is one of the primary sources of motivation. The fear of having to go without basic physical and social necessities is counted upon, along with open ended acquisitiveness, to drive our market economy. We contrive economic insecurity in hopes of creating a more productive economy.

But even this does not fully explain the contined dominance of perceptions of economic necessity in our affluent, quality-oriented society. We do, after all, have a "safety net" in place, intended to ensure that no one goes without basic food, clothing, shelter, and medical care. Why then do we worry so much about losing access to markets?

The reason the publicly provided safety net offers little economic security is that, to use it, we have to have first "failed" in a fundamental way, and then we have to be willing to accept the stigma of being on welfare. Even then, with our survival needs taken care of, our poverty will exclude us from participating in mainstream social and cultural activities. We will dress differently, live in different homes, send our children to different schools, and enjoy a quite different type of social life. We will be on the margins of the larger society, documented failures.

Scarcity as we experience it in our economy is social. We judge what we need by looking at what the larger society indicates is expected of a successful individual or family. We judge how well-off we are not by what we have but by what we have compared to what our neighbors have. We do not ask whether our children or ourselves are warmly dressed in clean clothes. We ask whether they are dressed appropriately given the cultural norm: during the fads of the mid–1980s, we outfitted our children in $30 or $50 leather high top basketball shoes when $10 shoes were available—and almost none of them played basketball. We purchased $30 or $50 nylon pants covered with zippered pockets for our kids, when sturdy $10 and $15 pants were available. Our closets and bureaus bulge with clothes, but we "have nothing to wear," meaning nothing currently stylish. If our home and its furnishings do not meet the social norm, no matter how functional and clean they are, we feel embarrassed and deprived.

It matters what we drive, not just that the car is dependable. The character of the vehicle is a symbol telling our neighbors something about us.

In hard times, men still pay $15 to $25 to get their hair cut. Women pay a lot more. We even send our children to the barber rather than cut their hair ourselves, because the kids might be embarrassed by the less than stylish results.

This is not an attack on style or the conformity of keeping up with the Joneses. We are social creatures enmeshed in a culture that provides the guidelines for an acceptable style of living. This is not something new; as far as we can tell, all people in all times have done this.

We do not stand alone and make an individual assessment of our physical needs. Rather, we learn as we participate in the larger society what the cultural symbols of success and status are and we enthusiastically seek them. If we do not, we are losers, dropouts, on the fringe of respectable society.

Our experience of scarcity, then, is tied to our position relative to others and the standards the larger society sets. This is very important because it assures that no level of material wealth will ever assure economic security to the participants in our economy. Vast increases in the quantity and quality of the goods to which we have access will still leave us worrying about whether we have obtained a large enough share to live like our neighbors. If we have not, we will feel deprived no matter how distant the biological basis of our needs.

Only full participation in the commercial market economy saves us from all of this. It is not surprising, then, that participation in that economy is looked upon as necessary for survival. That is how we survive with self-respect. We have to have a job, for without it, in our specialized world, we are lost. We have to have a money income at about average levels or we cannot participate as full members in the larger society. Necessity, in this sense, is definitely at stake in our participation in the market economy.

This does not contradict the lengthy argument above that our collective economic activity is not associated with survival and necessity. The focus earlier was on what the economy in the aggregate actually produces. It does not primarily produce survival goods or necessities. But the individual participant's point of view is quite different. A job and average income are needed simply to be respectable, whatever the larger society is pursuing. A telephone and color TV set and reasonably stylish clothes are needed, not because survival requires them but because full participation in the larger society does.

Our discussion above focused on what it was the larger society pursues in its economic activities. This included both the final mix of goods and services actually produced as well as the social and cultural "standard of living" that it establishes, which then becomes our individual economic targets—our "necessities." We need to belong and participate even more than we need to survive physically. That is why ostracism was a more extreme form of punishment than execution, and why Socrates committed suicide rather than leave his community.

In our society, then, consumption activities requiring high levels of income are used to document status and position. This leads us all to focus considerable attention on earning income and spending it. Apparently, however, that is not enough incentive to assure commitment to the commercial economy. Our society purposely adds insecurity in the form of unreliable job tenure and uncertain earned income flows. The combination of the two keeps individuals continuously conscious of the possibility of being deprived of social necessities.

Much can be said about this system of motivation. Most economists have praised it for tapping and taming a powerful individual force for social ends. Critics, including some economic anthropologists, have seen its reliance on social insecurity and open-ended acquisitiveness as contradictory and perverse (Polanyi, 1968; Hirschman, 1982).

That debate lies far beyond the focus of this particular book. What is important for our present purposes is to understand how the motivational scheme around which a capitalist economy is organized creates a feeling of economic insecurity, which leads most participants to experience economic activity as a struggle to survive even though it is actually a culturally dictated pursuit of quality. Our ordinary economic language, with its emphasis on necessity and survival simply reflects this individual experience. What these last two chapters have sought to do is go beyond that individual experience and look closely at what we are actually doing in our collective economic activities. Only then can the pursuit of environmental and social quality be put in the proper economic context.

7. Conclusions

The last two chapters have made a few fundamental points over and over again. They have tried to draw lessons from our daily experience within our own economy to demonstrate that what our language and culture suggest about the nature of the economy is simply not correct. The repetition of these points was assumed to be necessary in order to break away from the folk wisdom that obscures the obvious. Here, in summary, we will simply restate those points.

i. The pursuit of aesthetic attributes not associated with survival is basic to all economic activity.

ii. Biological necessity plays only a very small role in guiding economic activity. It is the pursuit of quality, not necessity, that dominates.

iii. The subjective, diverse, and disputable nature of the individual judgments of quality creates no insuperable problems for either the producers of these qualities or those who pursue them.

iv. Subjective values not only dominate our consumption decisions and, therefore, what is likely to be produced, but they also determine how productive our economy is likely to be in transforming available resources into useful goods and services. Here too, in production, subjectivity creates no impossibly complex problems for economic decision-makers. We have dealt with the qualitative and subjective in production just as pragmatically as we have elsewhere in the economy.

The more general point we are moving toward is, of course, that the pursuit of environmental and social quality is fundamentally an economic pursuit no different than the vast majority of things we pursue through our commercial market economy. The pursuit of environmental and social quality is not different and noneconomic because it involves aesthetic, subjective, or qualitative judgments. Almost all economic activity involves these. Nor is the pursuit of environmental and social quality different and noneconomic because it is not necessary for human survival. That is also true of almost everything our commercial market economy produces and sells. The diversity of preferences regarding the environment does not make the pursuit of environmental quality a social problem rather than an individual or commercial problem. Diverse preferences characterize our food, clothing, furnishings, and entertainment purchases too, but that does not make these purchases noneconomic.

If it is not the aesthetic, subjective, "luxury," or disputable nature of environmental concerns that distinguish them from those we regularly pursue in the commercial market economy, the explanation for the different way we handle environmental pursuits must lie elsewhere. We turn to that explanation in the next chapter.

CHAPTER FOUR

The Economic Pursuit of Quality in a Noncommercial Setting

1. Introduction

The previous chapters have established the aesthetic, qualitative, and subjective nature of the goods and services that our private businesses produce and that we as consumers pursue in the commercial economy. This certainly suggests that the pursuit of quality can be an important economic activity. That, in fact, is what drives the commercial world we so often view as synonymous with the economy.

But simply because some economic activity involves the pursuit of quality does not establish that all pursuits of quality are economic in nature. In particular, many might doubt that the pursuit of, say, environmental quality, an attractive neighborhood, or a rich culture are economic. In fact such pursuits, however lofty, may well be seen as antieconomic in the sense that they can be pursued only at some cost to the economy in the form of reduced profits, productivity, and employment.

This chapter focuses on the pursuit of quality outside the market or commercial economy. It seeks to understand what it is that leads us to label as economic the pursuit of aesthetic goals when people buy stereos, restaurant meals, and concert tickets, but to doubt the economic character of peoples' pursuits of clean air, beautiful vistas, or stable communities. Both sets of pursuits are subjective. Quality is the dominant goal. And the judgments involved are passionately disputable. But this does not prevent the commercial economy from encompassing the one set just as well as it may neglect the other.

This chapter explores that paradox. It begins by asking what it is about environmental goods that makes them ''noncommercial.'' It goes on to establish that environmental goods are nonetheless economic in character. We then turn to the variety of techniques economists have developed to establish and even measure the economic value of environmental goods.

2. Commercial Versus Noncommercial
Economic Activity

It is clear that we pursue similar qualitative objectives in quite different ways. Pleasant aromas can be pursued by buying expensive French perfume or cologne, by purchasing an inexpensive "air deodorant" or an expensive air-filtering and -conditioning machine. Alternatively, we can seek to improve the ambient air quality by reducing the levels of various air pollutants in the airshed in which our community is located.

We can pursue beauty by buying the materials and services to decorate the interiors of our homes and landscape the surrounding lot. Relatively inexpensive paint or grass seed may be purchased or very expensive objects d'art. Alternatively, we may seek to save the trees that line our streets, improve visibility by reducing smog, or protect natural vistas and open space from degradation.

The character and quality of our social interactions are important to us. We may seek to enhance these by patronizing certain private recreation clubs, night clubs, or commercial entertainment events where there are likely to be people with whom we feel comfortable. Alternatively, we may seek to protect or modify the social and cultural character of the neighborhood in which we live.

Sound is important to us. We pay more for homes and apartments that limit the amount of noise from other peoples' lives that impinge upon our own. We may buy expensive stereo systems and increasingly sophisticated recordings of the type of music that appeals to us. Alternatively, we may seek to save the songbirds in our neighborhood or reduce the level of noise from automobile traffic or airplanes or general commercial congestion.

Our objectives in each of these situations are quite similar. The object of our pursuit is not what distinguishes our activities in each case. But there is something about the social context within which we pursue our objectives that leads us to commercial organizations for help in some cases and public or political organizations in others.

What characterizes environmental goods and forces us to pursue them in a different manner than the other quality-dominated goods we purchase in the commercial economy, is that in general no market exists where the environmental goods can be bought and sold. Aside from medical oxygen tanks or oxygen-dispensing machines in the Tokyo subways, one cannot simply go to a business and buy clean air. Similarly there are few businesses selling scenic vistas; those that do (for example, travel agencies) usually do not own, nor can they protect, that vista. However much we may value wild songbirds, it is unlikely any business could produce them in a natural setting and make a profit. Although we can hire guards for our homes and apartments, most of us do not see private bodyguards and private police forces as a feasible way to deal with crime and other threats to our physical security.

The fact is that there are very valuable goods and services that businesses do not produce and that we therefore cannot buy within the commercial economy.

The value of these goods to us is identical in character to the value of most of the goods and services we do buy from private businesses. It is aesthetic satisfaction, comfort, convenience, health, security, recreation, entertainment, cultural enrichment, and education we seek both when we shop and when we pursue a variety of qualities in our social and natural environments.

A hard-nosed pragmatist might well respond to this assertion by challenging the real importance to us of something for which we do not have to pay. One obvious explanation for the failure of private businesses to provide a particular good or service is that not enough people really put a high value on it. If we did, businesses would spring into existence to provide it. In this view, the lack of a private "environmental industry" is evidence that the values at stake do not pass a certain threshold of importance and are noneconomic for that reason.

But this assumes that all goods and services that people value can and should be produced by private businesses and sold on the commercial market. A little reflection will show that this simply is not and cannot be the case. There are some valuable goods that by their very nature cannot be prepared for sale by a private business, except at an extremely unreasonable cost to all of us. Other valuable goods could be bought and sold on the commercial market but, for a variety of reasons, we as a people have decided they should not be. In these two situations, the absence of commercial businesses producing and selling certain goods cannot be taken as evidence that the goods are not of sufficient economic value. There are no such businesses because, even conceptually, there cannot be, or because we quite purposely, in the pursuit of other objectives will not allow there to be.

a. Excludability and "Public Goods"

A private business can make money producing and selling a good only if that business can exclude from enjoying it those who do not pay for it. If the firm cannot do that, it will fail to cover its costs or earn a profit and will go out of business. More realistically, it will never come into existence.

Excludability is thus a prerequisite for any good or service to be produced and sold by a private firm. But all valuable goods and services do not have this characteristic. Consider clean air. If the air quality in the city in which you live is improved significantly by an enterprising business so that your eyes no longer sting or burn, the frequency of your respiratory distress is reduced and your life expectancy is extended, that firm has provided you with a service at least as valuable as what you might have obtained from a private doctor with the expenditure of hundreds or thousands of dollars. But how can that firm make you pay for the benefits you received? The doctor could make you pay by excluding you from her or his office, expertise, and care. But the firm cannot make you stop breathing "its" clean air. It cannot be assured of an income and will fail as a commercial business. The failure is not due to the lack of economic value in its services. It is due to the nature of the good: its natural "publicness." Public goods, those from which people cannot be excluded, cannot be produced at a profit by private firms.

There are other, less familiar examples of such valuable public goods. Let us jump ahead and consider a common but, within the language and concepts of a commercial economy, a more challenging example of a public good. It involves the preservation value of a good that individuals do not even intend to use themselves.

We know that some people place high value on historical and cultural artifacts. Those who can afford to do so often spend thousands or even millions of dollars to purchase and protect works of art, for example. We know that such preservation is economically important to at least a part of our population. Otherwise the prices attached to these goods would not be bid up as high as they are. Commercial markets do not, of course, adequately protect all or even most art. Nonprofit institutions such as museums devote major resources to such preservation activities, but some preservation activities cannot produce a private possession that can be purchased and sold, even by a nonprofit organization. Consider the preservation of an endangered species of wildlife in its natural habitat.

If the preservation of a rather primitive piece of pottery or sculpture from a people and culture lost millennia in the past has substantial economic value, it is certainly possible that the preservation of the grizzly bear or condor or bald eagle in its natural habitat has significant economic value, too. Yet how does a business or collector capture that value and exclude others from enjoying it if they did not help pay for it?

The good at issue is not viewing the animal or having it in a private zoo. The good is knowing that the species is prospering in its natural habitat. If some business does arrange for this to happen, all those who take value in this will automatically enjoy that value, whether or not they contribute financially to bringing it about. They cannot be excluded from enjoying the knowledge that the species has been preserved. Preservation of a wild species is a public good. A private firm could sell viewing rights on a "game ranch" or hunting rights on privately owned property, or one could go to a private zoo and see these animals. But seeing a captive animal may not be what the interested people are pursuing. They may wish to protect wildlife in its natural habitat not because they currently wish to see or hunt or pet those animals. They may simply wish to keep, say, the bald eagle in existence in just the same way others might want a medieval cathedral or a pueblo dwelling preserved. Not because they plan to use the eagle or cathedral or pueblo, but because the survival of that thing is important to them.

Economists recognize several such nonuse values with labels such as "existence value," "bequest value," and "option value." The point here is that the pursuit of such things does have an important economic aspect. People do spend large amounts of money on them and probably would be willing to spend more if success was more assured. But there is no way a private producer of such preservation values can keep others from enjoying the benefits of preservation, for others can automatically take value in knowing that the object of concern has survived. This creates the same problem that would exist if people did not have to pay when they went shopping. Public goods are important economic goods, but private businesses cannot provide them because of the inability to charge the beneficiaries for producing them.

b. Social Limits on Commercial Activity

Sometimes the commercial production of a desired good or service is possible, but society refuses to let it be produced and provided in that manner.

Consider voting rights. We could allow citizens to sell their votes. We could also allow the decisions of public officials such as judges, legislators, and governors to be bought and sold. No technical problem stands in the way of this. But we label this bribery and have very strong criminal penalties for those who engage in it.

Many people strongly desire babies or children but cannot produce them themselves. Other people would like permanent, compliant servants. Commercial businesses could certainly provide both of these if the sale of babies and children were legal and if slavery were legal. But we have laws that prohibit both of these viable commercial activities.

Or consider sex. Even though the legal barriers to the commercialization of sexual activity have been relaxed somewhat, most of the population believes that personal or intimate favors of any sort that are provided for payment are not as valuable as voluntary or spontaneous personal favors. A compliment from a paid flatterer does not have the same value as a compliment freely offered. Purchased sex is not the same as love to most people.

These examples may sound extreme; but the attitudes that bring them about are not unusual. There are very broad and important aspects of our lives from which we choose to exclude commercial activity at least partially. We do this not because nothing of importance is at stake but because something of *too much* importance is threatened by the market.

Again, consider basic food, clothing, shelter, medical care, and education. As pointed out in Chapter One, we have largely removed the provision of "survival amounts" of these goods from the commercial economy. Our society, like almost all previous societies, has decided that all citizens have a right to survive. We do not, in general, throw people out in the streets to die. Instead, we acknowledge what economists have labeled "merit wants," wants that should be filled regardless of whether the individuals involved can pay for them. We have at least partially removed physical survival from the commercial economy. We have done the same for schooling, access to local parks and to certain cultural events, and many other goods and services.

Shifting the provision of these goods from the market to noncommercial agencies does not prove they are non-economic. It cannot be that food and medical care for the poor are noneconomic while their provision through commercial businesses to the more well-to-do is economic. Both are economic. The values at issue are identical. The insitutions that provide for them are different because we have concluded that purely commercial forces are not reliable or appropriate for the distribution of certain valuable goods.

For both public goods and merit goods, the failure of commercial activity to provide us with what we want does not necessarily mean that the government has been chosen to do the providing instead. It is often to nonprofit, nongovernmental organizations that we turn. Such organizations play a major role in our economy running schools, hospitals, museums, and galleries, protecting wildlife, taking care of the needy, and more. Earlier in this century, nonprofit groups did pioneering work establishing cooperative insurance, savings and home-financing enterprises, proving the viability of such enterprises on a mass scale (Ginzberg, 1965). They include organizations as diverse as the New York Stock Exchange, Chambers of Commerce, and labor unions. The services provided include basic research, publications of books and magazines, and promotion of local economic development. One cannot possibly conclude that these are noneconomic goods and services, produced outside the private, for-profit sector because they are of low value. They are produced by government or private nonprofit enterprises for quite other reasons.

3. The Private Economic Pursuit of Environmental Quality

The substantial economic value associated with environmental goods and services is most easily demonstrated by considering some well known economic facts.

a. High Rent Neighborhoods

Consider the structure of our major urban areas. Although most of them are plagued by air pollution, crime, congestion, noise, and general urban grime, not all parts of the area have these characteristics. Some neighborhoods and communities have quiet, park-like streets where the threat of crime is quite remote. In these neighborhoods air pollution is much lower than in the urban core. These communities are anything but ugly. Residents take pride in the appearance of their homes and in landscaping their lots. They have nice parks and good schools.

If you were to provide this description of an urban neighborhood to someone and ask for a label, one cynical repsonse might be "the high-rent district." That label underlines an important aspect of our economic behavior. We are willing to pay considerably more for housing in neighborhoods we judge to have high-quality environments. An identically sized lot and a house of similar quality will bring a quite different price in a congested, polluted neighborhood compared to what it will bring in an attractive neighborhood.

This is familiar knowledge to anyone who has shopped around for housing and to any real-estate agent. Innumerable statistical and economic analyses have also confirmed it (Diamond and Tolley, 1982). The fact is that to a certain extent we can purchase the natural and social environment we wish by paying more for housing and moving to a preferred neighborhood. People do this on a regular enough basis, guided by preferences that are common enough, for definite patterns of housing costs to have emerged depending upon the qualities of the neighborhood.

This is important for several reasons. First, everyone is likely to admit that the sale of housing is an important economic act. The fact that in buying a home we are also paying dearly for a mix of neighborhood qualities or amenities underlines the economic importance of those qualities. Further, the subjective, aesthetic, or disputable nature of those environmental qualities does not baffle homebuyers or real-estate agents. Prospective residents of an area can look at its environmental and social qualities, look at the premium they have to pay to obtain those particular qualities, and decide if they are worth that price. They do it by the thousands, daily. It is no different a process than buying a stereo system or an automobile even though it is an environment that is being "purchased."

b. The Flight to the Suburbs

Since the Second World War this private pursuit of higher-quality environments has transformed our cities. No one would dispute the economic importance of the shift of population from our urban centers into ring upon ring of suburbs on what was once farmland at the urban fringes.

This movement of tens of millions of people required a dramatic change in how we use land, how we build homes, how we travel, and where we work and shop. And suburban development, in turn, has changed the character of our center cities. Almost all of them have gone through periods of blight and decay. Those that have recovered now serve quite different economic functions than they did before suburbanization. The move to the suburbs was clearly a major economic event in the history of our urban areas. All those who participated in it or had to adjust to it were forced to make major economic decisions.

But why did we move to the suburbs? On the face of it, we were acting in an economically irrational way: we moved away from jobs and away from convenient shopping. We added considerably to the time we had to spend commuting as well as to the cost. We often had to pay more for housing (Bradford and Kelejian, 1973). By and large, we took on all of these additional costs for one reason: to obtain more attractive social and natural environments. We were buying environmental quality. The shift to the suburbs was a flight from certain negative urban qualities out of which, with rising incomes, people increasingly could afford to buy their way. These included things as basic as larger lot and home sizes at a lower price than was available in "high-quality" urban neighborhoods, reduced congestion, noise, and urban grime, more socially homogeneous neighborhoods, natural amenities such as trees and open spaces, better schools, less corrupt political institutions, and cleaner air.

Millions of Americans evaluated these very complex mixes of urban and suburban qualities and invested tens of thousands of dollars in the pursuit of the mix they found most attractive. These were economic decisions of great importance in their lives. The subjective nature of these qualities did not confuse them. A very consistent pattern of movement evolved as the population systematically pursued the neighborhood qualities most attractive to them that they could afford. The pursuit of quality was already quite familiar to them from their experience in the supermarket and the department store, and the environmental character of neighborhood qualities added no insuperable additional problems.

c. Go West (and South) Young Man!

As dramatic as the shift of our population has been within urban areas, from center city to suburb, there has been an equally dramatic movement away from the population centers of the Northeast to the South and West. In addition, there has been a shift away from our dense metropolitan areas to the smaller towns and rural areas of nonmetropolitan America.

In some ways this change is even more dramatic, for it involves not just relocation within a familiar urban area but movement over thousands of miles. Such migration decisions are important economic decisions. They determine money income, job opportunities, and the demand for housing, land, and commercial services.

But why is our population relocating in so dramatic a way? The casual response usually offered is that people are going to where the jobs are. But that explanation is at best only half true. Why did jobs suddenly spring into existence in the deserts of Arizona and southern California, the mountains of Colorado and Utah, the hills of Texas, Arkansas, Tennessee and North Carolina, and the swamps of Florida? In general, there was no discovery of some industrial raw material in these areas that attracted factories and then people.

Besides, in a market economy, it is not only workers who migrate to pursue jobs. Businesses also pursue a cheap, high-quality workforce. Both the demand for labor and the supply are important. We have here a dynamic chicken-and-egg problem that is not clarified by repeating an assertion based on one half of the causal forces.

To add to the mystery, the areas people are leaving—the Northeast and metropolitan areas—are high wage areas. On the other hand, the areas to which people are moving, the South, the West, and nonmetropolitan areas, are low-wage areas. From a financial point of view, people are moving the wrong way! In addition, the areas to which they are moving have higher unemployment rates (Graves, 1980). Something perverse is taking place—or so an unreasonable narrow definition of economic rationality would suggest.

But consider economic activity as it has been described above, as focused largely upon the pursuit of various qualities. If regions differ significantly in the natural and social environmental qualities that people find important, some areas will be more attractive than others. If this is true of restaurants, home interiors, and neighborhoods, why should it not be true of geographical areas? There are dramatic differences in temperature, snowfall, humidity, topography, rainfall, access to oceans, lakes, and mountains, city size and age, and many other characteristics.

If the bundle of environmental qualities found in some areas is judged superior by a substantial number of people, migration is the likely result unless something else inhibits or blocks such a move.

If, for instance, people prefer warm, dry air to moist, cold air, or seashores, lakesides, and mountains to featureless plains, or new, growing towns to old, decaying ones, they would presumably be willing to pay something for the preferred qualities. That payment or sacrifice can take the form of higher land and housing prices or lower wages, and the acceptance of the risk and psychic costs associated with migration.

Attractive places will tend to draw more people. This will increase the local labor supply, which will have two effects: it will tend to depress wages and raise the unemployment rate. Unattractive places will have the opposite experience: higher wages will have to be paid in order to hang on to the work force or attract a work force, while competition for workers will keep unemployment down.

People voting with their feet can "buy" attractive bundles of environmental and social qualities by accepting lower wages. Alternatively, they can be "bribed" into accepting an inferior environment with higher money income. It is the mix of money income and environmental amenities that determines peoples' economic well-being (Power, 1980; Rosen, 1979; Porell, 1982; Graves and Linneman, 1979; Henderson, 1982).

This explains people migrating to areas of lower wages and higher unemployment. It is no more economically irrational than giving money to a salesperson in order to buy something in a store. If, in return, one gets a valued good or service, the sacrifice of income is perfectly rational. That is what purchasing something is all about.

Over the last two decades, Americans by the millions have been "purchasing" new environmental qualities by moving out of our major cities and relocating at great distances to previously rural areas, to the Sunbelt, to the coasts, and to the mountains and hills of the South and West. This again represents fundamental economic decisions that focus, at least in part, on the pursuit of environmental qualities. People have not had unusual difficulty deciding what sunshine, warmer temperatures, lower humidity, mountain views, and less pollution, congestion, and crime are worth. As with almost all other economic decisions in their lives, they evaluated complex bundles of qualities, weighed each against the necessary sacrifice of income, and made an economic choice.

The existence of preferred, high-rent neighborhoods, the flight to the suburbs, and the shift in population to the Sunbelt and nonmetropolitan areas all indicate that people regularly make economic decisions about the pursuit of environmental qualities. This should not be surprising. If people care about the cleanliness and appearance of their homes and spend scarce income in maintaining and enhancing them, why should we not expect the same behavior toward the aesthetic character of their communities? If people put great effort and money into the pursuit of tasty, attractive food, why should we not expect them to do the same in the pursuit of air that does not make them wheeze and cough or water that does not stink? If people spend hundreds of billions of dollars on recreation and entertainment, why should they not be willing to sacrifice similar amounts to protect natural areas used for recreation, or to move closer to high-quality recreational areas?

These examples are not offered as evidence that individuals and commercial markets left to themselves can adequately provide the environmental qualities people seek. As pointed out earlier and as will be discussed in more detail below, many of the qualities that are important to us are public in character and are unlikely to be provided efficiently or effectively through private market transactions. Migration in pursuit of a better mix of qualities may, for instance, cause these very qualities to be degraded, both in the areas gaining population and in the areas losing population. The costs associated with such ineffective private efforts may be quite high. The examples above of private efforts at improving environmental quality are offered only to document, however incompletely, the practical economic importance of those qualities to people.

4. The Absence of Information and Control

The value of environmental quality is an economic value no different in character than that of any other good or service. The difference between the pursuit of quality through private commercial businesses and the pursuit of environmental quality through other means is not a difference in objective but one of information and control.

When we seek a particular aesthetic experience at a restaurant, we usually know what we will have to sacrifice to obtain it. There will be an explicit price tag on it. Because private businesses usually do not provide environmental services, there is usually no mechanism by which we can learn the cost to us of any particular change in environmental quality. Nor is there a mechanism by which we can regularly and easily indicate what such a change in quality would be worth to us. That information on environmental costs and values is not regularly exchanged. There is no mechanism in place to make it so. As a result, even though we as individuals have a reasonably clear idea of what a particular improvement in the quality of our surroundings would be worth to us, there is no way to pass that on to those who make decisions about the quality of our surroundings.

Similarly, we are not told what it is likely to cost, per interested person, to obtain a particular change or improvement. All involved have to act in the absence of the convenient information that prices ultimately provide in a commercial context. In this situation good decisionmaking is much more difficult.

This is not a unique economic situation. An entrepreneur often does not know at first what people will be willing to pay for a new product. If the production process is new, the production costs themselves may be uncertain. This does not halt development. The entrepreneur ultimately has to take the risk, testing both the market and alternative production processes. The market then evaluates those decisions.

Environmentalists often face similar situations. They see a resource being undervalued and act to take advantage of that situation, putting the resource to a use they consider of higher value. An environmentalist seeking to protect a natural area that faces development for timber, minerals, or housing is similar in many respects to the businessperson who seeks to develop the area. Each sees something valuable to other people that might be lost unless they act. Each sees his proposed use as having the higher value. The environmentalist sees wildlife, scenic beauty, or recreation, all of which in fact are valuable to people. The developer sees lumber or minerals or home sites, which are also valuable to people. Each sees the other's use as a lower-valued use that wastes the area's potential. The point is that the environmentalists are acting as economic entrepreneurs: they see an important resource opportunity about to be wasted and act to see that these resources are committed to the use that they believe will provide the greatest value. The exact value of that resource in alternative uses may be somewhat unclear and the opportunity costs uncertain for both groups, but it is not irrational for either of them to act to protect their access to those resources.

The difference between the actions of the private business entrepreneur and the "environmental entrepreneur" is not that one initially has exact information and the other lacks it. Both act in the face of uncertainty and incomplete information. The difference lies in the possibility that for the environmentalist, there is no holding to account, no checks and balances along the way. The developer will ultimately have to reconcile at least the private costs and benefits the market reveals about his operation. Such an automatic reconciling may not exist for environmental resources, because for them there is nothing similar to the market evaluation of costs and benefits.

Besides information on value and cost not being conveniently available, there often is no mechanism to control the use of environmental resources. When you decide to pursue the complex set of qualitative services your favorite restaurant provides, you know someone is responsible for deciding on the details of that environment and product. Someone is in control.

This is often not the case with the social and natural environments. Until recently, anyone could release almost anything into the air and water we share. In the absence of zoning or covenants, property owners could do whatever they wanted to with their land and buildings. Scenic vistas could be obscured, or destroyed in piecemeal ways. Wildlife could be eliminated. Outdoor recreational opportunities could become scarcer. City congestion, noise, and pervasive grime could build. In the process, things very important to peoples' well-being could be destroyed. But no one could be held responsible, and private individuals could not easily do anything about the loss except move away.

What is often missing in the pursuit of environmental qualities is what economists would call property rights. The restaurant owner is in control because she or he owns the restaurant and can exercise considerable influence over what happens within it. Customers or workers who would disrupt the ambiance that she or he is trying to create can be excluded.

But environmental goods and services are often public in character, and such excludability is not practically possible, or they are merit goods from which we have decided not to exclude people. These characteristics of environmental goods and services can diffuse or destroy control and reponsibility. If this happens, the resources may be misused and the economic pursuit of the qualities these resources can provide becomes much more difficult.

The absence of information and control makes the economic pursuit of quality in the social and natural environments more difficult, but it does not make it any less economic. We simply have to use our intellectual and social imaginations to assure that the information is gathered and that control and responsibility are imposed.

5. Measuring the Value of Environmental Qualities

The discussion above attempted to demonstrate the economic importance of the pursuit of environmental quality and its importance in determining land and housing values, where people live, and the number of people competing for jobs in an area. It also suggests how we can measure the value of some of these environmental qualities to people.

To pursue environmental qualities privately, people regularly engage in market-related activities: they buy homes in particular locations, paying more for "better" sites: incurring moving costs, accepting risk, and perhaps facing lower incomes. They travel to high-quality recreational areas, spending money on transportation, food, and shelter. They take particular jobs only if the additional wages cover the costs of living in that particular area and the problems associated with that particular job. We can analyze that market activity to determine how important those qualities are to people compared to things they pursue in the commercial economy.

Economic valuation consists of establishing what it is that people will voluntarily sacrifice to obtain something else. That sacrifice is the cost they are willing to pay. It indicates clearly the particular value they place on the good or service.

People go through this valuation process daily as they purchase goods or consider purchasing them. They simply ask, "Is it worth it?" The more complete question is whether the money, time, and convenience that must be sacrificed is justified by the value to the individual of the good or service obtained. They also go through this process in evaluating environmental qualities. People regularly have to decide whether the income associated with a particular job is sufficient to justify moving, working overtime, or even risking life and limb. Similarly, they have to decide whether the enjoyment of a particular recreational or cultural experience is worth the travel, cost, and time, and whether a neighborhood's location, schools, social character, etc. justify the cost of living there. Trade-offs are at the heart of economic activity. In a market economy like our own, almost everyone is familiar with this type of economic decisionmaking from at least their pre-teenage years.

Economists draw on the extensive experience almost all of us have with such trade-offs to establish the economic value of goods and services that are not bought and sold directly in the commercial economy. The intent is not to commercialize everything, but simply to tap the fairly sophisticated evaluation skills we spend a lifetime developing. The use of dollars as the unit of value is not an implicit assumption that only money matters. Dollars are used because most of us have a fairly good idea of what a hundred or a thousand dollars is worth to us personally, what we would sacrifice or refuse to sacrifice to obtain another hundred or thousand dollars. We know this because our daily experiences in the commercial economy indicate what comfort, convenience, and quality could be obtained with that additional money. Money does not have to be all that matters. It just has to matter enough that we regularly pay attention to it and know its value to us. There are very few for whom this is not true.

Economists tap this experience with the commercial economy in two ways to establish the economic value of non-commercial goods and services. First, they analyze commercial activity for clues. Second, they question people directly about the value of environmental qualities in a way that mimics a market experience.

a. Measuring Noncommercial Economic Values: The Clues from the Market

As pointed out above, people need not accept the social and natural environment in which they happen to find themselves. They can pursue a more attractive environment by moving, by traveling, or by changing jobs. Economists analyze the statistics on such behavior for clues to the economic values individuals place on various environmental qualities.

Consider property values: if a home is located in a noisy, congested, polluted area with high crime rates, low-quality schools, and dubious social character, we would expect its value to be lower than if it were located in a quiet neighborhood far removed from polluting industry, adjacent to a park and near a good school. Of course many other factors, such as ease of access to jobs and shopping and the age, size, and quality of the house, would affect the value as well. What the economist attempts to do is statistically hold all of the other characteristics of a home constant while varying one environmental quality at a time and watching how this affects property values. The result is an indication of the price people have demonstrated they are willing to pay for a measurable improvement in a particular environmental quality such as noise. Homes near expressways, airports, railroad tracks, and aircraft approach paths do have lower values. The evidence is clear. With careful analysis, the economist can estimate what we are willing to pay to escape a certain level of noise, or how much lower housing costs have to be to get us to accept an increase in the noise level.

That economists might be successful in doing this should not be surprising. Land developers make their livings by estimating what people are willing to pay for environmental amenities. Access to ocean or lakeside property, for example—even merely visual access, in the sense of a view of the water—is worth a lot to people. One finds a simple, direct relationship between property values, distance from the shoreline, and the absence or presence of a view (Pollard, 1982). If land developers can informally determine what a bundle of environmental qualities is worth to people, economic analysis should have some success at it, too.

Take the case of outdoor recreational opportunities. The natural environments that support such activities are usually located at some distance from urban centers, and it costs us something in terms of time and travel expenses to gain access to them. Even if there is no admission charge to use a particular recreational area, the cost of getting there limits use of the area. If one asks people at recreational areas where they came from, one finds, not surprisingly, that the rate of use falls off in a regular way with distance. The way in which use changes when travel costs vary tells us something about the strength of people's preference for a particular recreational area. We have, in travel costs, an indication of the sacrifice people are willing to make to use the area. From that, through statistical analysis, we can obtain a statement of the economic value of the area for recreational purposes (Freeman, 1979).

An analysis of wage rates can convey important information, too. Most people would prefer jobs that entail little physical danger. If we can, we avoid dangerous jobs unless the pay associated with them convinces us that it is worth the risk. Given two similar jobs of quite different risk, the increase in the supply of labor to the safer job will depress wages, while the shortage of labor in the more dangerous job will cause its wage to rise. Differences in wages will tend to compensate workers for differences in risk (Olson, 1981).

Many things complicate this: unemployment, limited job opportunities, lack of knowledge about the risks. Small but cumulative long-term risks may be evaluated differently than dramatic short-term risks, and so on. But it still may be possible to observe the value people put on threats to their lives by observing how much pay they will sacrifice to avoid those risks or how much of a "bribe" they insist upon before they will take on those risks. A statistical analysis of the wages associated with jobs of various riskiness may reveal the economic value workers put on their own safety.

This analysis of wage rates can be carried further. As noted above, people may sacrifice job opportunities and income to live in an area they like. An area with attractive social and natural environments will tend to draw more people. This will tend to depress wages. The opposite will happen in areas people prefer to avoid: a labor shortage will cause wages to rise. Wage difference will compensate people for difference in the quality of the natural and social environments. A sophisticated analysis of the geographic differences in wage rates may tell us something about the economic value of the various bundles of environmental qualities that different areas provide. It will not be easy, because many, many other things vary between areas. But there may well be important clues as to the values of various environmental qualities buried in observed regional wage differentials (Rosen 1979; Power, 1980).

b. Measuring Noncommercial Economic Values: Simply Asking People

Until recently, economists prided themselves in being behavioral scientists who puzzled out the internal logic (or lack of it) in human activities simply by studying that behavior in summary form, as reflected in market-determined prices, quantities supplied and demanded, income flows, employment rates, etc. People revealed the logic or meaning of their economic activities through their behavior, not by what they said. Economists have traditionally conducted their craft as if talk was cheap.

As long as economists limited themselves to the analysis of activities conducted within the context of commercial markets, this approach worked tolerably well. Commercial markets are, after all, information-gathering and distributing mechanisms: they assemble information on what all participants wish to purchase and what they wish to spend. Similarly, they collect information on what it costs to produce various goods in particular ways. This constant gathering of information and the incorporation of it into prices allow a market economy to proceed without a planner guiding or directing it (Hayek, 1945).

But when we turn to goods and services that are not bought and sold on a commercial market, it should not be surprising that we cannot always depend upon valuations revealed by the market: there may be no market to do that job.

This has forced economists to turn increasingly to personal-survey techniques to gather data. Words may be cheap, but some information is better than no information! Over the last half-century, other social scientists have developed ways of systematically and accurately polling a population to determine its attitudes. Economists have begun to draw on some of those techniques to obtain information on the economic value of nonmarketed goods and services.

The general approach taken by economists in these personal surveys is to simulate the evaluation process the individual would go through if the environmental good or service had been sold on a commercial market. The point, again, is not to commercialize something that is not and possibly should not be commercial, but to draw on the respondents' extensive experience with economic evaluation.

An example may help here. Often, undeveloped river sites that could be dammed and used to generate electricity are also important for the production of other values: fish, wildlife, scenic beauty, recreation, and water quality. A hydroelectric dam may convert a free-flowing river, complete with rapids and falls, into a fluctuating reservoir with dirty, bathtub-like rings around it. Electricity is gained, but other things are lost.

The problem comes in evaluating what is gained and lost. Electricity is relatively easy to evaluate because it is regularly bought and sold in commercial markets. This is not because it is a more "practical" or "objective" economic good than, say, scenic beauty. It is because it is easy to exclude people from the enjoyment of electricity if they do not pay for it. The enjoyment of the scenic beauty of a public waterway may be more difficult to control if the river is to remain public. It is even more difficult to keep people who do not even use the river for recreation from taking satisfaction in knowing that a beautiful work of nature had been preserved.

The value of electricity is similar in many ways to the environmental values that may be threatened in its production. Electricity is preferred as an energy source in the home because it provides clean and convenient light and heat. It allows us to operate our television sets and stereos, to enjoy appealing meals, wear attractive clothes, and enjoy relaxing hot showers and baths. These are all subjective qualities whose value we have to determine every time we purchase an appliance or pay our electricity bill. If we can make such judgments about electricity, we certainly should be able to do the same about the services provided by a free-flowing river.

The economists might phrase his or her evaluation questions in the following way: "A dam and reservoir that could increase the supply of relatively cheap electricity may be built on this section of the Colorado River. It would flood part of the Grand Canyon. The pictures I am showing you are the scientists' best approximations of how the dam will change the character of the canyon. If the users of electricity are willing to pay somewhat higher electric bills, the dam could be avoided and the character of the canyon could be kept more or less as it is today. Would you be willing to pay a somewhat higher electric bill if such a payment would assure that the Grand Canyon was preserved? If yes, how many dollars more a month would you be willing to pay for electricity so that this dam would not have to be built?''

The intent is to phrase the evaluation question in a familiar way and make explicit the trade-off at issue. Significant amounts of other information about the person responding would be collected at the same time in order to allow the economist to test for biases of various sorts in the responses and adjust for them if that is appropriate.

Rather than leave the evaluation question open-ended with respect to how much the person would be willing to sacrifice to preserve the free-flowing river, the economist might ask about a specific monthly increase in the electric bill but vary the amount randomly as different people are questioned. Alternatively, the amount may be raised or lowered from an initial randomly chosen level until it reaches the amount the particular person being interviewed thought appropriate.

The evaluation question need not assume that it is current users or "nonusing enjoyers" who would have to make a sacrifice to preserve the river or canyon. Instead, the question can be phrased in terms of the electric utility and its customers making the sacrifice. One could ask those who currently enjoy the canyon as it is, "How much would have to be paid per year before you would voluntarily agree to the damming of the river?'' Or, to avoid a question that converts a public good into a private good: "The electric utility is willing to compensate for the fish, wildlife, and other environmental losses caused by the dam by paying to restore the dewatered and heavily polluted reach of the river 200 miles up (or down) stream. How much per year would the utility have to contribute in your name to this effort before you would voluntarily agree to this dam?''

The question need not be phrased in terms of dollars, either. The compensation offered for the dam could be miles of river elsewhere, which would be reclaimed and improved or a number of fish- and wildlife-habitat improvements, or assured protection for other reaches or rivers.

In some situations the economist may be able to go beyond simply asking questions to simulate a market-like evaluation. The economist may actually be able temporarily to create a commercial setting. For instance, if one wanted to know what the ability to hunt for big game in a particular area was worth to people, one could offer to buy up the hunting licenses from a carefully chosen random sample of people and see what price they demanded. Or one could experiment with access fees and see how use varied with the level of the fee. Such experiments could work only where exclusion from enjoyment of the environmental good was possible. For many public goods it would not be possible; even where it was technically possible, it might be politically impractical because of peoples' strong feelings about the right to access and the unfairness of exclusion, especially exclusion on the basis of inability to pay a high access fee.

The key to success in such exercises is to phrase the question realistically, in terms familiar to the respondent. The economist wants to simulate a situation where, in return for the sacrifice of one valuable good or service, the person obtains another. The loss and the gain that the respondent reports are equivalent, and establish the size of the economic value in question.

Although this approach is fraught with difficulties and the danger of bias, sophisticated design of the interview to include multiple cross-checks can eliminate many of the problems or at least provide some warning that those problems remain. The net result, while not perfect information, is at least some important information about the value of environmental resources.

CHAPTER FIVE

Profaning the Sacred? Economic Valuation of the Natural Environment

1. An Intrusion of the Commercial Mentality or the Development of Social Rationality?

To many even the suggestion that we might try to measure scenic beauty in dollar terms seems silly. This reaction is based on the feeling that such a thing cannot be done, and that, even if it were possible it should not be done.

In Chapter Four we have tried to indicate why it not only can be but is done regularly by homebuyers, land developers, tourists, recreationists and others. Here we wish to deal with whether it should be done.

The chief objection to stating noncommercial values in dollar terms is that this represents an intrusion of the commercial mentality into realms from which such attitudes have been excluded. That mentality includes the conscious weighing of personal gain and loss and the quantification of value judgments, in short, a selfish, calculating mind.

Our poets and pundits have well expressed this objection:

> An economist is one who knows the price of everything but the value of nothing. (Anonymous)

> . . .

> High Heaven rejects the lore of nicely calculated less or more (Wordsworth, ''Inside of King's College Chapel'')

Christ did chase the money lenders from the temple. The Protestant Reformation was partially fueled by revulsion against the sale of God's favors in the form of indulgences. The taking of bribes is a serious crime in almost all societies. And whatever its legal status, prostitution is rarely an elevated profession. There are some fields of endeavor where commercial pursuits undermine and degrade the values that we are pursuing rather than satisfying them: family and community relationships, religion, public trust, loyalty, and the protection of human life itself.

In a very real sense, commerce is seen as profaning, making common, what is special or sacred in these areas. The hesitance to express environmental and social values in dollars is often tied to this legitimate feeling of sacrilege.

2. What Is an "Economic Value"?

Before evaluating the danger posed by the application of economic tools to noncommercial aspects of our lives and values, it is important to understand what it is the economist is trying to do. Much of the fear of the use of economic tools outside of the market place is tied to a misunderstanding and serious exaggeration of economic valuation.

a. Economic Evaluation Need Not Involve Any
Private, Commercial Activity

To put a dollar value on, say, improving wildlife habitat or protecting scenic beauty is not a prelude to privatizing it and selling it to the highest bidder. Buying and selling are not the objective and need not be involved at all. The objective is simply to get a relative feeling for how important such things are to people so that we can decide how much effort should be put into them. We know that an infinite effort, sacrificing all other objectives, is probably inappropriate, as is zero effort. But in between zero and infinity is a very broad range of choice which economic valuation seeks to help us narrow. Economic valuation does not necessarily involve commercial activity. It does not extend market activity to yet another realm. The effort is undertaken precisely because commercial activity has not adequately handled the resources in question. It is a substitute for commercial activity.

There are those who think that rather than having publicly funded economic analysis guide public decisions about the use of environmental resources, it would be better to try to extend commercial activity to these areas. If that could be done, they argue, the market would automatically do the evaluating and no public-policy decisions would be needed. Their idea is to extend and perfect markets rather than use public decisionmaking in place of markets (Baden and Stroup, 1981). We will not evaluate here this proposed solution to the misuse or waste of environmental resources. It is important to understand, however, that economic valuation is not a prelude to this solution. It is undertaken because this commercial solution is not acceptable or possible. If it were acceptable and possible, commercial activity and markets would automatically do the valuing and determine the use of environmental goods. Public decisionmaking would not be necessary.

b. Economic Values Need Not Involve
Only Individual Self-interest

Human beings value things for a broad range of reasons other than the desire to possess and use them personally. This is true in some very important economic activities. Parents, for instance, regularly sacrifice current consumption in order to provide for the future well-being of their growing children. Parents regularly make substantial gifts to grown children and leave them bequests. Those are not simply the result of parents miscalculating and failing to consume all of their wealth before they die. People care about the well-being of future generations and act economically to provide for it. The substantial investments we make in education, parks, churches, museums, basic science, long-lived public works, etc., also attest to the importance we place on goods that are not for our immediate personal benefit.

The motives or values behind such economic activities are not just individual whims or preferences. They are expressions of shared social values. But this is also true of our preference for clothing, food, and most other things. The prominence of beef in our diet and blue denim in our casual clothing are not tied to the individual preferences of isolated households. These, too, are reflections of much broader values.

Economic valuation seeks to give explicit expression to these common values, which otherwise might be ignored or misstated because they are not commercial in nature. Those values can be individual use values, but they can also be of a social or collective nature.

c. Economic Values Are Not Necessarily
Use Values

It is quite possible that people with no intention or desire to currently use, say a natural area, may still place an economic value on it and its protection. Others may value the same natural area because they use it to fish, birdwatch, or hike. Economic values can be either use values or non-use values.

The character and prevalence of such non-use values can be illustrated with an example. The grizzly bear is an endangered species in the lower forty-eight states. Because grizzlies range so widely and do not interact well with human beings, they need large tracts of wild land for habitat. The availability of such land is steadily shrinking.

Some people like to visit areas known to be inhabited by grizzlies because the bears' presence indicates that the area is truly wild and untamed. They may even hope to see a grizzly bear or two, at a safe distance, in their travels in the back country. For them, the grizzly has a use value.

But most of us do not feel better knowing there are grizzly bears in an area where we are hiking, fishing, or camping. Their existence does not enhance our visit; the fear and tension caused by proximity to the bears may actually detract from its value. To such individuals, no doubt the majority of Americans, the grizzly bear has no use value or a negative use value.

Despite those fears, large numbers of people who never want to meet a grizzly bear in its native habitat may be quite willing to sacrifice the commercial benefits that might come from development of that habitat—copper, silver, oil, gas, timber, downhill skiing, etc.—to protect the grizzly. They would be willing to pay the higher prices that could result when development restrictions limit supplies of these commercial products. They might be willing to accept less varied or lower-quality or more congested skiing if that would protect grizzly habitat. Such willingness to sacrifice commercial products to obtain something else is clear evidence that an economic value is at stake.

Economists have identified three such *non-use* economic values:

• *Existence values*, or the pleasure and satisfaction of merely knowing that some resource or quality continues to exist or is enhanced. In the example above, many people who never wish to meet a grizzly bear may take considerable pleasure in knowing that some of these magnificent animals can still find a wild home. Habitat wild enough to support these symbols of our early frontier may be seen as a valuable national heritage even if no humans regularly use the area.

• *Option values*, or the value of keeping alternative possibilities open. Flexibility is valuable. The narrowing of future choices is costly. For that reason, an economic value can be associated with keeping an option or options open. People who have no intention of currently using grizzly habitat may want to hold open the possibility that at some point they would want to use those wild lands. Or there may be some concern that use values unknown to us now would be permanently eliminated if the grizzly habitat is destroyed and the bear becomes extinct. These are related to use values but involve no current use or certain future use. Finally, we do not know with certainty what value future generations will put on the grizzly or on the commodities that could flow from commercial development of grizzly habitat. Yet extinction is irreversible. Delaying development keeps our options open until more or better information is available. Keeping options open has an economic value, as shown by modern commodity markets that buy and sell options and by the higher value of contracts that have options built in.

• *Bequest values*, or the pleasure or satisfaction associated with providing for future generations' well-being. We regularly seek to provide for future generations in both the public noncommercial and the commercial market sectors, and can clearly do so when it comes to the quality of the natural environment as well. To continue with the grizzly-bear example, we may place value on assuring future generations that at least some parts of the nation have remained sufficiently wild to allow this species to survive.

Narrow utilitarian use values are not the only basis for economic values. We will see from the quantitative studies reported in the next chapter that nonuse values often are far more important.

d. Economic Values Are Relative, Not Intrinsic

Economists do not try to determine what a thing in and of itself is ultimately worth. That is a project far beyond economics. Economists are quite willing to leave the exploration of such intrinsic values to anthropologists, philosophers, and theologians. Economists have a much narrower goal: to measure what a small amount of one thing is worth compared to a small amount of another thing. Economic valuation always involves comparison. The economic value of a thing *is* the amount of some other thing you would be willing to sacrifice to obtain the first.

Note that this sidesteps the question of intrinsic value. If people indicate they are willing to sacrifice a certain amount of improvements in their homes to support better public schools through property taxes, economists do not ask why people value public education in this way. They do not ask what the "real" value of that education is. They simply note that people, on the average, have in fact been willing to sacrifice, say, 50 square feet of living space in exchange for the availability of education to all the children in the community. That is a statement of the minimum economic value of publicly available education to those people.

Note also that the economic value can be stated without the use of money units. In this example, we used square feet of additional living space. Instead we could have used additional days of vacation, or additional meals eaten at restaurants, or anything else with which people are familiar.

It is not only in estimating economic values outside of the context of commercial markets that this exchange rate or exchange equivalence is used. Early American colonists measured the commercial value of things in terms of bales of tobacco or cotton. In prisoner-of-war camps, cigarettes have often been used to state the value of things. Ounces of gold or silver have been used for millenia to express economic values.

The use of the dollar as a unit of measure for economic value is only shorthand, a matter of convenience. Originally the dollar itself stood for a certain fixed amount of gold into which it could be converted—say 1/35 of an ounce. That is, the dollar was an amount of another valuable good, ounces of gold, in terms of which the value of still other goods was expressed. The dollar is now the measure of value for anything that can be purchased commercially within the United States economy. Through daily experience most of us have a very good idea what values can be satisfied through purchases in that commercial economy. That is to say, we know the exchange value or exchange equivalent of a dollar.

When we express noncommercial, social or environmental values in dollar terms, all we are doing is comparing the importance of things obtainable outside the commercial economy to things obtainable within the commercial economy. That gives us a familiar point of reference that may help in our judgments and decisions. We obtain valuable things and qualities both within and outside the commercial economy. We often must choose where to direct our limited efforts in the pursuit of the qualities that make our lives meaningful and satisfying. Valuation in dollar terms seeks to bridge the two domains in which we pursue quality. If that bridging is successful, then the dollar value placed on goods and services in both the commercial and noncommercial realms will indicate the relative capacity of additional amounts of any of those goods and services to contribute to our well-being.

e. Economic Values Are Incremental Values, Not Total Values

One of the most common objections to the economic valuation of environmental resources is that, say, clean air or the survival of the grizzly bear is "priceless." Most economists would agree with this objection in one important way, but would simultaneously insist that it misunderstands the limited nature of an economic value.

The earth's atmosphere obviously is priceless in the sense that neither human beings nor most other forms of life could survive without air. But an economist would not attempt to measure the value of the entire atmosphere. The economist would only attempt to measure the value of a small improvement in the quality of the ambient air.

Most people feel a moral revulsion, or at least uneasiness, at putting a dollar value on a human life. A human life is considered priceless in the sense that no price tag is appropriate. Most economists would agree with that. They do not try to substitute economic values for moral values. They do, however, study the importance to us of risks and threats to our health and safety. All of us evaluate daily whether particular risks are worth the comfort, convenience, or thrill that incurring the risk allows. We voluntarily put our health and safety at risk in the pursuit of other objectives. Because we do, there is evidence available about the economic value to us of small changes in the risks we face. That is what the economist evaluates.

If, for instance, it is observed that people regularly accept an increase in the risk of great bodily harm of one in a million in order to save fifteen minutes of travel time by driving faster or taking a shorter, more dangerous route, the economist can say something about the economic value of safety: the economic value of fifteen minutes is a one-in-a-million risk of great bodily harm, or a change in risk of one in a million is worth fifteen minutes. This can easily be put in dollar terms by asking how much money people are willing to sacrifice to obtain fifteen minutes of leisure time. That may be the wage they would have been paid—say, two dollars if the wage is eight dollars an hour. Then an additional one-in-a-million risk of great bodily harm is worth two dollars as indicated by peoples' behavior. This can be stated in summary form: the economic value of avoiding a serious accident that does great bodily harm is two million dollars. That is the economic value of safety to the individuals observed.

Now someone may object that we have crossed the line into the moral realm by putting dollar values on human safety. But recall that the economist is only evaluating small changes in the statistical likelihood of bodily harm. That is something we all do daily without facing a moral dilemma. The economist is simply reporting back on the judgments implicit in those decisions.

Life *is* ''priceless'' but safety, in the statistical sense of risk, is not. It is the latter with which economists deal. This is not a trick or an evasion. It is fundamental to what we mean by the economic value of any good. When an economist interprets the market price of sugar to reflect the economic value to consumers of another pound of sugar or the loss of one pound of sugar given how much they are already consuming, these qualifications are being made for a very important reason. To assert that the economic value of sugar is, say, 25 cents a pound is not to claim that any consumer would sacrifice $1 million for the privilege of consuming 2,000 tons of sugar. After obtaining a few pounds, most of us would pay nothing for additional pounds. Nor does it mean that if there were almost no sugar available, people would only pay 25 cents per pound for it. We know that people would pay outrageous amounts of money in those circumstances. To say the economic value of a pound of sugar is 25 cents is only to say that we currently observe people making their decision about whether to buy more or less sugar at the 25-cent price, and that we therefore know this must represent the value to them of the *last units* of sugar being purchased. The same is true of the value of improvements in life expectancy or safety. To say that our expenditures to protect our lives or the wages we demand on risky jobs imply a value of, say, $1 million per life does not mean that for $1 million we would accept execution, or that no more than $1 million should be spent to save an individual life. Both interpretations are gross misinterpretations of the concept of economic value. A $1 million value of life means only that we are willing to pay $1 to avoid a one-chance-in-a-million risk to our life given the risks that currently surround us. Small changes from the current situation are the ones with which economists regularly deal, not fundamental changes.

The extinction of the grizzly bear or bald eagle is a moral problem of considerable dimension. So is the life or death of any particular person. But an increase in grizzly-bear habitat of, say, 5 percent, or an increase in the bald-eagle population of 10 percent is what the economist would try to evaluate. These may represent a less serious moral dilemma than the question of extinction. Similarly, an improvement in life-expectancy rates by some small fraction does not raise the same moral questions as a life-or-death decision about a particular person.

Alternatively, economists could consciously and explicitly ignore the moral considerations associated with species extinction and consider only the direct use value of a species in, say, developing disease-resistant plants or a new medicine. This latter problem could be addressed in terms of the impact of species extinction on the probability that some needed germ plasma will not be available and a less productive or more costly alternative will have to be used instead. By taking a risk-analysis approach similar to that used above in the economic evaluation of risks to human life, by limiting the analysis to use values, and by looking at situations where there are substitutes available, the economist could cast even the analysis of extinction in terms of small changes from the status quo (Brown and Goldstein, 1984). But in the case of extinction the economist would be purposely ignoring some of the important, probably even dominant, values at stake. The economic analysis would be limited in scope and seriously incomplete as a guide to decisionmaking.

Economic valuation is a matter of small increments or decrements, not "total" values. For instance, no economist would attempt to estimate the value of all the gold or water in the world. Those are speculative or philosophic problems that would quickly baffle the economist. If there were only one ounce of gold in the entire world, what would it be worth? Would it be "priceless"? If there were an unlimited supply of gold, would it be "worthless"?

An economist will, however, try to determine what an additional ounce or ton of gold would be worth, or an additional million gallons of water, in a particular place at a particular time. These are economic questions because they deal with small increments of supply. Questions of "total value" are not economic questions and have to be left for others with skills and tools quite different from those of economists.

It is because economists limit their analysis to small changes from the status quo that they can avoid the very difficult philosophic and moral questions associated with survival and extinction. It is important to keep the scope of economic value in mind in evaluating the legitimacy and appropriateness of what the economist is attempting to do.

f. Economic Values Are Not Statements of the Economist's Values

Often, when people read that some expert has determined the economic value of a particular environmental good, the reaction is, "says who?" The impression is that someone is telling the rest of us what our values ought to be. Worse still, it is suspected that someone is trying to substitute her or his own values for our own in important decisions. An estimated economic value of a noncommercial good is taken as the opinion of the estimator.

This is not what economists do. Their estimates of economic value are not complex statements of their personal values. Rather, they are estimates of how the general population actually values the good in question. This is not based primarily on personal opinion or guesswork, but on the analysis of empirical data detailing how people behave with respect to those goals. Economics is an empirical science. Although economists' values motivate, guide, and can distort their analyses, they are not what economists report on.

g. Economic Values Do Not Prejudge Environmental Rights

One of the aspects of economic valuation that makes many noneconomists suspicious of the entire approach is the economist's traditional emphasis or "willingness to pay." Confronted with this way of stating the importance of an environmental good, many bristle: "Why should I pay *anything* for what I already have? Let the bastard who's trying to take something away pay! If anything, I should be compensated for my loss."

This response is not just an assertion of a particular view of fairness. It is correct economics. In a situation where something is being taken from people, the correct measure of value *is* the amount of compensation that would lead these people to agree to the loss. Willingness to pay is an inappropriate measure of economic value in that situation.

Economists' traditional emphasis on willingness to pay is not tied to an implicit prejudging of who has the right to use or enjoy environmental services. It flows from a more general view of the human condition: that when resources are scarce, we can do one thing only at the cost of not being able to do something else. We have to sacrifice some valuable opportunities in order to pursue any particular economic value. Those trade-offs, those sacrificed opportunities, are the basis for economic valuation. The very meaning of economic value is tied to those sacrifices: the economic value of anything is indicated by the value of the things we are willing to sacrifice to obtain it.

Willingness to sacrifice alternative possibilities and willingness to pay sound similar, but they are not the same. In any particular situation, a focus on willingness to pay raises questions of who should be paying whom. Now we are talking about possible conflicts between individuals, not simply describing the unfortunate conditions scarcity imposes upon us. In any particular situation it very much matters who is going to bear the cost of a change. It matters both because questions of fairness and rights are raised and because the decision on who has what rights to environmental goods affects the measurement of the economic values at stake.

Some might think that quite similar answers would be given to the questions "What would you be willing to pay to continue fishing here?" and "How much would you have to be paid before you would agree to changes that will effectively make fishing here impossible?" In fact, economists have long believed that except under extreme circumstances there should not be much difference in the response to these two questions. Ability to pay—that is, income level—certainly puts a cap on willingness to pay, while it does not limit willingness to accept compensation in the same way. So someone who is poor but receives substantial value from an environmental resource might well give dramatically different answers to these two questions. But even in this situation economists believed that the divergence between the two answers should be limited to a relatively narrow range.

Besides, economists were suspicious of the open-ended nature of the compensation question. If one had to gather this information by actually surveying people, economists thought, asking about willingness to pay would put people in a more realistic and disciplined frame of mind. They would have to think about sacrificing part of their limited income when stating the economic value of something to themselves. But the compensation question had no upper limit on possible responses. Economists, possibly showing their doubts about the reality or importance of environmental goods, feared that this open-endedness would encourage exaggerated and inaccurate responses: "The sky's the limit!"

Experimental data coming from both psychologists and economists indicate quite clearly that willingness to pay and willingness to accept compensation are quite different concepts to people. People value what they know and have in an entirely different way than something they do not have but are trying to obtain. Thus, for instance, if you distribute raffle tickets of equal value and then study peoples' willingness to trade those tickets, you will find that you have to pay them much more to give up a ticket than they themselves are willing to pay to get a ticket to start with. That is a well-tested observation of how people value things. It suggests that when we are evaluating threats to environmental resources that people now enjoy, we should not be using a willingness to pay conception of value but a compensation measure. Use of a willingness-to-pay approach will lead to substantial underestimates of the real value to people of that environmental good. The difference between the two approaches can be *very* large. Compensation value can be two to ten times willingness to pay (Knetsch and Sinden, 1984; Knetsch, 1984)! This is important to keep in mind when, in the next chapter, we explore the available data on the quantitative importance of environmental goods. Most of that information is based on willingness to pay and in that sense may seriously understate the values at issue.

3. The Dangers of Economic Valuation

Economic valuation does not introduce commercial activity or values into non-commercial fields. It does not challenge intrinsic or moral values because it deals with a much more narrow and limited aspect of value than do philosophers and spiritual leaders. Economic valuation seeks to offer immediate practical assistance to decisionmaking by sidestepping the larger question of the "real" value of things. Its focus is restricted to the relative value of small changes from the status quo. In that sense economic valuation is very limited in its ambitions and pretensions. This is both its strength and its weakness. That narrow focus allows economics to concentrate its analytical power on particular, practical problems. At the same time, by avoiding fundamental philosophical, political, and moral problems, economics becomes uncritical of people's preferences and values. It is, in that way, directionless and unguided; at best, it is a tool and nothing more. At worst, it is philosophically biased by its long association with the interests of the commercial economy.

Having insisted on the usefulness of the economists' approach to protecting environmental and social goods, it must be admitted that economic valuation does impart some aspects of the commercial frame of mind into noncommercial areas. This may in fact make it dangerous to the values we seek to protect. It may still profane the sacred.

It does this in at least three ways. First, it insists on comparing our judgments in noncommercial activities with our judgments in commercial activities. Second, it assumes the existence of some common dimension in all values. Third, it is quantitative and calculating.

a. Is Nothing Sacred?

Economic valuation uses as a reference point the values we regularly obtain by participating in commercial activity: earning income and purchasing goods and services. The value of noncommercial qualities is established by comparing them to the qualities we pursue in the market. That comparison is central to the economic valuation process, but it is at least possible that what is pursued outside of commercial activity is simply not comparable to what we seek through the market. If that is the case, we may both demean the noncommercial values and misstate those values when we put them in economic terms.

All societies have limited the domain of the market to those areas where it was felt that free rein could be given to the competitive pursuit of private interests. When broader issues were at stake, issues going to the heart of the character of the society, a market solution was regularly rejected. This suggests that we carry within us at least two different types of values: self-interested ones tied to our personal desires and public or social ones associated with our moral or social convictions.

These distinctions are as old as our political and moral traditions, dating back to ancient Greece and the origins of the Judeo-Christian tradition. They are embodied in our laws and codes of ethics governing public officials. Public officials are expected to separate their private financial interests from their public responsibilities. They are expected to put on a different hat when they step into the public arena. We all are expected to have separate categories in our minds labeled "private, household" and "want" on the one hand and "public, social," and "conviction" on the other. Different behavior patterns and modes of thought are considered appropriate to the two different settings.

In the past, societies have made major efforts to keep the private, selfinterested aspect of our thinking and behavior under control, confined to narrow spheres of activity. This is the reason that in many societies, including medieval Europe, only those who were not members of the community could engage in unrestricted commercial activity: Jews in Europe, Moslems in West Africa, Indians in East Africa, etc. Such calculating, self-seeking behavior was considered socially dangerous and at least amoral if not immoral. Full members of a society were expected to think and act in terms broader than their personal interests.

But economic analysis makes no distinction between private desires and public convictions. It merges them into "interests" or "preferences." That may well not be the way people actually look at the world or, more importantly, it may not be the way people should look at the world if they are to maintain a productive society. Maybe we need two separate valuation processes, one for satisfying private interests and another for analyzing public interests. Economics, by using the commercial market as a reference point, may implicitly be importing a private, individualistic perspective into what ought to be a public or social process (Sagoff, 1981).

At best, this builds confusion into the evaluation process economists advocate. People's private, commercially-oriented activities are used to evaluate their preferences for public conditions and environments. Expressions of personal desires in the marketplace are used to approximate their moral convictions. When people are interviewed about the intensity of their convictions about public conditions, they are intentionally encouraged to respond with reference to their private desires in commercial markets. Economists mix the private and the public, desires and convictions, indiscriminately.

What impact this has on economists' estimates of people's "public" values is unclear. It might seem to understate them systematically, because those values are suppressed by the very way economists phrase their questions and limit their study of human behavior. But those "public" values may, in a given situation, add to or subtract from the total economic value. All we know is that economists' estimates are inaccurate because an important part of our preferences is implicitly suppressed or confused in the estimating process itself.

This potential noncomparability between social and private values is just one example of the dangers of directly comparing all qualities that are important to us. Economic valuation assumes everything is comparable to everything else. Within the limited realm of problems economists address, nothing is immune from scrutiny. Economists would be perfectly willing to estimate the economic value (relative, incremental value) of a cow to a Hindu or of consecrated bread to a Christian. To most noneconomists such efforts would simply be silly. No reliable information would result from comparing noncomparables. These examples may represent another extreme, but the point is more general. People may not directly compare all valuable things to each other in making their judgments. If that is true, economists cannot assume that they do and expect accurate or meaningful results (Lutz and Lux, 1979, chapter 3).

How much noncomparability is there in our actual evaluation processes? Public values do spill over and influence private values. People do seek consistency between their social values and their private lives. People do boycott stores and products to express social values. They do adjust purchasing patterns to match their moral and social values. There is interaction between different types of values; whether there is enough to justify the economists' approach, we cannot now say. Whether the actual degree of comparability between different types of values is socially or morally appropriate is a question beyond the scope of this study.

b. Is There a Common Denominator to All That We Pursue?

The statement of economic values in dollar terms or any other terms assumes that however complex the pursuit of quality or the mix of qualities we seek, the economic value of those qualities can be stated with reference to a single measure. The assumption is that there is some common denominator to the qualities we seek or our enjoyment of them, that allows us to construct a simple, one dimensional, quantitative measure of their relative capacity to affect our well-being. Some may simply not believe that this is true. Forcing of the comparison of all qualities into these terms may be seen as both destructive of the qualities being pursued and inaccurate.

Economists seem to assume that our entire experience takes place in some uniform psychic medium whose characteristics are similar for all members of a society. This allows one person's evaluation of fine wine to be compared to his or her evaluation of diapers and visits to the doctor's office. The value of these can be ''added up.'' This uniform psychic fabric then allows this person's aggregate values to be combined with other people's evaluations of still quite different qualities into a larger social aggregate. That is exactly what economists do when they evaluate air quality in a neighborhood or national park: the value of improved air quality is introduced into the individual's personal budget considerations to be compared with everything else on which the person spends money—hairpins, newspapers, aspirin, orange juice, and so on. From this comparison comes an individual statement of economic value. The same is done for thousands of other individuals and the resulting statements of economic value are arithmetically combined to produce a single numerical statement of economic value that claims a certain amount of precision.

In developing the theoretical basis for this process, economists have actually talked in terms of a psychic unit of measurement, the ''util'' (for utility). For many decades, discussion of economic valuation in such terms has been unfashionable. But the presumption of some such common denominators still underlies the aggregation of economic values across qualities and people. We may use dollars as units that sound less mythical and more concrete, but economists are still making a very questionable assumption about people's evaluation processes. Little or no empirical or theoretical analysis supports that assumption.

c. A Social Calculus or a Commercial Intrusion?

Economic valuation is a quantitative process of adding up benefits, subtracting out costs, and calculating the bottom line. In that sense it mimics the behavior of the merchant, the calculus of profit and loss.

This is not surprising. Economics emerged as a separate discipline while seeking to explain the hidden social logic of the market economy. Economists have been enamored of how well the market allocates resources. They have devoted most of their efforts to explaining how consumers, business firms, and societies can squeeze the most out of their limited resources. They seek to apply the maximizing logic of the business firm to the larger society in order to improve the use of social resources.

Economists may assume that a society as a whole has objectives and preferences as simple as those of the business firm. They may also assume that the society is neutral about the means used to attain its objectives. The economists' conception of society is that of an organization with a simple objective that can be pursued single-mindedly using all the resources available.

This conception of the larger society as just one big shopkeeper seeking to maximize "profits" may not jibe very well with most of our beliefs about political and civic virtue and the pursuit of the public interest. It is possible that citizens do not want their political and social institutions to be calculating in this way. They may want to see commercial and noncommercial institutions run in entirely different manners.

It should be clear that economic valuation is not a neutral process. Economic analysis is not just a tool. The approach of the economist has embedded in it particular, maybe even peculiar, assumptions about human beings and their societies. Economics carries significant philosophical baggage that needs to be evaluated before the results of economists' exercises are embraced as accurate or useful.

We will not attempt to assess here the dangers posed by these aspects of the economic-valuation process. (See Kelman, 1981, and Lutz and Lux, 1979.) Implicit in all of them is a criticism of how well the commercial market economy itself performs in helping us obtain the qualities that make life satisfying and meaningful. As we pointed out in Chapter Four, our pursuit of quality is not limited to the noncommercial realm. It also dominates our commercial activities, there we constantly compare the importance and cost to us of diverse and disparate qualities. We are also ultimately forced to reduce that comparison to a common dimension: dollar cost and available income. In doing all of this on a daily basis, it is hard not be "calculating."

If this is destructive of the pursuit of quality in the commercial realm, it is certainly also likely to be so outside of that realm. If it is somewhat distorting but useful in allowing us to pursue what is important to us in the commercial realm, that may also be true in other areas of human activity. It is on that tentative basis that we will proceed to attempt to quantify the substantial economic importance of noncommercial environmental and social values.

CHAPTER SIX

Beauty and the Beast: Quantitative Evidence on the Economic Importance of Environmental Quality

1. Introduction

In the previous chapters we have tried to make several points. First, we have insisted that the pursuit of quality is a dominant objective of all economic activity, including activity in the commercial marketplace. Second, we explained why, in many situations, commercial businesses cannot adequately provide the goods and services we want and why we feel uneasy depending on commercial activities to provide certain valued things. Third, environmental qualities, social and natural, often are among the things the commercial market cannot provide in the way we wish. Finally, despite the failure of commercial markets to provide these environmental goods or to value them adequately, there are tools that will allow us to estimate their economic value.

What we wish to do in this chapter is use those tools to provide some feeling for the relative size of these environmental values. To do this we will attempt to measure their relative importance in terms of both what we would sacrifice to obtain them and the commercially available goods and services we would demand as compensation for their loss. That is to say, we will attempt to state those values in dollar terms.

We deliberately begin with the most "aesthetic" of these environmental qualities, scenic beauty. We then turn to environments that are usually characterized in moral or cultural terms: wildlands. We follow that up with one of the most "practical" aspects of environmental quality, its capacity to keep us healthy and alive. We consider the economic damage done by air pollution in raising morbidity and mortality rates. We also look at crime and the value of security from it.

2. Beauty: The Economic Value of Visual Quality

In those criticisms of environmental preservation that pose as economic, one of the most common targets is the concern with visual appearance. Environmentalists, we are told, want things to look pretty even if it costs people their jobs and income. We are reminded by critics that beauty is subjective; the implication is that it cannot be worth the sacrifice of jobs and hard cash. It seems almost as if the proof of hard-nosed realism in the face of environmental and social concerns is to attack as fuzzy-minded the aesthetic basis of those concerns and stand firmly in favor of any economic activity that generates jobs and money income.

This dismissal of the economic importance of the visual quality of the world around us is completely in conflict with what both the commercial market and everyday behavior tell us.

a. The Impact of an Attractive View on Land Values

Scenic vistas are not things of little economic value. Home, hotel, and office sites with an attractive view command a very high premium. The availability of that view dramatically changes the value of the land, rental prices, and the height and character of the buildings. For instance, an analysis of residential rental values in the Chicago area revealed that if other characteristics are similar, proximity to Lake Michigan and a view of the lake from an apartment building caused rental costs to rise 26 percent compared to otherwise identical apartments without these advantages. With people spending 20 to 25 percent of their income on housing, this represents a sacrifice of 5 to 6 percent of their income in the pursuit of this particular form of visual quality (Pollard, 1982).

This strong economic demand for scenic beauty also had a major impact on the character of the city's buildings. Buildings with a view of the lake were two to four times as tall as other buildings, so that that view could be more fully exploited and marketed. Another preferred view had an effect as well. Buildings in the central business district, the Loop, that lacked a view of either the Loop or the Lake averaged 17 stories in height, while those with a view of either of the Loop or the Lake averaged 30 stories. Buildings with a view of both the Loop and the Lake had an average of 54 floors (Pollard, 1982).

These are hard-nosed business people who build or rent these buildings. They recognize the economic importance of scenery and act on it without hesitation or confusion. Similarly, the hundreds of thousands of people who live in the apartments with views do not complain daily about having to sacrifice a major chunk of their family income to have that view. It is important enough to them that they sacrifice other things they could be purchasing. One could dismiss them as the affluent elite who can afford such things, but if it is only a lack of income that keeps the rest of the population from expressing similar preferences, it is unclear that this undermines in any way the economic importance of such views. It may be that only the rich can afford gold and diamonds, but that is hardly evidence that gold and diamonds do not in fact have a high economic value.

b. The Economic Value of a Shoreline

Property close to a lakeshore is also sought after for the aesthetic environmental qualities the lake provides. Property on the lakeshore itself is so valuable it is often sold by the foot rather than by the acre or fraction of an acre. That high value carries over into the surrounding neighborhood. The closer a house is to the shoreline, the higher its value compared to a similar house located a greater distance away.

An analysis of housing prices in Seattle quantified the value of proximity to a lakeshore. The sale price of homes bought and sold in the vicinity of Green Lake, Haller Lake, and Lake Washington were analyzed to determine the way closeness to the lakes influenced the value of the house, all other things (like house size, age and quality) held constant. On average a house within 300 feet of Lake Washington cost $19,000 more than a similar house half a mile from the Lake. Having a park buffer along the shoreline added to this value. The wider the buffer, the higher the additional value to homes in the vicinity. Thus around Green Lake, houses on the side with a 300 foot park buffer sold on average for $4,400 more than similar houses on the side with only a 100 foot buffer (Brown and Pollakowski, 1977, pp. 274–75; all dollar values in 1985 dollars).

An analysis of property values along Lake Michigan revealed the same pattern. Land on or very close to the lakefront sold at prices twice as high as land just 500 feet inland. As the distance from the lake increased to 1,500 feet, the value of the land fell to a fifth of that of the lakefront land (Grimes, 1983, p. 154). It takes about six minutes to stroll 1,500 feet! Anyone living at that distance who wished to visit the lakeshore could easily do so. Despite this easy access, people were willing to pay a very high premium to live as close as possible to this particular natural environment. It is highly unlikely that the millions of people in the United States who have purchased immediate access to such natural areas at considerable cost to themselves are all deranged environmentalists. More likely, they are normal citizens who are expressing the high economic value they place on this particular type of environmental good. If more of us had the incomes they have, more of us would be able to make similar expressions of the economic value of such natural environments.

c. The Economic Value of Clean Air
in Residential Neighborhoods

Visual quality is not just determined by the availability of scenic vistas. Air pollution can, among other things, drastically change visibility by creating a more or less dense haze that blocks or obscures and generally diffuses sunlight.

The chemical content of the pollution can also cause discomfort, making the eyes smart and water.

This could be treated as a minor inconvenience except for the fact that that is not how people treat it when they go about purchasing or renting a place to live. Consider the Los Angeles area, famous for its air pollution. Not all of the metropolitan area suffers equally from the pollution. Because of the city's rolling terrain and the presence of the Pacific Ocean, some neighborhoods regularly have good air quality while others suffer. This allows a pairing of neighborhoods with similar housing and socioeconomic and community characteristics but significant differences in air quality. Statistical analysis can then be carried out to isolate the impact of air quality on property values when other characteristics of the property are held constant.

Such an analysis indicates that, when buying housing in higher-income neighborhoods, families were willing pay about $284 per month more for better air; for lower-income neighborhoods, the figure was about $84 per month for the same air-quality improvement (Brookshire et al., 1982, p. 173; dollar values in 1985 dollars). The air-quality improvement represented a reduction of about 60 percent in both nitrogen dioxide and suspended particulate. If one assumes that low-income folks have the same ability to enjoy clean air as their more affluent fellow citizens but simply do not have the income to express that desire as strongly when bidding in housing markets, then the value of clean air in the high-income neighborhoods might be taken as indicating the relative economic importance of clean air when money is no object. In a public-policy setting where access to clean air is at stake, this higher value may be the most appropriate one to use.

The Los Angeles region is not known as a stronghold of bleeding-heart liberalism. Rather, it has become a symbol of a late-20th-century lifestyle built around materialism and commercialism. Nor is what was recorded in this study (and dozens of similar studies) an expression of political preference or idle aesthetic judgments. Southern Californians spend considerable shares of their income pursuing clean air: $284 per month is $3,400 per year and $102,000 over the life of a 30-year mortgage! Clean air obviously has considerable economic value to these people, and presumably, to most of the rest of the population.

Analysis of property values in various parts of Boston reveal a similar pattern. The less pollution, all other things held constant, the more homebuyers are willing to pay for homes of similar character and quality. In heavily polluted neighborhoods, the data indicate that high-income households would be willing, on average, to pay $8,370 for an 11 percent reduction in pollution. Low-income households were willing to pay $4,185 for the same reduction (Harrison and Rubinfeld, 1978; adjusted to 1985 dollars).

Instead of determining what people are willing to pay in higher property values to obtain cleaner air, we can analyze the way salary levels for highly mobile occupations vary geographically with the level of air quality, all other things again being held constant. One such study analyzed university professors' salaries. It adjusted statistically for the character of the school, the characteristics of the town besides air pollution, and the experience and characteristics of the professor. It then isolated the impact of different levels of air pollution on salaries, calculating the additional income that would have to be provided to the average professor to compensate her or him for a decline in air quality. In areas with high air quality, a full professor would require, on average, $2,240 per year to accept a significant increase in pollution, an increase equal to the average variation in pollution levels across the nation. Assistant professors would require on average $1,100 per year to accept that sort of deterioration in air quality (Bayless, 1982; adjusted to 1985 dollars). An analysis of a much broader range of jobs in urban areas indicated that workers in St. Louis would be willing to pay close to $1,800 to obtain a 30 percent reduction in sulfur dioxide in the ambient air (Cropper and Arriaga-Salinas, 1980; adjusted to 1985 dollars).

These results are based on data from 1960 and 1970, when knowledge and concern about air pollution may not have been what they are today. For that reason, these may be underestimates.

If these results are applied to the entire working population, we are clearly talking about tens or hundreds of billions of dollars nationwide.

d. The Economic Value of Visibility in National Parks

The examples above of how visual quality is reflected in market prices certainly indicate that scenery or a clear view is an economic resource of considerable value. Other studies of human behavior reinforce this conclusion. When atmospheric visibility is high, participation rates in a broad range of outdoor activities increase significantly and the number of television sets in use falls to a low level (Tolley, 1983). Since it is unlikely that clean air damages TV sets or TV reception or that it causes the quality of programming to deteriorate, this change in behavior can only be interpreted to mean that clean air is a preferred good of some value to people.

That value cannot always or even usually be expressed well in commercial markets. Often it is impossible or very costly to exclude people who do not pay for it from enjoying scenery or clear air. Just as important, there are social or economic reasons for not wishing to do so. In that situation economists must turn to carefully constructed survey techniques to quantify the economic value of visual quality.

During the 1970s, when it became apparent that population growth, availability of natural resources, and low population density made the Southwest a prime candidate for energy development, concern was expressed about the impact of this development on some of the nation's most visited parks and recreational areas: Grand Canyon, Zion National Park, Mesa Verde, Glen Canyon and Lake Powell, among others. This led to a whole series of studies seeking to quantify the economic impact of decreased visibility from air pollution and the economic damage due to changes in the natural desert landscape, such as power-plant smokestacks, smoke plumes, transmission lines, and huge cooling towers. All of those studies estimated significant economic losses associated with declines in the visual quality. (See Randall, 1984 and Schulze et al., 1981, for summaries of these studies.)

The Grand Canyon was threatened by two changes as a result of thermal electric generation in the area. First the dispersed effluent in the air would reduce visibility. The horizon would be significantly foreshortened and much of a scenic vista could be lost. Second, the plume from a power plant's smokestacks could dominate the otherwise natural view from the edge of the canyon's rim.

Because Grand Canyon is a national park that draws visitors from across the country and seemed likely to be valued by visitors and nonvisitors alike, the study of the economic value of its visual quality was extended to residents in four sample cities: Albuquerque, Denver, Los Angeles, and Chicago.

The analysts sought to determine the maximum a household would be willing to pay in the way of higher park entrance fees or higher utility bills to maintain the parks' visual quality at its current level. To obtain this information, the analysts used photographs developed by scientists to show the effects of various levels of energy development on the view from, for instance, the rim of Grand Canyon. The average willingness to pay to protect air quality was reported as $4 to $5 per household per month for the Grand Canyon alone. When surrounding parks (Zion and Mesa Verde) were included, the willingness to pay was $7 to $10 per household per month. When the results from this sample of the population were carefully applied to the entire population, using the socioeconomic characteristics of the sample population, the estimated economic value of air quality in our southwestern national parks was over $6 billion per year (Schulze et al., 1983, pp. 167–170). If this annual value were to be capitalized into an investment value, the scenic vistas in these parks would be worth $70 billion to $133 billion. This is not the sort of economic value one wants to trivialize as subjective, judgmental, or "merely" aesthetic.

It is important to note two things about this result. First, only about 1 percent of the value of clean air over these parks is associated with current users of the parks (Schulze et al., 1983, p. 172). The vast bulk of the value was associated with other Americans who considered these parks national treasures even though they had not recently visited them. This split between current user values and non-use values is extreme because we are focusing on very unusual and well-known natural areas. But it underlines the importance of non-use values in estimating total economic value. In a more typical situation, the relative importance of non-use economic values will depend on the uniqueness of the natural environment at issue. If close substitutes are considered available, if the particular area is just one of many similar areas, use values are likely to dominate. When, on the other hand, we are dealing with well-known, irreplaceable natural areas, we can expect non-use values to increase in relative importance.

Finally, note that these surveys dealt with willingness to pay, not willingness to accept compensation. Since we are considering a change that takes from the population a valuable thing it now has, we know we should be asking how much people would need to be given before they would agree to the degradation of air quality in the parks. We also know that this value would be considerably larger than the $70 billion to $133 billion cited above.

e. The Economic Value of Wilderness

In the conventional discussions of the economic impact of protecting a natural area against development, the emphasis is on preservation's negative economic impact. This is especially true of statutory wilderness classification, which involves a formal commitment to restrict all human activity. This restricts tourism development, besides locking up timber, mineral, grazing, and water resources. The general population may strongly support such protection for moral, cultural, or aesthetic reasons despite this economic loss. But the economic dialogue casts such wilderness classification in an anti-economic light: we are purposely restricting or eliminating economic activity and sacrificing the economic values that could flow from it as we pursue other noneconomic objectives.

The problem with this characterization of wilderness, as we have noted over and over again, is that it ignores the enjoyment people derive outside of the commercial realm from the protection of natural areas. That enjoyment is real and valuable and is dependent on decisions about the use of scarce resources, and is therefore, economic. Just as people want the timber in wilderness to make aesthetically pleasing homes whose style connects with our cultural traditions, they also want the wilderness of those areas. Both provide aesthetic and cultural satisfaction. Both are economic. We do not have to build our homes of wood. We could use concrete and synthetic materials, as most of the affluent societies of Western Europe and Japan do. For cultural and aesthetic reasons, and because wood is readily available and relatively cheap in North America, we prefer wood. As an urban industrial country molded relatively recently by our struggles to push back the wilderness, the few wildlands remaining also have important cultural and aesthetic meaning. This presents a conflict between two sets of economic values, one commercial and the other largely noncommercial, not a conflict between economic and noneconomic values.

Economists have tried to quantify the direct, noncommercial economic values associated with wilderness. These include the value of these lands for recreational purposes: backpacking, hunting, fishing, cross-country skiing, wildlife observation, mountaineering, etc. But the economic values provided by wilderness also include non-use values: those associated with the pleasure of simply knowing such lands exist and providing options and opportunities for future generations. One analysis focused on the economic value of Colorado's remaining roadless, undeveloped wildlands. At the time of the study (the summer of 1980), 1.2 million acres of wilderness had already been designated in Colorado, about 2 percent of the state's area. Another 1.4 million acres had been proposed for wilderness status out of Colorado's 10 million acres of wildlands. Considerable controversy surrounded the decision on how much of this land should receive wilderness protection. The study was designed to help in that decisionmaking.

Because non-use values need not be connected to recreational or tourist use or to any other commercial or market-related activities, we cannot study people's actual market choices in order to measure these values; we have to turn to survey techniques. The Colorado study, after clearly explaining the land-use decision that needed to be made, asked heads of households to state the maximum amount their households would be willing to pay each year to protect various amounts of wilderness in Colorado. They were then asked to divide this stated value between recreational use, existence, and option and bequest values. These "bids" from the sample population to protect wildlands were combined with socioeconomic data and analyzed.

Wilderness-recreation use values were also estimated using market-related behavior, namely the willingness to incur the costs associated with travel to a wilderness area. As distance from an area increases, the costs associated with making use of the area also increase. By studying how usage varies with distance, we can determine the intensity of demand for that area's recreational potential. The travel costs tell us something about the sacrifices people actually make in order to enjoy a wilderness area for recreation.

For Colorado residents the pattern of travel costs indicated that wilderness recreation was worth $18.50 per visitor day. If this value is aggregated over all Colorado wildlands—in-state as well as out-of-state users—the annual recreational value associated with 2.6 million acres of actual and proposed wilderness was $28 million per year. For all 10 million acres of roadless wildlands, the recreational value was $77 million per year. These annual values are being enjoyed now and will continue to be enjoyed by a growing population. The present value of these streams of annual future recreational values came to $710 million for the 2.1 million acres of wilderness and $2 billion for the $10 million acres when a 4 percent discount rate was used.

Clearly there is a substantial direct economic value associated with recreational use of wilderness. But the non-use values revealed by this analysis were much larger. These preservation values were estimated to be $24.75 per Colorado household for the 2.6 million acres of existing and proposed wilderness and $46.20 per household for all $10 million acres of wildlands. In addition, it was estimated that to households outside of Colorado who were less familiar with these areas and lived farther from them, preservation of the 2.6 million acres was worth $1.37 per household while preservation of the full 10 million acres was worth $2.19 per household.

When these non-use preservation values are aggregated over the entire U.S.

population, following the socioeconomic characteristics of the sample, the total annual value of preserving Colorado wilderness was $135 million per year for the 2.6 million acres and $295 million per year for the 10 million acres. These annual values, too, will continue to be enjoyed each year and will grow with the expanding population. The present value of those future streams of non-use preservation benefits is $3.1 billion for the 2.6 million acres of wilderness and $5.1 billion for the 10 million acres if a 4 percent discount rate is used. Note that these non-use values are 2.6 to 4.4 times larger than the recreational use values.

The total economic value of preserving Colorado wilderness when both recreational use values and non-use preservation values are taken into account is $3.8 billion for the 2.6 million acres of existing and proposed wilderness and $7.1 billion for all 10 million acres of unroaded wildlands (Walsh et al., 1982; all dollar values in 1985 dollars).

These are anything but trivial values. They easily outstrip the value of these lands for timber production. It was for that reason that in 1984 the Colorado state government officially opposed U.S. Forest Service plans to significantly increase the level of roaded timber development in the unclassified wildlands. Colorado pointed out that three-quarters of the value produced on U.S. Forest Service lands in Colorado was recreation-related. Only 15 percent was timber related. If the non-recreational preservation values were included, the figures would be even more lopsided.

It is important to understand that the economic value of the Grand Canyon and Colorado wildlands are direct economic values enjoyed by people, not "tourist dollars." We have not discussed tourists' spending at all nor its potential impact on local economies. Those are not the type of economic values associated with natural beauty that we have been discussing.

Our exclusive focus on the value associated with direct enjoyment of a natural area is based on several considerations. First, it is often the local population, not tourists, that makes the heaviest use of the surrounding natural environment. That is not true for unique national treasures like Grand Canyon, but for most natural environments it is. There is absolutely no reason to ignore the value the local population obtains from these areas. This is especially true given the likelihood that the local population moved there, or resists moving away, because it places a high value on what is unique to that area. The local population may value local environmental qualities more highly than non-residents.

Second, as pointed out above several times, it is not only users, local and non-local, who take value in preserving natural treasures. The general population with no current plans to use a natural area may still value maintaining the area's qualities. As we have seen, these non-use preservation values may be much larger than the values obtained from use, only a part of which is tourist use. This is especially likely to be the case if the natural area has unique features.

Finally, tourist expenditures are not all benefits. These expenditures primarily offset the costs the tourist imposes: the gasoline consumed, the food eaten, etc.

Thus tourist expenditures mix cost and benefits together in a not very useful way. Some measure of net value to tourists and to the community in which they spend their money is needed.

Tourism is not the only or even the major source of economic value associated with the preservation of natural areas. The direct, noncommercial enjoyment of those natural areas is likely to be far more important.

3. The Beast: The Economic Cost of Sickness, Crime, and Death

a. Air Quality, Disease, and Life Expectancy

Depending on its cleanliness, the air around us can either limit or enhance our access to the beauty of the landscape. But there is more at stake than beauty. That air can also be the beast that sickens or kills us.

Health, like beauty, can be labeled a subjective phenomenon, a mere matter of our internal feelings of well-being. As with beauty, however, it is not clear what insight is gained from such a description. Almost all economic activity is driven by such subjective feelings. But that can be no justification for ignoring something as important to us as health.

Again, all we have to do is look at what we already spend on health care to assure ourselves that substantial economic values are at stake. In 1980 we spent $287 billion on health care in the United States. The percentage of the economy's production we devote to maintaining or enhancing our health increases each year. In 1950 it was 4.4 percent, in 1960 it was 5.3 percent, and in 1980 it was 9.5 percent (U.S. Department of Commerce, 1983). This upward trend has continued, with no upper limit in sight.

If air quality affects our health and life expectancy and both of these have value to us, there is clearly economic value at stake in the way air or water or food pollution affects our collective health.

We now have almost two decades of studies establishing the connection between chronic exposure to relatively low levels of air pollutants on the one hand and sickness and reduced life expectancy on the other. Sulfate particles, sulfur dioxide, total suspended particles, and nitrogen oxides have all been implicated (Freeman, 1979; Chappie and Lave, 1982; Ostro, 1983a and 1983b; Mendelsohn and Orcutt, 1979). Lave and Seskin estimated that implementation of the Environmental Protection Agency's mid-1970s air-pollution standards would reduce mortality and morbidity in the United States by 7 percent. They pegged the economic value of this at $48 billion (1977, dollars adjusted to 1985). Chappie and Lave, using more recent data, concluded that a 50 percent abatement of particulates and sulfates would lower total U.S. mortality by 6.9 percent (1982, p. 371). Mendelsohn and Orcutt (1974) estimated that in 1970, 140,000 deaths— 9 percent of all deaths in the United States—were related to sulfate pollution.

Ostro found that higher pollution levels increased the likelihood of sickness serious enough to cause people to miss work and drastically reduce their routine activity. A 25 percent increase in pollution led to a 12.5 percent increase in the expected level of lost work days and a 7.5 percent increase in expected reduced activity days due to illness (1983, p. 376, and 1983b).

We know air pollution damages our health and life expectancy. What we want to address here is the economic value of this damage. By that we emphatically do not mean only or primarily the lost wages associated with lost work days or the cost of medical care. Besides these costs there is the discomfort and suffering associated with disease and death. Even if society agreed to cover everyone's lost wages and medical bills while they were sick and after they died, very few people, if any, would become indifferent to disease and death. There is a much larger loss involved than wages and medical expenses. As we will see, pain and suffering are by far the dominant costs, being many many times larger than the value of lost wages.

It is important to remember that we are not dealing with the imminent death of an individual or the costs associated with a particular person becoming ill. Rather, we are dealing with increases in the statistical likelihood that members of a given population will get sick or die. It is changes in the morbidity and mortality rates of a large population that are at issue, not the death or illness of any specific individuals.

One place where individuals make market-like decisions about what they will sacrifice to avoid increased threats to their lives and health is in the job market. Some jobs have a near-zero likelihood of a serious accident. Others have high rates of accidents resulting in serious injury or death. Economists have statistically analyzed the wages paid on different jobs to try to isolate the effect of job safety from the other determinants of wage levels. One would expect workers on risky jobs to have to be compensated through higher wages for taking on that risk, and that is exactly what one does find. A 10 percent increase in the probability of a nonfatal accident raises weekly earnings by 9.1 percent. Workers on jobs with average risk—a one-in-thirty chance of a nonfatal accident—receive $1,700 per year more in wages than those on totally riskless jobs. The wage premium paid to accept a 1-in-10,000 chance of death, compared to a job with near-zero risk of death, was found to be $850 (Olson, 1981, pp. 173 and 178; dollars adjusted to 1985).

These wage premiums that workers require before they will take on the risk of injury and death can be translated into statements of the economic value of safety or health. If workers must be paid $850 per year to take a 1-in-10,000 chance of death while on the job, then 10,000 workers, one of whom is likely to die on that job, would collectively have to be paid $8.5 million to accept the risk. That is the value to these workers of a "statistical life," or the cost to them of a "statistical death." Similarly, if workers require $1,700 in higher wages to take on a one-in-thirty chance of an accident serious enough to cost work time, one can say that thirty workers, one of whom is likely to be so injured, collectively judge the cost of such a "statistical injury" to them to be $51,000. Given that the average lost work due to such an accident is fifteen days, the compensation demanded by workers is $3,400 for each day their health is so damaged they cannot work. This can be compared with the lost wages of, say, $90 per day. In this example, the compensation required is thirty-eight times what would be needed just to compensate for lost wages. Put differently, lost wages make up less than 3 percent of the cost of a serious accident. Remember, these values come from compensation workers actually demand and get before taking risky jobs.

These compensating wage payments for differences in job safety are almost certainly incomplete. Workers are not fully compensated for all the risks they face, some of the compensation may be provided in nonwage form not picked up in these wage analyses, and some workers may not be compensated at all. The bargaining strength of various groups of workers, the extent of labor surpluses (unemployment) in various labor markets, and various barriers to workers seeking higher-paying jobs (discrimination) all may work to reduce compensation for risk. In that sense, these estimates may be low (Dorman, 1985). In addition, these payments at best compensate only the worker, not his or her relatives or close friends. It is not only the individual worker who suffers from his or her injury or death. Others will likely be willing to pay to avoid their own risk of loss from threats to that worker's life and health. Needleman (1976) has estimated that this would add 25 to 100 percent to estimates tied only to the compensation workers themselves demand.

The distinction between accidents and disease should be kept in mind. Accidents involve sudden damage to the body. Illness—say from chronic air pollution serious enough to cause loss of work—may come and go; early death due to air pollution is usually the result of cumulative damage. We may consider the sudden trauma of an accident to be more threatening and frightening. On the other hand, the mounting feeling of debility and the long, painful dying associated with degenerative diseases may be judged more of a burden than a sudden accident.

Finally, the risk of sickness or disease from pollution may be evaluated differently than the risk we take on the job. The latter may be looked on as a risk voluntarily assumed, while the former is seen as imposed without our permission, a threat over which we can exercise little control. For that reason we might demand greater compensation before we would feel that we had been "made whole" from air pollution damage. Clearly, there are reasons to believe that the economic costs associated with risks of injury and death on the job are not necessarily the same as the economic costs associated with the risk of sickness and death due to air pollution. But in order to get a feeling for at least the order of magnitude of the costs involved, we will apply these accident values to air-pollution morbidity and mortality.

If, as reported above (Ostro, 1983a, p. 376) a 50 percent reduction in air pollution leads to a 25 percent reduction in lost workdays and a 15 percent reduction in days of reduced activity due to pollution-related illness, the average number of sick days would decline by 15 to 25 million per year for the entire population. If the values assigned to nonfatal accidents (discussed above) are applied to this reduced illness, the economic gain associated with the reduced sickness would be $51 billion to $85 billion.

In addition, there is the loss associated with pollution-related deaths. If, as reported above, there are 140,000 additional deaths (Mendelsohn and Orcutt, 1979) due to pollution each year, the economic loss suggested by the compensation for accepting risky jobs is $1.2 trillion. Even if these estimates are off by a factor of two, five or ten, it is clear that there are substantial economic costs associated with the damage air pollution does to our health.

Note that these economic losses have little or nothing to do with lost worker productivity, lost wages, or the burden of medical expenditures. These are primarily the direct costs imposed on people in the form of pain, debility, and reduced quality of life. This is important because our ordinary language so often ties economic costs only to commercial losses of one sort or another, such as lost wages or increased medical costs. These are only a small part of the economic cost. Most of us would not volunteer to get cancer even if someone covered our lost wages!

This point has significant policy implications. Congress and state legislatures have been urged recently to limit the damages awarded in wrongful-death and injury cases to "economic losses." "Economic" is incorrectly defined in this situation as lost wages and medical expenses. Pain, suffering and mental anguish are specifically misdefined as noneconomic. This is grossly incorrect. We regularly sacrifice substantial resources to avoid pain, suffering, and mental anguish. These things have a dramatic influence on economic activity. It makes no sense at all to label them noneconomic; they are very important economic qualities.

Finally, to economists, it is important that the procedure used above to generate ballpark estimates of the cost of polluted air is conceptually incorrect. The cost to the average individual affected was used to estimate the total cost. If everyone had identical preferences and we were talking about a relatively small change in the current situation, this might not be objectionable. But that often will not be the case.

There is evidence, for instance, that some people are less risk-averse than others. Increased risk does not bother them as much as most other people. They may tend to take the more dangerous jobs, reducing the observed wage premium to below what the average person would demand. In such a situation we would have to be very careful how we aggregated the costs across the population, or we might overestimate or underestimate the cost. This is a general warning that applies not only to these risk estimates but also to the estimates of travel costs, compensating wage differentials, interview-based estimates, property values, etc.

Similarly, the cost associated with significant changes in the status quo may not be closely related to the costs experienced in the current situation. Large increases in pollution may do more than proportional damage. Dramatic improvements in air quality may not bring proportional benefits, as the later improvements may be less valuable than the initial ones.

To obtain accurate estimates of the costs involved, economists would try to take both of these considerations into account. That requires significantly more information on the variety of preferences the population holds and on how individuals' evaluations might change as the quality of the environment around them changes.

b. The Cost of Crime and the Value of Security

The threat of crime against our person or property imposes a substantial economic cost on all those who feel that threat. Put the other way around, being able to live in a community where the threat of violence to ourselves or the violation of our homes is negligible has a substantial economic value.

Once again, the cost and value we are talking about are not primarily associated with property actually lost to criminals, or the medical bills associated with a mugging, or the funeral expenses of a murder victim. These are real enough but are small compared to the dominant costs. This can be easily demonstrated by asking whether, if free insurance fully covered all of these costs, we would be indifferent to burglars breaking into our homes, thugs attacking us on the street, and murderers periodically taking the lives of our friends and neighbors. Obviously we would not. There is some substantially greater cost associated with crime than these residual costs. Any accurate economic analysis of the value of security against crime would fully evaluate these other costs.

One place to start this economic analysis of the impact of crime is to look at the changes in behavior the threat of crime forces upon us. In the absence of crime we would engage in a preferred set of activities. Because of crime we have to abandon or modify these and engage in other activities we would have preferred to avoid. We sacrifice things we want and take on costs we do not want. An economic analysis would seek to evaluate all of these adjustments to see what the total loss to us is.

These adjustments to crime include significant changes in lifestyle. We avoid going out after dark. We avoid traveling through certain neighborhoods. We do not use the parks and open areas that were supposed to be neighborhood amenities. We are suspicious of or even hostile to strangers and to neighbors we do not know well. As a result, we do not get to know many people in our communities. And, of course, we have to teach our children to do the same. The damage this does to the character and spirit of our community is significant. We lose something that is very important to us. In addition, we have to carry the psychic costs of fear with us as we engage in our daily activities.

We seek to protect ourselves against some of this by investing, if we can afford to, in home-security equipment, by hiring private security guards (doormen) to protect the entrances to our apartment buildings or exclusive neighborhoods, or by moving to areas with low crime rates.

These private, market-oriented activities provide us with some evidence of how important security from crime is. If peoples' choice of residence is influenced by the desire to avoid the threat of crime and the costs associated with it, property values should vary with crime rates. People will be willing to pay more to live in higher-security areas where the lifestyle, psychic, and out-of-pocket expenses (higher insurance rates, higher tax rates for police expenditures, higher private-security costs, etc.) associated with crime are lower.

Careful statistical analysis of the factors that determine property values is needed to quantify the impact of variations in crime on property values. Areas with high crime rates also often have other problems, such as pollution, congestion, low per capita incomes, and high population densities. The economist must analyze a wide range of neighborhoods with different mixes of characteristics in order to isolate the impact of crime rates.

Such analysis shows what we would expect. The crime characteristics of neighborhoods influence the likelihood that families will be willing to move into them, especially families with children. One study found that high-income white families with children were two to three times more likely to choose a low-crime neighborhood when moving. High-income black families with children were four times more likely to choose low-crime neighborhoods (Katzman, 1980).

Such choices play an important role in the decline of urban neighborhoods. As the population of higher-income families flees an area, property values decline, the commercial vitality of the area deteriorates, and the property-tax base shrinks. This reduces the level and quality of public services available there, making it even more unattractive. School quality, street maintenance and cleanliness, upkeep of parks, etc. deteriorate. A blighted, decaying neighborhood develops.

A statistical analysis of property sales in the Chicago metropolitan area indicated that families buying and selling average-value homes put a value of $4,650 on increased security against crime. Seven-and-a-half percent of the value of the home was determined by the crime characteristics of the community. For higher-income families the value of security from crime increased rapidly. A 25 percent increase in income was associated with a 65 percent increase in the value of lower crime rates. This would boost the value to $7,700 (Diamond, 1980, all values in 1985 dollars).

A more complex analysis of the impact of crime rates on property values in Boston found that a 10 percent variation in total crime rate led to a 16.7 percent variation in property values (Naroff, 1980). For residential homebuyers purchasing a medium-valued home for $73,000 in 1985, this would imply that a 10 percent reduction in crime was worth over $12,000. An earlier study of Boston homebuyers' behavior indicated a smaller impact: a 10 percent reduction in crime raised the price homebuyers were willing to pay by about 7.5 percent (Hellman, 1979). Even this would indicate that this modest improvement in security from crime was worth $5,500 on the median-priced home in 1985.

When these values of a 10 percent reduction in crime are applied to all the property in Boston's central business district, they suggest that this small reduction in crime would be worth $250 million to $550 million.

An analysis of the impact of burglary and vandalism in residential neighborhoods on property values in Minneapolis indicated that each 1 percent increase in residential burglary was associated with a decline in the average value of an owner-occupied home of about $1,000. Just one more act of vandalism per 1,000 population was associated with a more than $300 decrease in property value. The differences in residential property values between the high- and low-crime neighborhoods attributable to these crimes were over $12,000 per home for burglary and almost $10,000 per home for vandalism (Gray and Joelson, 1979, p. 53; 1985 dollars).

Aggregating these values over the entire population is difficult. Peoples' concern over crime varies, and initial reductions in crime rates may be more valuable than further reductions. But if the security from crime associated with significant reductions in neighborhood crime rates is worth at least $5,000 per household, as the above results suggest, the aggregate economic value of such security from crime to America's 90 million households totals $450 billion.

Our behavior when we collectively evaluate what we are willing to pay for our homes indicates this security is an important economic matter. So do our private and public expenditures on protection and crime control. We annually spend almost $40 billion on our criminal-justice system (U.S. Department of Commerce, 1984a, p. 183). In addition, it has been estimated that we privately spend $10 billion a year on security guards, locks, burglar alarms, security weapons, and the like (Kalalik and Wildhorn, 1977; 1985 dollars). Protection and security from crime clearly have a very important economic aspect. It is not just a "social" problem.

4. Conclusion

This chapter has sought to provide empirical, quantitative estimates of the economic value of some familiar environmental qualities that are usually treated as noneconomic or even anti-economic: visual quality, beautiful vistas, clean air, and reduced crime.

These substantial economic values, just a small part of the value we obtain daily from the social and natural environments, are not produced by businesses for sale in the market. Yet their economic importance is clear.

If we were to analyze systematically the myriad of noncommercial environmental and social qualities that make communities attractive places to live and work, their economic values would rival those of major segments of our commercial economy.

To ignore these noncommercial economic values in the pursuit of whatever increases the dollar volume of income or business receipts would be anti-economic, in the sense that it would assure waste of significant economic resources and leave us all worse off.

The values developed above were not intended to be exact. It was the relative magnitude that we were trying to establish. Much more careful analysis would be required to provide firm estimates, especially in the aggregating of the values over large populations. That more technical analysis lies beyond the scope of this book. Here we are only trying to establish that real and substantial economic values lie outside the world of business. Those values, like all economic values, are largely associated with the pursuit of quality.

Until our common economic conceptions incorporate this aspect of economic reality, public economic policy is likely to be seriously biased or perverse, wasting extremely valuable resources in a misguided pursuit of limited commercial gains.

In the following chapters we turn to an analysis of public economic policy in the context of this broader definition of economics and the economy. Our focus will not be on the national or international economy but on the economy in which we live, the local economy. For it is here that the familiar folk economics is most narrow and distorted. We begin in the next chapter with the way in which the local economy is usually understood in public discussions.

CHAPTER SEVEN

The Economic Base: Distracting Vision, Distorting Reality

1. Economic Development and the Pursuit of Quality

In the previous chapters we have examined the dominant role that the pursuit of quality plays in almost all economic activities. We have shown that almost all economic actors—consumers, producers, migrants, workers, employers, etc.— are guided by subjective, qualitative objectives. Quality is not a vague, aesthetic notion foreign to normal economic activity.

But most of the discussion has focused on individual, private decisions: the expenditure of income on a variety of consumer goods, migration, the purchase of a home, the hiring of new workers, the development of new technology. But we do not pursue economic well-being only through private activities. Even in our private-enterprise economy, we also pursue economic well-being collectively, through a variety of public economic-development policies. These public policies seek to enhance our economic well-being by influencing the type of economic changes that take place in the communities where we live.

This and the following chapters seek to deal with the degree to which these policies accurately take into account the noncommercial, qualitative nature of many of the determinants of our economic well-being. We do that individually, but does the public policy carried out in our names?

This and the following chapter will document the ways in which a crude, quantitative emphasis has come to dominate and pervert local economic-development policy. We begin in this chapter with a critique of the dominant way in which the local economy is conceptualized: the concept of the economic base. In the next chapter we discuss the quantitative objectives and policies that tend to make up almost all economic-development programs. And finally, in Chapter Nine, we discuss appropriate development strategies that take into account the noncommercial and qualitative aspects of our economic objectives.

2. Simplifying Economic Reality

The popular perception that the economy is a very complex, hard-to-understand set of relationships is well founded. In any modern economy, because of the great degree of specialization in production and the broad range of products that are regularly bought and sold, the web of interconnections between producers and consumers is extremely fine. We are all dependent on multiple chains of suppliers stretching back through a maze of alternative paths.

Some of our very first analytical economists, the Physiocrats of 18th-century France, saw the need to model in a quantitative way these interconnections among producers and between producers and consumers. They chose an input-output type of model to track the flows of goods through the economy and impose the conditions of balance that were necessary if waste and disruption were to be avoided. That type of model survives today in more complex form as one of the basic tools of economic analysis.

Faced with such complexity and detail, comprehension of the economy can proceed only if some basic order can be perceived. If broad patterns of connections and some causal ordering can be uncovered, it is possible to see beyond the myriad events and relationships and begin to make sense out of the complexity.

That is the function of economic models: to bring order and direction to our observations, so that we can comprehend the underlying logic of the system. That understanding can then inform public policy, warning it against actions that will disrupt or guiding it in actions that can improve economic performance.

Economic models are necessary, but they are not neutral. They do not simply let us see more clearly. They shape our vision, our perception of reality. That is not a drawback; that is their function. Any model is an attempt to strip away unnecessary complexity and focus on key relationships and primary forces. Models are designed to distract us from those things that are not crucial or central. As the word suggests, models "mold" what we see and guide the questions we ask.

As necessary as this is, if we are going to avoid standing paralyzed and confused before an infinitely complex reality, bombarded by undifferentiated sensory inputs and information, modeling can also be dangerous. Since the model controls what we see, the questions we ask, and also the policy handles available to change what we see, it can be seriously distorting. It is like a pair of complicated spectacles that sets the focus of our vision at a certain distance. A microscope is not very helpful in navigating a car or an airplane. Radar and radio telescopes will not help much in fighting a new disease. It matters where the model focuses our attention. Dysfunction, distraction, and distortion can result from an inappropriate model even though that model may accurately depict one aspect of reality.

This chapter will look at the concept of the local economic base as such a distracting and distorting model. The intent is not to argue that there is no economic base or that economic-base theory is wrong. Rather the intent is to show the dysfunctional way in which that particular vision distracts us from steps that could improve the well-being of our communities and diverts us into ineffective or self-defeating efforts.

3. The Economic Base: An Overview

The vision of the economy that the economic-base approach seeks to provide is straightforward and legitimate enough. It seeks to isolate the kernel of the economy, the driving force. If that can be done, and that core is much smaller and simpler to comprehend than the economy as a whole, we have substantially reduced the magnitude of the conceptual problem we face. We can focus our attention on that economic core rather than on the periphery. In addition, isolating the main causal force will help us order events and direct policy measures to where they will be most effective. Instead of wrestling with symptoms, we can work on causes.

In the abstract, this approach is not only unobjectionable, but it seems sensible and likely to be productive. With no preconceptions, let us pursue this quest to discover the base of a local economy.

At its most general level, the economic base would include all those things and activities in a local area that contribute in some primary way to the economic well-being of the residents. The economic base certainly should include all of the primary sources of local economic welfare.

This general statement, however, is easy prey for the narrow definition of "economic" discussed in the previous chapters. If economic well-being is taken to mean only those valuable things obtained through commercial businesses, it is easy to see how the economic base could be envisioned as simply the primary sources of jobs and income.

In fact, that is exactly how the local economic base is understood by most people, including most business economists. Since money income is the lifeblood of the commercial economy, the focus is usually on what brings money income into an area. Since it is assumed that the local population cannot print money or mint coins, attention shifts to commercial activities that bring money into the area. Although income can flow into an area as a result of government grants and transfers, or from retirement funds or from distant corporations' dividend and interest payments, income usually flows into an area only in exchange for the goods or services that the area has supplied to the outside world. It should not be surprising, then, that the economic base has come to be viewed as the part of the local economy that exports goods to the larger economy and as a result, "injects" income into the local economy. That income then gets spent and respent, putting people to work and making it possible for the population to support itself. In this view, the ultimate source of almost all of the populations' jobs and incomes are these export-oriented business activities. The economic base consists primarily of that segment of the commercial economy. This way of looking at the local economy does simplify and focus our thinking. Since manufacturing, mining, and agriculture, especially for export to the larger economy, are likely to make up only a quarter or a third of local economic activity, the size of the "basic" part of our economy on which we must concentrate is significantly reduced. In addition, with the causal imagery of outside money coming into the local economy and triggering successive waves of spending and respending, it provides us with a way of ordering and understanding the myriad economic interconnections.

It is this widely held view of the local economic base that this chapter will examine in detail.

4. An Approach As Old As Economics

This general approach to the economic base is not new. It is as old as economics itself. The French Physiocrats argued that land, and the labor that worked the land, were the primary economic resources. All other economic activity simply processed the wealth that farmers, loggers, miners, and fishermen brought into existence. Manufacturing, trade, and government activities were basically derivative and unproductive. They simply took a share of the wealth created by the primary workers. This was not a surprising economic vision for a country of peasants and landed gentry living on sprawling rural estates who looked with suspicion on the commercial urban areas.

In England, where a rising mercantile class was successfully challenging the landed aristocracy, a somewhat different vision of the primary economic activities emerged. In England the emphasis was heavily on exports: wealth and well-being came from exporting all that England could produce, the minimization of imports, and the accumulation of the ultimate embodiment of wealth, gold bullion.

With the industrial revolution came a greater emphasis on manufacturing. In Britain, the "workshop of the world," this fit nicely into the emphasis on exports. But the physiocratic vision had to be modified: it was hardly tenable to label the increasingly dominant form of economic activity, manufacturing, as unproductive.

The classical economists, starting with Adam Smith and carrying through to Karl Marx, accepted the productive/unproductive dichotomy, but manufacturing was welcomed into the productive fold. Economic actors who seemed merely to support productive manufacturing, mining, and agriculture—such as financiers, commercial middlemen, those providing personal services, and government workers—were labeled unproductive. They created no new wealth. They were parasites, living off the wealth created by those who sweated in the fields and factories. These economic visions, over two centuries old, should strike a familiar chord. They emphasize the primary importance of those commercial activities that produce things, especially things for export. Manufacturing, mining, and agriculture are the economic base; all other commercial economic activities are secondary or derivative, possibly even unproductive. In this view, noncommercial resources or activities do not even deserve the label "economic."

That is still the common vision of the economic base. Especially in our smaller cities and nonmetropolitan areas, building the local economic base means expanding the manufacturing or mining sector while protecting agriculture. The insights of the very first economists have had an impressive staying power.

5. The Economic-Base Model

We begin a more detailed explanation of the economic-base approach to analyzing the local economy by focusing on a rather primitive version of it. Most professional economists would reject this primitive model as too crude to be of much help and potentially misleading. At the same time, however, it is the model most often used by local planners, business economists, and others analyzing the impact of major business developments on the local economy. Although shunned by professional economists in favor of a more complex and detailed approach, it seems to dominate public perceptions of what makes the local economy tick. Simply for that reason it is worth discussing in some detail.

Consider a local economy consisting of many businesses and households. If an existing business or a new business increases its sales outside the local economy by, say, $2 million, it will have to increase its local purchases of labor and other inputs. This $2-million export leads to the creation of new jobs and the infusion of new income into the local economy. The entire $2 million is unlikely to stay in or even circulate through the local economy, however. Most locally produced goods make use of equipment and inputs imported into the local area, which have to be paid for by dollar outflows. Likewise, local firms may be owned by people living outside the area or may be financed by funds borrowed from outside. This will cause profit and interest payments to flow out of the local economy. Let us assume that half of the value of the $2 million in new exports is paid directly to local residents for their labor services or other inputs produced locally.

This means that $1 million in new income will flow into the pocketbooks of local households. These households will spend that income in a variety of ways, and the money will begin to circulate through the local economy. Households may not spend all of their incomes. They may save some of it, and if what they save is lent to people outside the area, it immediately leaves the local economy. But other people may be borrowing from outside, creating a partially offsetting counterflow of income. To keep the explanation simple, we will assume that the local savings are borrowed and used locally or that the savings flowing out are exactly offset by outsiders' savings flowing in.

As the households spend their new income at local businesses, the dollar volume of business increases and those businesses expand, hiring more people and purchasing more inputs. Again, what is purchased is not all made locally. Some part of the new business income flows out of the local economy as payment for imported goods or as profits and interest paid to outsiders. If two-thirds of the value of what is locally purchased is locally produced then two-thirds of a million dollars, or $667,000, flows again into the pocketbooks of local households while $333,000 "leaks" out of the local economy to pay for imports. This additional household income of $667,000 will again be spent at local businesses, leading to a further expansion of those businesses and creating even more jobs. Again, one-third of this will pay for imported goods and services, but two-thirds, or $445,000, will go to local households as payment for their work or products. This will trigger another $445,000 in household spending and further expansion of local businesses. When the leakage to the outside economy is accounted for, two-thirds of this or an additional $296,000 will flow to local households. This will go on and on, each cycle creating a somewhat smaller expansion.

Table 7.1 and Figure 7.1 show this expansion and its cumulative impact. The expansion goes on until the full $1 million in additional income injected into the local economy has been used to pay for imports from the larger economy. By then total household income will have increased a total of $3 million, three times the initial increase in income and one-and-a-half times the initial increase in export sales. These numbers, 3 and 1.5, are called the income multipliers. They indicate the ultimate impact of the increased export sales on the local economy. In this very simple model, the multiplier is easily calculated as the reciprocal of the fraction of local income that is spent on imports. In our example this was one-third, hence the multiplier is 3.

Before going on, note the basic logic of this economic model. The expansion stops when all of the new income injected into the local economy has gone to purchase imports. This indicates the only function of exporting goods from the local economy: to get the income necessary to import that which is not easily produced locally. The average need to import determines the number of people that can be supported by a given level of export income. If, on average, one-third of household income goes to purchase goods not made locally, any given dollar of export income can support $3 of household purchases. The smaller the import needs—that is, the more self-sufficient the local economy—the fewer the export dollars needed to support the local population. If the local economy spends only one dollar in ten on imports, each dollar of export earnings can support $10 dollars of expenditures in the local economy. The multiplier is much larger. The logic of the model underlines the fact that imports are the objective, not exports. Import needs make exports necessary. A reduction of import needs has an expansionary impact just as an increase in exports does.

But this way of looking at export activity begins to be more than a bit convoluted and distorted. The less an area depends on imports, the less it needs to export to support its population. But the export-base model will describe this quite

Figure 7.1
**The Export-Base Model: The Circulation Within and Leakage Out of Additional Income
Injected into the Local Economy**

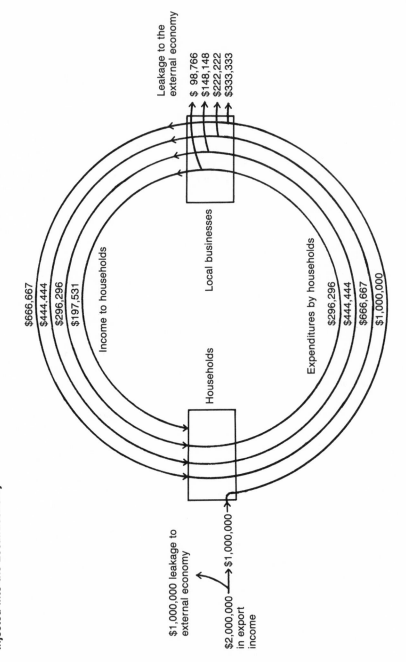

Table 7.1

The Export-Base Model: The Multiple Impact of Additional Income Injected Into the Local Economy

Assumptions:

Initial increase in exports:	$2,000,000
Payments for imported goods and services used to produce the exports:	$1,000,000
Net injection of income into the local economy:	$1,000,000
Fraction of local expenditure going to imported goods:	one-third

Cycles of local spending	Change in household income	Leakage out of local economy
Initial increase in household income	$1,000,000	$ 333,333
Second-round increase in household income	666,667	222,222
Third-round increase in household income	444,444	148,148
Fourth-round increase in household income	296,296	98,765
Fifth-round increase in household income	197,531	65,844
Sixth-round increase in household income	131,687	43,896
Seventh-round increase in household income	87,791	29,264
Eighth-round increase in household income	58,528	19,509
Ninth-round increase in household income	39,018	13,006
Tenth-round increase in household income	26,012	8,671
Remaining rounds	$ 52,026	$ 17,342
Total increase in household income	$3,000,000	$1,000,000

differently, for the lesser dependence upon imports will increase the multiplier and suggest that exports are all the more powerful and important. This is certainly a perverse aspect of the export-base vision.

To use this model, of course, we have to know what the multiplier is or what fraction of local spending goes directly or indirectly for imported goods and services. One shortcut usually taken to get around the need for such detailed data on our spending patterns is to divide the local economy into two parts: export-oriented and locally oriented. If we make the assumption that the dollars flowing in from exports make all locally oriented commercial activity possible, we can calculate an average multiplier. We can simply take the total income earned in the local economy and divide that by the income earned in the export-oriented sector; we are assuming that the export sector stimulates all income. That means the multiplier is simply the ratio of total income to export income.

This model's simplicity and power should be clear. It suggests that we need only focus our attention on the one-third to one-fifth of the economy that is export-oriented. That minority drives the rest of the economy. And a simple multiplication relationship exists between the two. If an export-oriented firm locates or expands in the area, we can predict the impact on the overall economy by simply finding out what the payroll will be and applying the multiplier. The same can be done to determine the impact of an export firm shutting down.

To translate this income information into job information, we simply need to know average wages in the export firms and in the locally oriented firms. In our example above, if the export firm paid workers $20,000 per year, fifty new jobs would be created in the export firm. The additional $2,000,000 in induced local income would provide 200 new jobs if the average wage paid in locally oriented firms were $10,000 per year. This would be a total of 250 new jobs associated with the creation of fifty jobs in the export-oriented firm. The job multiplier is 5 even though the income multiplier was only 3, because of the assumed lower wages in locally oriented firms. The additional income injected into the local economy can support more local job creation when wages are low.

This simple model allows us to project the impact on jobs and income of any change in the economic base. We need only minimal information and the ability to engage in a little arithmetic. This may explain its appeal to public decision-makers, the business community, and the general public.

6. Local Economic Development
Versus Export Growth

The economic-base model is often presented not only as an explanation of how certain types of changes in the economy get translated and amplified but as a theory of local economic development. Regions develop when they have a product the rest of the world wants. The entire regional economy develops around that export demand: the more diverse and rich the export demands, the more diverse and rich the regional economy. Regions without such exportable goods are simply part of the undeveloped hinterland (North, 1955 and 1956).

This approach has some basic commonsense appeal. A powerful economic force is specified as the engine of economic growth. But equally commonsensical reflection underlines its gross limitations. The world as a whole cannot export to anyone. The United States, for most of its history, has exported very little. Does this mean the world economy cannot develop and that the United States economy has had only limited development potential? Obviously not. The fact of the matter is that improvements in technology, improvements in the quality of the work force, improvements in our knowledge and organization, savings and investment, entrepreneurial spirit, and attitudes toward work and consumption drive economic development. These are the internal forces that propel economic development. Export markets are not necessary, though they can certainly stimulate the development of these forces.

There are other important internal economic forces as well. Increases in population and changes in its rate of growth and age structure will have a profound impact on the economy. Changes in the pattern of goods and services on which we spend our incomes will also transform the economy. Changes in workforce participation by young people, women, and the elderly have a major impact on economic patterns. The economic-base model, with its focus on exports, ignores or takes for granted all of these dynamic forces which have propelled the economic transformation of both the world and local economies over the last several centuries. Exports cannot be said to have caused such fundamental change.

Consider just a few of the recent structural changes that can drastically modify the role of exports in the local economy. Technological change and productivity growth diffuse throughout the national economy. This, combined with migration, causes per-capita incomes to rise significantly nationwide, in the "undeveloped" hinterland as well as in the metropolitan centers, regardless of export activity. As a result, all local economic development has had an autonomous trend unrelated to regional specifics. In fact, this autonomous, nonlocal trend has been the main determinant of local incomes. We have a reasonably uniform standard of living in all parts of the country, regardless of patterns of export activity. Changes in local per capita income are highly correlated with national trends, not with local-development forces. Also, consider the changes in our consumption patterns. In the very early years of our history, agricultural and handicraft activities dominated. By the early twentieth century they had given way to manufacturing as the dominant form of productive activity. Now, in the late twentieth century, manufacturing is declining in importance and services are playing an increasingly important role. These trends have a major impact on the multiplier emphasized by the economic-base vision. Early, self-sufficient agricultural and handicraft activity with limited reliance on export markets would have suggested very large multipliers when exports were not very important. In our own era, as consumption patterns shift toward services, most of which are locally produced, the same thing happens, the measured multiplier grows larger. But the economic-base model does not explain why the multiplier is increasing or by how much it will increase in the future. It does not explain the economy's direction. In addition, as pointed out above, it has the perverse characteristic of increasing the apparent importance of exports precisely when their actual role shrinks in importance.

Finally, as an area grows for whatever reason, the local market expands and the area can profitably produce a broader range of goods and services. With growth, a region becomes more self-sufficient and its imports decrease. Locally oriented activities expand. This, too, increases the measured multiplier, for there will be more local jobs for any given level of export employment. That is, import substitution will increase the export multiplier. Exports will not have caused this change in economic activity, but the model will attribute these changes to exports nonetheless.

The point is that the economic-base model ignores everything but changes in the export sector and it does not even attempt to explain why those changes in exports take place. They are just random shocks that trigger waves of adjustment.

Meanwhile, what to the export-base theory are autonomous and unexplained trends roll on, transforming our regional and local economies. This is not a very useful way to look at local economic development.

7. The Economic-Base Model as a Model of Short Run Economic Shocks

The economic-base approach is so primitive that many professional economists see it only as a tool for forecasting the impact of short-run economic shocks on a local economy. For the short run, over a year or two, the primary sources of economic growth can perhaps be ignored. For instance, if a large factory begins operation or a power plant is constructed or the military closes a base, the economic base approach may predict the short-run impact of these events on local jobs and income. Some researchers initially found convincing empirical evidence that the economic-base model was useful for this limited purpose (Williamson, 1975).

This would be a relatively modest undertaking that left to others an analysis of the long-run forces operating in the local economy. But the economic-base model does not even seem to do this very well. The problem is that its vision of money being injected into the local economy and then being spent and respent as it circulates does not specify how long all this takes. Does it take a year for the full impact to be realized, or less or does it take many years? When economists have tried to measure empirically how quickly the predicted multiple impact will follow an external shock applied to the local economy, they have come up with widely divergent answers. Some have found lengthy time lags, four to twenty-five years, and have emphatically stated that the economic-base approach is worthless for predicting short-run impacts (Moody and Puffer, 1970; McNulty, 1977; Tiebout, 1956). Where careful statistical searching revealed a measurable short run multiplier impact, the multiplier often has been small, only 1.5, and most of the changes outside of the economic base could not be explained by changes in the economic base (Henry and Nyankori, 1981). Finally, whatever multiplier may be measured, it may well change significantly from year to year and certainly will differ from one area to another (Richardson, 1978). Thus, factually, we cannot have much confidence that even in the short-run the economic-base approach tells us something about how our local economy will change in response to external shocks. The multiplier seems to be unstable and unpredictable.

There are many reasons why it may take some time before additional jobs and income are generated locally as a result of export expansion. Local businesses may have some excess capacity, which would allow them to serve the new customers without hiring additional workers. Even after that excess capacity is fully utilized, expansion is likely to depend on the businesses' longer-term expectations about whether the additional spending is temporary or permanent. In either case, the additional hiring may be delayed for a significant time. This will slow each cycle of expansion and possibly stretch the total expansion out over a lengthy period. Households, like businesses, also do not react instantaneously to increases in income. Households tend to plan their budgets and expenditures based on long-term expectation of their reliable level of income. Higher levels of income have to be around for some time before household spending shifts fully upward and triggers the full cycle of expansion.

The second problem with using this simplified economic-base model to project short-run adjustments to shocks is that each part of the economy is linked to the rest of the economy in quite different ways. The description provided above of how changes in the base affect changes elsewhere in the economy focused on only one linkage, that of the expanding firm hiring more workers and those workers spending that income. But many other linkages are possible. The expanding firm may need other inputs that can be obtained locally: electricity, natural gas, semi-finished products, and raw materials. Likewise, as the expanding firm markets its increased output, it may use local businesses for transportation, wholesaling, retailing, further processing, etc.

Export-oriented firms can be more or less tied into the local economy. Their impact on the local economy will be greater or lesser depending on these link-ages. At one extreme, a highly automated firm might obtain almost all of its inputs, including its machinery, skilled labor, and raw materials from outside the local area and ship out its product in company-owned trucks. An expansion of such a firm might have very little impact on the local economy. At the other extreme would be a business that buys most of its inputs locally from other businesses, is labor-intensive, and sells its output through local businesses some of which process it further into different products for export. Such a business would be linked extensively to many parts of the local economy, and any signifi-cant changes in its level of activity would have repercussion throughout that local economy.

These variable linkages mean that a single multiplier may not be appropriate for all firms in the economic base. The use of an easily calculated average multiplier will not do. For some extensively linked industries such as agriculture, we know this is the case. Often one can find no statistically reliable relationship between net farm income and the level of economic activity in farm-related communities. The net income of the farm household does not even begin to account for all of the connections the farm as a business has with the local economy. In addition, because farm income is notoriously unstable, both farm households and the businesses that depend on them have learned to ride the fluctuations in some stable way. Both groups implicitly average good times and bad and adjust their spending, purchases, number of employees, size of business, etc. to this average. That means the local economy does not adjust immediately to this year's level of farm income. There is a lag and a smoothing process.

Farms are not unique in this regard. They are just a dramatic example and a warning about the limits of this simplified economic-base model. That model does not tell us when the impact of expansion will take place nor, reliably, what the size of that impact will be. That makes it of questionable value as a short-run predictor of the economic impact of changes in the "export" base.

Most of these problems with the economic-base model have been recognized for decades. They are the reason most academic economists have abandoned this approach to local economic analysis. In its place, economists have developed detailed regional economic models that in effect model each type of industry separately and use region-specific data. Each industry's connections with the rest of the economy are traced by tracking from where it gets its inputs and to where it markets its output. This allows all of the direct and indirect impacts of one industry's expansion on all the other industries to be measured. Each industry, then, can have its own multiplier, which is tied to the particular ways in which it connects with the local economy.

Such elaborate input-output models can also be tied dynamically to national macroeconomic models that project trends in industrial expansion. Such detailed dynamic regional models can then project the expected character of the changes in the local economy (Miernyk, 1984).

This more sophisticated approach is the one the academic economist would always choose if it were possible to do so. But such a detailed approach is usually not possible. It demands enormous amounts of detailed local economic data, which may simply be unavailable. In addition, it requires the development of a very complex computer model, which needs to be constantly tended and updated. Most local areas, even most states, do not have the data, resources, or economic and econometric skills to develop this type of detailed analysis. Instead, they fall back on a simpler model, often to the primitive economic base model. Simplicity and public understanding are, after all, the chief attractions of this crude approach.

8. Who Is Pushing Whom? Causality and the Economic Base

The economic-base model attempts to focus our attention on those forces in the local economy that are the primary causes of economic change. The model suggests that it is mainly changes in export income that cause changes in the rest of the economy. Given the difficulties discussed above in estimating the size of the impact that changes in the export base have on the rest of the local economy, one might wonder whether the economic-base approach has directed our attention to reliable causal forces. It certainly is possible that the development of a broad array of sophisticated local service industries is what makes a local area an attractive place for manufacturing firms to locate. In that situation, it is the nonbasic, "derivative," or service industries that cause export activity to increase rather than the other way around.

In fact, a significant number of regional economists have insisted for several decades that this is the real direction of causality. They have focused on the cumulative causation triggered by population growth in a particular area. As population grows, the local market for various types of goods and services increases, local production, rather than importation, becomes possible. That local production of import substitutes in turn creates a demand for more local economic activity, and a still richer mix of local businesses comes into existence. The more diverse and complete the range of economic activity found locally, the more attractive the area becomes for other firms that both produce for the local market and export. Note that this, too, is a theory of multiple waves of economic expansion, but not of expansion triggered by exports. The development of locally oriented economic activity drives the expansion. Exports are a result, not a cause (Richardson, 1973; Tiebout, 1956).

This suggests that economic analysis offers two quite different views of what causes local economic development. One emphasizes exports as the driving force. The other emphasizes import substitution and the development of a broad range of locally oriented economic activities. Of course, it is perfectly possible that both sets of forces are operating together and reinforcing each other. Export growth may draw population, which creates the market for expanded local markets that bring a broader array of local businesses into existence. This may attract additional export firms and a larger population, which in turn stimulates further expansion of locally oriented firms. And so forth.

The economic forces could, logically, run in either direction, or the causality could be bidirectional, with feedback from both export-oriented and locally oriented expansion maintaining cycles of growth. Logic alone cannot tell us which of these approaches is better or whether both are equally important. Only empirical analysis can help us determine that.

One analysis of the economies of eight southeastern states tested the direction of economic causality between export and locally oriented activities. Two divisions of local economic activity were tried. First, the economy was divided between export-oriented and locally oriented economic activity. Then a division between service industries and nonservice industries, including manufacturing, mining, and agriculture, was tried.

The results were not encouraging for the economic-base approach. Of the eight states, in only two were earnings in exports causally related to the level of locally oriented economic activity. In three of the states, causality ran in the other direction: changes in locally oriented economic activity caused the changes in export activity. In one of the states, causal forces seemed to be operating in both directions.

When economic activity was divided between services and nonservice, "basic" activities, the causal forces appeared to be strongly bidirectional. In five of the eight states, changes in service activities helped explain changes in nonservice activities. But in six of the eight states, changes in nonservice activities also helped explain service activities. In the majority of the states, then, the economic forces were operating in both directions. Growth in service activities played a very important role in determining overall local economic growth. Manufacturing and other traditional export oriented activities were not the primary economic forces (Giarratani and McNelis, 1980). Others have also found evidence that "local" economic activities may drive the overall economy rather than just adjust passively to export activities (Shahidsaless et al., 1983; Green, 1966; Richardson, 1973). Some analysts insist expansion of service industries is what leads all modern economic growth (Riddle, 1986). The failure of the primitive economic-base approach to explain economic growth in these states may be due to the use of statewide data. States are not always, or even usually, integrated economic units. Within each state there are often reasonably separate local economies, tied into regional economies that cross state boundaries. It is possible that the economic-base model would do better if it focused on true local economies rather than political units that may take in bits and pieces of many different local economies. U.S. Forest Service economists have tested the economic-base model of growth in a small local economy in Northwest Montana. They obtained similar results to those reported above: the direction of economic causality was not primarily that of changes in the basic sector causing changes in the rest of the economy. Causality was again bidirectional. Changes in the service and retail sectors also caused changes in the export sector. Economic growth was not a simple process in which the export-oriented businesses led the rest of the economy (Connaughton, et al., 1984).

9. Defining the Economic Base

The economic-base model has one more intractable problem: specifying the basic economic activities. Without completing that step empirically, one has no explanation of anything. We have to be able to specify which economic activities are the "primary" activities that supposedly drive all others in the local economy.

Often this problem is solved intuitively by simply specifying those industries which obviously produce for export: manufacturing, agriculture, and mining. To these are added "autonomous" inflows of income from federal spending, major construction projects, and income earned outside the local economy. All other economic activities such as services, retail and wholesale trade, local construction, and local government are labeled derivative or secondary.

But this usually breaks down very quickly. Some manufacturing, agricultural, and mining production may well be for the local market, not for export. In addition, an area may be a regional trade center or tourist attraction, and part of the spending on services and retail and wholesale trade may not be local in origin at all. These industries may actually be part of the economic base.

That means that all economic activities are partly basic and partly derivative.

But how much of each? Two approaches have been taken to this problem. One method assumes that all regions have similar consumption patterns per capita. National averages are used to establish how much of the dollar value of each good and service is "needed" to serve the local population. The value of all production in excess of this average is assumed to be exported and to be part of the economic base. Besides assuming that all areas have identical consumption patterns, this approach also assumes that all areas have identical productivity and that areas do not both export and import the same type of good or service. None of these are safe assumptions. Use of this approach has led to clearly spurious results (Gibson and Worden, 1981).

The other method is to specify a minimum level of locally oriented economic activity that is needed in each industry to support the local population. All activity in excess of this is then seen as part of the economic base. This minimum level can be estimated by studying economies of similar size and taking the lowest level of economic activity found in each particular industry as the minimal requirement for local needs. All activity above this level in other areas is assumed to be externally oriented and part of the economic base. This approach is also built around heroic assumptions including the assumption that almost all areas export but none of them import.

Clearly, major definitional problems plague the economic-base model. Practical, commonsensical solutions have been developed to give empirical content to the basic/derivative dichotomy, but each of these, because it is ad hoc, adds an undetermined amount of arbitrariness to the application of the model. This may explain some of the difficulty in getting reliable and stable results using the model.

This difficulty in defining the base of the economy can lead to some seriously misleading conclusions. The focus on exports can lead to an emphasis on manufacturing, mining, and agriculture; locally oriented economic activities such as retail trade and services can then be dismissed as not of primary importance in determining how the overall economy performs. They can be seen as simply following export activity, without any power to stimulate the economy themselves. But this may be wrong, even within the context of the economic-base model. A city may grow primarily because it has become a regional trade, cultural, political, or recreational center. Nothing at all may be exported. The city's stores, services, government offices, and entertainment facilities may simply attract people who then spend money. Careful economic-base analysis would pick this up, but the imagery of the export base might well hide this reality and inappropriately divert attention toward traditional manufacturing.

10. A Distorted Vision

The economic-base model is stark and dramatic: our wealth and well-being come from working the earth, clawing at its surface or digging into its bowels to pull or coax from it the stuff of our survival. With our sweat and ingenuity and craft we mix those basic raw materials into useful things. Then we send those useful things away in return for colorful pieces of paper or drab accounting entries called money.

But drama is not what we seek in an economic model. We seek useful guidance in public policy. And when the economic-base model is phrased in this way, its major weaknesses become apparent.

How can our well-being be tied to sending the useful things we make away for others to enjoy? Why do we want these colorful pieces of paper, even if they could, as of old, be converted into a shiny metal, gold? What about the ways the Earth or our community directly nurtures the local population and contributes to its well-being? Why are the things we do for each other that make life comfortable, convenient, and satisfying not counted as contributing to our welfare in a primary way? The vast majority of us, two-thirds to three-quarters of us, are not employed directly in producing things that are shipped to distant markets. Most of us are employed providing services and goods to each other in the area where we live. We educate each other, take care of each other's children, provide entertainment, transportation, meals, government services, and medical care. We operate stores, which provide ourselves, not people at distant locations, with goods—some locally made, many imported from afar.

Those imports, not exports, are the things that are important to us. For they are the goods we enjoy directly. Sending away our valuable production is not an economic good in itself. It is an economic "bad," for we lose something unless the exports allow us to import something even more valuable to ourselves. We want these colorful pieces of paper (as, in an earlier period, we wanted the shiny metal), not because they contribute to local economic activity but because they allow us to go outside the local economy to obtain things that would otherwise be difficult or impossible for us to produce locally.

It is imports that contribute to our welfare, not exports. We export only in order to get the money that will allow us to import. We seek that outside money not because it puts us to work, but in order to put others to work in distant places, producing the things we want but cannot easily make ourselves.

Meanwhile, the comfort and convenience and variety in our lives are tied to what we do for each other in the local economy and the way in which our natural and social environments nurture and stimulate us. Most of our commercial economic activity actually involves "taking in each others' wash," not producing for distant markets. These local service activities are what makes life civilized.

But the economic-base vision, with its emphasis on making things for export, its emphasis on importing only money, and its dismissal of the productivity and value of locally-oriented economic activity and resources, distracts us from this reality. Instead, it pictures a highly distorted reality partially tied to our past and heavily influenced by ideology.

11. Intellectual Inertia and Ideology

Our frontier history partially explains the intuitive appeal and staying power of the economic-base model. In settling what to us appeared to be an empty and often forbidding continent, we did wrestle with the earth to survive. Isolated on a foreign continent, thousands of miles from familiar centers of civilization, we were on our own. If we could not get what we needed at any particular location, we would have to leave. This folk history is one we all learn in school, and it is retaught to us in our novels and films.

In our rural areas we still seem to be on the frontier, closely in touch with and dependent upon the earth. If we could not raise food, harvest timber, or extract minerals, we would be forced to relocate to more productive areas. If these basic economic activities in our hinterlands are faltering or failing, the rural areas will give up their population to our cities, just as they always have done. To avoid this, we must either revitalize those basic activities or supplement them with relocated export-oriented manufacturing. We must chase after the footloose smokestacks. All this, too, has its roots in our common understanding of our history and the emigrations from the countryside, which ultimately brought most of our families to the metropolitan areas.

But folk history and intellectual inertia are not the only reasons we continue to accept a distorting model of economic reality. Economic models adjust to the dominant political reality, and in that sense they incorporate a significant amount of ideology. Earlier, in a rural, land-based political system, our economic models assured us that land-based economic activities were the vital ones. Urban-based trade and manufacturing were of secondary importance or simply unproductive and parasitical. In the Great Britain of the 17th and 18th centuries, with an island mercantile economy focused on international trade and the financing of imperial wars, the economic models assured people that exports were vitally important, that imports needed to be restricted, and that the accumulation of gold bullion— the basis for financing foreign wars and expansion—was the foundation of national prosperity.

With the rise of an industrial society, the economic vision had to change if the rising capitalist class was going to take its rightful place. Our economic models had to acknowledge the manufacturer's legitimacy, even primacy. Now it was mere mercantile activity, services and trade, that was labeled unproductive along with the meddling regulatory apparatus of the mercantile state. The real productive forces were industry and manufacturing, not trade, finance, and government.

So, too, has political power been enshrined in our contemporary economic-base models. The dominant commercial forces in the local economy, the national corporations that export to the larger economy, are singled out as the primary economic actors upon whom the rest of us depend. In largely rural areas where agriculture or mining or timber once dominated, the prevailing economic model helps shore up past privilege by continuing to emphasize these shrinking sectors of our economy. Finally, by emphasizing growth in the gross volume of income and population as a measure of economic-improvement, economic base models support the type of economic change most likely to benefit those in the local economy who own resources that are fixed in supply: private real estate, established banks, and well-located businesses. Such growth, whatever it does for the majority of the population, boosts the value of the assets of an area's most influential groups. It should not be surprising that the dominant economic model is so supportive of these groups' interests.

Although our collective history and the social influence of commercial interests may explain our continued dependence on a rather primitive model of economic well being, they certainly provide no intellectual justification for it. They do the opposite: they warn us that we may be looking at our local economies through an outmoded and politically biased pair of economic glasses. This is not just a matter of academic concern. If we want to be able to protect and enhance the economic well-being of the general population, we need an economic model that addresses that issue in a clear, contemporary way, illuminating the problems and directing us to the policies that can deal with them. The economic-base approach does not do that.

Instead, it turns our attention to an aspect of the local economy that local development policy cannot influence: the national and international markets for the area's exports and the business decisions of the huge corporations that usually control them. These are not useful policy handles except in a negative sense. Although local efforts are unlikely to influence distant markets and corporate offices, local policy decisions might raise the cost of operating in an area and drive the export-oriented firms out. The message from the export-base theory is, "Don't bite the hand that feeds you."

Efforts to protect or enhance local environmental quality might raise production costs. Improvements in local schools and public infrastructure might raise the tax burden on export operations in a way that makes them noncompetitive. Fair energy pricing, union wage demands, local zoning restrictions and health and safety codes all can be seen as burdensome to the goose busy laying the golden eggs.

In that sense the economic base model is not politically neutral. It empowers the already powerful and officially classifies the majority as unavoidably dependent upon the local business elite. It teaches that the local population needs to understand and respect that dependence or risk its livelihood. In this way it encourages hopelessness, fatalism, and despair. Someone else holds all the cards, it tells us. We as residents and citizens can only watch, respect, and adapt.

12. A Theory of Non-development: Instability and Dependence

The traditional economic-base view of the local economy is not a theory of economic development. It guides local policy in the opposite direction, toward dependence and instability. It tends to trap the local economy in a primitive, underdeveloped state.

a. A Guide For Instability and Dependence

Some ways of looking at the economy are just not very productive. They do not give us a feeling for where we are going or how we can get where we would like to be. But they are otherwise harmless.

That is not the case with the economic-base approach. With its emphasis on exports and the need to support the interest of the businesses that produce the exports, it guides local economy policy in a direction that undermines the area's real economic base and prevents real economic development.

Heavy reliance on exports creates dependence. A local area has almost no control over the national or international market for its products; as the demand for its exports fluctuates, the flow of income into the local economy fluctuates, and these fluctuations are amplified by the multiplier. During national recessions or periods of a strong dollar, demand for an area's exports plummets. The exports, touted as the primary source of local economic welfare, become the conduit through which instability in the national and international economies are imported. The more dependent the economy is on exports, the stronger its "economic base," the more it is at the mercy of random external events.

An export-oriented economy is an underdeveloped economy. It produces little of what it needs itself. "Colonial" is the word we used to use for such a situation of economic dependence. Yet this is the direction in which the economic-base vision, and policies based on it, would take our local economies.

b. Real Economic Development

Consider the forces that almost all of us would agree are the primary sources of economic improvement: rising productivity, technological innovation, improved labor quality, advances in basic knowledge, and more efficient use of resources. The economic-base approach says nothing about any of these. It simply assumes a given level of each, and sees changes in them as startling occurrences or autonomous trends.

Consider the major changes now taking place in our economy. The decline in traditional blue-collar manufacturing and the increasing importance of service industries reduces the role played by the export of raw materials and commodities. This change in the character of the things we seek from our economy, combined with improvements in transportation and communication allows a significant decentralization of population and economic activity. Rural areas need no longer be the hinterland. Small metropolitan areas need no longer be appendages of a few major metropolitan areas. The economic-base model is silent on these trends, which are transforming our economic geography.

Think about the areas we would all agree have sophisticated, developed economies: the metropolitan belts on the East Coast, Southern California, Texas, and the Great Lakes. But how many can name what it is these areas export? These areas produce such a variety of products, and consume so much of their own production, that no particular export industries in fact stand out. They simultaneously export and import many of the same products. They are not dependent on particular flows of exports or imports. Their ''economic base'' is not visible.

As Jane Jacobs has pointed out, economic development takes place around import substitution, not exports (Jacobs, 1984, p. 39). Export-oriented economies remain primitive, suffer through booms and busts, and go nowhere. It is only when an area begins making for itself what it once imported that a viable economic base begins to grow. Production for local use is what begins to weave the connections between local individuals and businesses that make them parts of a productive and stable economic community. The development of *local* dependencies is what economic development is all about. The strength of our local economy is tied to the richness and diversity of what we can do for ourselves and our neighbors, not what we export or import.

c. Reversing the Emphasis:
Locally-oriented Economic Activities

This suggests a drastically different picture than the economic-base vision provides. Instead of demeaning locally oriented economic activity as derivative or secondary, we should see it as the seed of a reliable local economy. Instead of seeing exports as the key to our future, they should be considered a temporary liability associated with the primitive state in which we find some of our local economies.

Economic-development policy should encourage import substitution and the development of a diverse set of local services. This will cut the leakage of local resources and increase the range of economic opportunities open to local residents.

Instead of chasing after new smokestacks to increase our ''export base,'' we should be supporting existing small firms in their competition with imports and the national market.

Ironically, even the economic-base model supports this approach. Leakages of income to finance imports bring to an end the multiple expansion triggered by the injection of new income. The greater the dependence on imports, the smaller the multiplier. Thus one can stimulate the local economy, provide jobs and income, by displacing imports just as one can by increasing exports. The advantage of the former strategy, as pointed out above, is that it reduces dependence and instability and allows a more sophisticated economy to develop. Import substitution does not just mean producing locally the bread that previously was imported. It is much broader than that. All locally oriented businesses seek to offer residents attractive opportunities to spend their income. To the extent they succeed in diverting expenditures to their businesses that otherwise would have flowed out of the local economy, they will have a stimulating effect similar to that usually assigned to a new export-oriented firm. Thus a bowling alley or dance studio, the type of "secondary" or "derivative" activities the economic-base model suggests cannot stimulate economic development, can indeed boost the local economy simply by holding onto income that would otherwise have left the area.

The availability of services may stimulate economic development in another way. The availability of day-care facilities and convenience foods makes it possible for more family members to work outside the home. At the same time, those services provide job opportunities outside the home. This allows the increased specialization and division of labor that have transformed our homes and local economies over the last two decades.

Finally, as noted above, the availability of a broad array of local services and amenities makes a community a more attractive place to both potential businesses and residents. These "derivative" activities can draw new economic activity to an area. Service-led growth is not only possible, it is the primary mechanism of real economic development (Riddle, 1986; Jacobs, 1984).

These types of economic development—created in a way often rejected as impossible in the context of the economic-base model—are not only feasible but attractive compared to chasing export-oriented smokestacks.

13. The Real Economic Base:
Local Quality and Economic Development

The real economic base of a local area consists of all those things that make it an attractive place to live, work, or do business. That means the economic base includes the quality of the natural environment, the richness of the local culture, the security and stability of the community, the quality of the public services and the public-works infrastructure, and the quality of the workforce. None of these are things produced by the commercial economy or produced for export. They are provided for outside the commercial economy. Yet they are the local area's economic base. This should reorient us and our local economic policies. Protecting the natural, cultural, and human-made environment is most certainly productive economic activity. It cannot be dismissed as noneconomic or anti-economic. Similarly, taxes that support public services, infrastructure, and the development of a high-quality work force are also economic, not a burden on the economy. They help finance the building of our economic base. Although this alternative vision turns the traditional economic-base model on its head, it represents a return to mainstream economic analysis. The economic-base approach focused on one set of external forces that influence a local economy, the demand for its exports. But this left unexplained the supply of exportable products to begin with.

The economic-base approach is concerned exclusively with external demand. It ignores "the other half of the scissors" of traditional economic analysis, supply. To understand why firms locate where they do, one cannot help but deal with what it is that makes a location attractive. We are forced back into dealing with the qualitative characteristics of an area.

In a few instances, one can give a quantitative answer: the area is the cheapest source of raw material for a particular product. But fewer and fewer firms are tied to resource deposits in this way. Changes in what is produced, development of synthetic materials, and improvements in communication and transportation have made it possible for firms to locate in a broad range of places. Automotive factories do not locate only in the Detroit area anymore; they shop around the entire nation looking for an appropriate location. The same is increasingly true of almost all manufacturing.

What then draws a firm to a particular site? Transportation costs and the size of the local and regional markets are still very important, but they only help in choosing a general region. Local qualities play a major role: the quality of the work force given the prevailing wage, the quality and range of commercial services available, the quality of the public infrastructure, the quality of the community as a place to live, the quality of the school system, the quality of the entertainment and recreational opportunities, the quality of the natural environment, and so on. Without making reference to these, one could never explain the geographic distribution of businesses and population location.

Businesses appreciate these factors for several reasons. First, they want to attract and hold a high-quality work force with relatively low wages. In addition, by drawing population to an area or holding it there, these qualities create larger markets for a broad range of businesses. Finally, businesses are run by people, and most people care about their communities, in terms of both the richness and diversity of existing businesses and the overall quality of life.

In this alternative vision, export-oriented business fades into the background as just another activity supported by the local economic base. Businesses are no longer the factor around which all local economic policy must revolve. Citizens seeking new skills, environmentalists seeking clean air or water, artists seeking attention to their work, school boards seeking support for their schools, neighbors seeking to protect the integrity of their communities are all engaged in economic activities. They are as relevant to the area's development as the downtown businessperson or the national manufacturing or mining firms that operate locally.

The advantage of this view of the local economy is that it directs public policy where it stands some chance of having an effect rather than to national and international forces. More important, it focuses our attention on things that are directly beneficial to us as well as important to the area's economic development. That opens up the possibility of a "must win" local economic policy. The measures taken to improve the local economic base can also directly improve the quality of our lives and the range of opportunities open to us.

CHAPTER EIGHT

The Self-Defeating Strategies of Quantitative Growth

1. Introduction: The Strategies for Growth

The last decade and a half have brought hard times to most American communities. It has been a time of economic disruption and reorganization, painful, and even demoralizing to many. Four recessions, including the two most serious downturns since the Great Depression, stalled the national economy in a lengthy period of almost no net growth. Persistent inflation, sometimes at double-digit levels, added to the economic confusion.

In addition to these national economic cycles, significant regional shifts added to the sense of breakdown. The industrial heartland, a belt stretching through the Great Lakes region into New England, entered a period of significant decline. Manufacturing activity declined nationwide as goods from other countries made significant inroads in American markets. In addition, consumer purchasing patterns shifted somewhat away from manufactured goods toward services. Compounding these problems in the traditional manufacturing states was a shift in the location of manufacturing activity, out of the "frostbelt" toward the South and West.

But even the South and West have faced economic disruption. The bust that followed the energy boom of the 1970s has left many western states reeling, and the near-collapse of metal and uranium mining and processing has compounded the problems. Even glamorous high-tech industries have not been immune to disruption and decline. Major electronic firms began laying off thousands of workers in the mid-1980s as the electronics boom stalled.

Almost all regions and communities have faced elements of economic decline over the last decade and a half. In response, cities, states, and regions have searched desperately for ways to shore up their economies. Out of these efforts has emerged a common set of public policies labeled economic development strategies.

These strategies emerged from the economic-base view of the local economy. The business community, most economic-development professionals, and the ubiquitous local economic-development corporations strongly endorse these strategies and reinforce that economic folk wisdom. That same view is a substantial part of what the general population "knows" about economics.

The central concern of this strategy is to attract industry to an area to offset the losses associated with both cyclical declines, such as recessions, and more permanent downward trends, such as a decline in manufacturing or mining. Such new industry, the folk wisdom tells us, will improve local economic well-being by:

• providing jobs for the local residents who are unemployed or underemployed;

• providing jobs for the young people so that they will not be forced to leave home;

• boosting per-capita income by increasing the number of high-paying jobs and the employment opportunities for multiple family members;

• drawing population to the area and increasing the overall level of expenditure in local businesses;

• decreasing poverty as more employment opportunities and a higher overall level of income boost the fortunes of the disadvantaged;

• increasing the local tax base and allowing government to keep tax rates low while maintaining or improving the quality and mix of public services.

The folk wisdom holds that the key to reaping all these benefits is the local "business climate." If the climate is bad, new firms will avoid the area and existing firms that are considering expansion may relocate. That climate can be improved, this popular strategy suggests, by, among other things:

• reducing taxes on businesses and on high-income individuals who are likely to invest in businesses;

• reducing the regulatory burdens local government imposes on businesses, especially environmental, land-use, health, and safety regulations;

• reducing workers' wage demands and eliminating other union policies that increase local labor costs;

• subsidizing capital costs through the issuance of tax-exempt industrial-revenue bonds, lending public capital at reduced rates, and directly subsidizing initial location or expansion costs.

These familiar strategies for "economic development" have two important characteristics. First, they are aimed at quantitative expansion in the dollar volume of business, dollar income, the number of jobs, and the number of people. That quantitative expansion is seen as an economic good by itself that automatically boosts the economic well-being of the local population. It is often invoked to override qualitative considerations such as neighborhood aesthetics, environmental concerns, the quality of public services, or the local "way of life."

Second, the strategy considers business activity as the sole or primary type of economic activity that needs to be expanded. Local economic well-being is seen as tied almost exclusively to the business sector.

Earlier chapters of this book have stressed the importance of both qualitative objectives and noncommercial goods, services, and activities in determining economic well-being. These are almost totally absent from the most common local development strategies, which should make us at least a little suspicious that something important is missing from these strategies. Because of this deficiency, the strategies may be seriously off the mark.

2. The Objectives and Measures of Economic Growth

The folk wisdom that dominates both the popular vision of and public policy toward local economic development centers on growth. That growth has dimensions, whose relevance to economic well-being are usually taken for granted.

• *An increase in the level of business activity.* Almost any local newspaper's description of how well the local economy is doing will focus on the overall level of business activity, how much the gross volume of business has grown. Concern is for more money changing hands, more money being made, more people being drawn into economic activity. A healthy economy is pictured as having continuous growth in the total dollar volume of business activity.

• *An increase in income.* This is closely related to overall business activity. One person's expenditures are another person's income. A business's purchases are income to other businesses and to individual suppliers of inputs. Among the most important such "suppliers" are workers; in fact, payments to workers usually dominate local income. Since people do not save all or most of their increased income, a rise in income leads to an increase in spending, which supports additional businesses and generates additional jobs.

• *An increase in the number of jobs.* This is a priority objective, not only because a job is usually the prerequisite for an income, but because useful employment is an individual and social objective by itself. The availability of more jobs can both reduce the pain and social disruption caused by unemployment and generate additional income that can support local businesses.

• *An increase in the total population.* Population growth is often taken as the key indicator that a region is prospering. More people means increased spending and an increased demand for all resources. The larger population is an increased market for local businesses.

Clearly, all of these economic growth measures and objectives are related. Additional jobs are needed to support a larger population. Wages are the chief source of local income. The circulation of that income through the local economy creates the total volume of business activity. It is no wonder that these objectives are often used interchangeably and that growth is discussed in general terms rather than in terms of a particular economic variable. ''Growth,'' often otherwise unspecified, is the most widely held economic objective because all of these economic variables seem to move together and contribute in their own ways to improved economic well-being.

3. Quantitative Growth and Economic Well-Being: The Missing Connection

Although the prevalent economic folk wisdom, public policy, and the business community see a close connection between quantitative growth and the economic well-being of the local population, professional economic analysis is far less conclusive. The connections between the quantitative growth of any of the growth objectives and economic well-being are anything but intuitive or obvious. Professional economic analysis supports none of these quantitative growth objectives as unambiguously connected to an area's improved well-being. Some of them are not even distantly related to economic well-being. Others can be reformulated so that there is at least the possibility of a positive correlation between their growth and improvements in well-being.

But before we can proceed to examine the connection between popular economic-growth objectives and economic well-being, we have to be more explicit about what we mean by the latter term. We will postpone a detailed discussion of this until the next chapter. Here it will be adequate to use the definition implicit in the folk wisdom. Improvements in local economic well-being consist of either or both of the following:

• improvements in the flow and quality of the goods and services available to the typical existing resident.

• improvements in the availability of satisfying economic activities to the typical existing resident.

With that definition in mind, we can proceed to examine briefly the relationship between each of the popular growth objectives and well-being.

a. Increased Dollar Volume of Business

The gross dollar volume of business, whatever its attraction to the business community or financial press as a measure of economic well-being, begins with a fatal flaw: it ignores the difference between costs and benefits and adds the two together indiscriminately. For instance, all the costs of goods purchased outside the local economy are counted as benefits produced by the local economy. In addition it double-, triple-, or quadruple-counts whatever benefits are there to be measured. The more local middlemen there are getting a good to people, the larger the exaggeration. Finally, it ignores the question of who receives whatever net benefits are generated. They may not accrue to local residents, and therefore may not boost local economic well-being.

If, for instance, government regulations required that all final commercial transactions in the local economy be supervised by businesses with offices in Washington, D.C., run by people with MBAs from Harvard, a new layer of commercial activity would be added to the local economy.

This would add to the cost of obtaining all goods and run many local firms completely out of business. It would also drain money out of the local economy. Clearly, local economic well-being would decline even though the dollar volume of business, counting the new "middlemen," increased.

At the very least one must net out of gross business volume the losses or costs associated with the activity. In addition, benefits must be counted only once, by focusing on net income or value added. Finally, income that flows out of an area must not be counted as a gain for that area. Since these adjustments would reduce this measure of growth to simply the growth in local income, we turn next to this second popular measure of local economic improvement.

b. Increased Money Income

Because growth in the local population's money income provides the means to obtain any desired goods and services, and because it is likely to be closely correlated with the availability of productive roles in the local economy, the assumed connection between income and local well-being is understandable. But there are several very loose links here. Most important is the interaction with population. If income grows but so does population, the income available per person or per household may remain the same or fall. This certainly would not represent an improvement in economic well-being for the individuals and families involved. At the very least, income growth must be measured on a per capita or per family basis.

c. Increased Per Capita Income

But even this major adjustment may not be enough. If our focus is on what further economic growth will do for existing residents of the area, we need to know if the additional income generated by that growth accrued to existing residents or to new arrivals. Since the objective of local economic growth policies is presumably not to boost the well-being of those living elsewhere, this is an important adjustment. At the very least, we need to be focusing on the average income of existing families or the per-capita income of existing residents.

The oil boomtowns of the West provide an example of this. Oil discoveries drew highly specialized and highly paid oil workers into the area—the jobs were too specialized for local residents. The sudden increase in the demand for almost all goods and services, backed by the migrants' high incomes, drove up local prices. News of the boom brought more job-seekers than there were jobs. Competition for less-skilled local jobs increased, putting downward pressure on wages in those lower-paying jobs. The impact of the new high-paying jobs on existing residents could easily have been negative, as their wages stagnated or declined while costs increased.

Finally, growth in income and population can be accompanied by increased costs of living. Housing costs may rise, for instance, as may the prices of many other goods and services, including taxes. Any increase in per-capita income must be adjusted or deflated to cover any changes in the cost of living. Inflation, local or national in origin, must be removed if real improvements in local well-being are to be measured.

It should be clear that simple growth in total local income need not be related to improvements in local economic well-being. Total local income can easily rise while local economic well-being deteriorates. Real income increases per capita to existing residents are what we should be looking at if we want an "obvious" measure of local economic well-being. Later in this chapter we will explore some of the less obvious problems with even this measure.

d. Increased Employment

An increase in the number of jobs, because it represents an expansion in the range of economic opportunity and provides an additional source of money income, may be expected to have some connection with local economic well-being. But, again, the connection is tenuous. The most important question is who gets the jobs. For the new jobs to benefit the local population, they must be higher-quality jobs than those currently available, and they must be accessible to local workers. If the jobs go to new migrants, or if the availability of the jobs draws migrants who increase the competition for both the new jobs and for the existing jobs, the current population may be made worse-off. Unemployment may actually rise, and the employment rate among the current population may fall along with wages.

Different jobs have different skill and experience requirements, which the existing population may lack. Competition for jobs in an expanding economy also takes certain skills and personality characteristics; that longtime local residents may not have these to the same extent as migrants who, as a group, are likely to be more ambitious and aggressive in their job search. After all, by moving into the area, they have already shown a commitment to aggressive job-seeking.

In addition, the wage level associated with the additional jobs available to the existing population is important. If only low-wage, "secondary" jobs open up and population is growing, per-capita income may not be much improved or may deteriorate. The character and mix of the new jobs, their accessibility to the existing population, and the size of the new population they draw to an area must all be analyzed before any conclusion can be reached about whether an increase in employment in an area has improved local economic well-being.

e. Increased Population

Professional economic analysis does not even hint that an increase in the number of warm bodies in a particular area is by itself an economic good. The shanty-towns that surround every major Third World city, teaming with the poor, drama-tize this. With growth in population most certainly come increased congestion, pollution, and crime. With it may also come increased unemployment, a decrease in the quality of local public services, increased incidence of poverty, rising tax burdens, destruction of a sense of community, and loss of local control by existing residents.

On the other hand, significant population growth may also bring increased diversity, a richer culture, a broader range of economic opportunity, more locally available goods and services, increased property and business values, an expand-ed tax base, and a more dynamic and exciting social life. Only detailed analysis combined with judgments presumably based on the preferences of the existing population, will tell us if any particular type of population growth in an area will improve local well-being. There is no reason at all simply to assume that it will.

Clearly, when we are looking at relatively open local economies, none of the popular quantitative measures of economic growth needs be connected to im-provements in local economic well-being. The intuitively obvious connections are not there. The economic folk wisdom may not be that wise.

However, adjustments in some of these growth measures may yield a reason-able quantitative indicator of economic well-being. The level of income of the typical existing resident, adjusted to changes in the cost of living, is the measure economic analysis would suggest is most likely to be connected with actual local economic well-being. It is to this economic indicator that we now turn our attention. Following that, we will turn to more detailed analysis of the use of the employment-growth indicator.

4. Lower Per-Capita Incomes as an Indicator of Superior Well-Being

Average family or per-capita income, adjusted for differences in the cost of living, certainly has an intuitive appeal as a measure of local economic well-being. By focusing on the real purchasing power of the average household, this measure might seem to be closely tied to what most of us mean by economic well-being. For that reason, it might be a reasonable target for local economic-development efforts: boost per-capita income to at least national averages, or toward those levels attained by the nation's most prosperous regions. A local per-capita income below national averages or below the levels attained in adjacent areas might be taken as a sign of economic ill-health, a lagging, unproductive economy that is depriving local residents of the affluence enjoyed elsewhere in the country. As intuitively plausible as this interpretation of regional differences in per capita income may be, it is seriously flawed by its exclusive focus on the goods purchased from businesses. Because this measure ignores what we as individual economic actors do not ignore—namely, quality and valuable goods and services that are not produced by businesses—it can provide precisely the wrong indication of economic health. When an area is a particularly attractive place to live, per-capita income will be low, falsely indicating that the area is economically inferior. The way in which local quality and noncommercial goods reverse the economic meaning of per-capita income will be the focus of this section.

We want to explore the conditions under which differences in per-capita income can be used to indicate differences in local economic well-being. Per-capita income is regularly used in this way. Often no more need be done to demonstrate the inferior status of people living in the Mountain or Southern states or most rural areas than to point to the fact that their per-capita incomes are 20 to 50 percent below those in the urban areas of the Pacific, Mid-Atlantic, or New England states. Similarly, economic-development strategies often consist of no more than the intent to attract high-wage industries to an area so that per-capita income can be boosted.

Neither the attractiveness of these higher wages nor their assumed impact in raising per capita income is usually challenged.

The use of high per-capita income as both an economic growth objective and a measure of local well-being has two implicit assumptions. In an economy where the labor force is mobile, per-capita money income could serve as a measure of local economic well-being only if the following assumptions hold:

• People do not care where they live and work.

• Businesses do not seek to minimize their labor costs. Instead, guided by moral feelings, tradition, or some other consideration, they set wages well above what they would otherwise have to pay to get the workers they need.

Stated explicitly, both of these are so patently false that grave doubts have to be raised about the use of even this one remaining quantitative growth objective. This may be hard on business economists and those who seek simple approaches to complex social issues, but it will not surprise most others. The empirical evidence indicates that the vast majority of people reject these assumptions as they make their everyday economic decisions.

Let us begin with the second assumption: What is it that determines the level of wages paid by firms in a particular area? The general assumption is not that business firms are driven by a basic sense of a ''just wage.'' Rather, firms in a competitive market economy pay only what the market requires in order to get and hold the work force they need. If workers with particular skills and work experience are in short supply, firms will have to raise wages in order to compete for those workers. If such workers are not available in sufficient numbers, wages will have to be set high enough to lure others to the area.

On the other hand, if the workers needed are readily available locally, if there is an adequate supply or even a surplus of such workers, there will be downward pressure on their wages. Businesses will be able to get away with paying less.

Business firms do try to keep labor costs low. They relocate plants to different areas of the country and even overseas in the pursuit of lower labor costs. They use recessions and periods of economic crisis to drive hard bargains with their workers. It is therefore not outrageous to propose that business firms pay higher wages only when they have to in order to get the workers they need. If firms are paying higher wages in one location than in another, one has to ask what market forces are making them do it.

That brings us to the first assumption. One reason firms may have trouble obtaining the workers they need cheaply is that workers and their families do not want to live where it is most profitable for the firm to be located. In Chapter Six, we discussed the extensive empirical evidence that families sacrifice considerable purchasing power to live in especially attractive places. They spend tens of thousands of dollars pursuing location-specific preferences. People care where they live.

Given that we know this to be true, it should not seem unlikely that people might also sacrifice income by accepting lower wages to live and work in a particular area in the same way they might sacrifice income by paying a higher price for a lot and home. Similarly, before they are willing to live and work in an unattractive location, they might insist on higher wages just as they might accept living in an inferior neighborhood only if the price of housing was unusually low.

This possibility can be initially discussed in a context that everyone should find realistic. When the cost of living in a particular area is unusually high, as in Alaska or Hawaii, the purchasing power of wages is reduced. If the same wages are paid in an area with a high cost of living as are paid in an area with a low cost of living, the workers in the high cost area will have a lower standard of living. In this situation, almost everyone would agree that the similarity in money wages does not imply a similarity in economic well-being. One group of workers is clearly better off. With our work force as mobile as it is, firms in the high-cost area will have difficulty holding on to their workers unless they raise their wage levels to cover the higher cost of living. Only with money wage levels raised will workers be as well off in the high-cost area as workers elsewhere. Higher wages are necessary in that area to provide workers with a level of economic well-being equal to that found elsewhere.

The higher wages are necessary to compensate workers for the higher cost of living. The higher money wages are not a sign of something that is unusually good about that area but a sign of something that is unusually bad, namely the unusually high cost of living. We could not use the higher wages as a sign of superior economic well-being without making a very basic, and serious, error. This is not a theoretical problem. We know that the cost of living in some areas is much, much higher than the cost of living in other areas. In 1984, Bureau of Labor Statistics data indicated that the annual costs of maintaining a moderate standard of living varied by as much as 40 percent between various American metropolitan areas (for example, Honolulu versus Dallas or New York versus Atlanta). The differences would be even greater if low-cost nonmetropolitan areas were compared to high-cost metropolitan areas (Cebula, 1983, p. 3). Not surprisingly, firms operating in high-cost areas pay wages substantially above the national average. In weighing the actual economic well-being of people in those areas, we have to take into account the fact that some of that higher money income does not contribute any increment to economic well-being but simply compensates for high costs. This adjustment is no different than the one we must go through in comparing wages paid in 1950 with wages paid in 1985. We know the cost of living rose by a factor of four during that period, and that if this were ignored we would draw very erroneous conclusions about relative well-being in the two periods.

But there is no reason to believe that only geographic differences in the cost of living lead to such compensating wage differentials. Any characteristic of an area that the general population tends to judge negatively will lead to wage differentials that compensate but do not enhance economic well-being. At the extreme, we could imagine an employer trying to attract a qualified work force to the Antarctic wastes or to disease-ridden swamps in the tropics. Some "bribe" would surely be necessary over and above the wage that would ordinarily be paid for, say, employment in a typical suburban community.

A similar situation could develop if a particular area is an especially attractive place to live. Such areas will draw job-seekers. Migrants who receive no job offers will struggle to find some way of remaining there. This will create competition for jobs, which will depress wages. Employers will find that they do not have to offer as high a wage as they expected in order to hold the work force they need. Over time wages will fall below national averages for the same types of work.

Those lower wages might be interpreted as a sign of economic disadvantage, but that would represent the same error. The lower wages are offset by the advantages of living in that particular area. They are a measure of the area's other advantages, not of economic disadvantage.

This can be put more generally. If the labor force is mobile, if areas differ in their living characteristics and if the general population evaluates these characteristics in similar ways, money wages will vary across regions in ways that have nothing to do with differences in economic well-being. Those differences in money wages will merely compensate people for the differences in regional characteristics, in such a way that workers in each area will judge themselves to be about as well off overall as they would be anywhere else. In judging their economic well-being they will take into account the nonmarketed advantages and disadvantages of living in particular areas as well as the money income they can earn.

It should be pointed out that differences in local costs of living and quality of life may not be unrelated or separable. Many people find warmer climates attractive, and warmer climates certainly reduce heating bills, the cost of heating equipment, the investment in the thermal integrity of the home, and the cost of winter clothing. Per-capita incomes may be low in warmer areas both because people prefer the warmth and because the cost of living is lower.

Also, in general, if an area is an attractive place to live, wages will be lower than otherwise. This will reduce the cost of locally produced goods and services, lowering the cost of living there. It may not be possible to separate out the part of the lower incomes that compensate for cost-of-living differences and the part compensating for differences in living conditions.

5. People Care Where They Live:
Preferences for Living Environments

Wages and income will adjust in a particular pattern to compensate for differences in local living conditions only if there exist within the general population common preferences that influence migration. If preferences for living conditions are random or at least very diverse, then for every individual who prefers one type of living condition, there may be another who prefers something quite the opposite. In that case, those preferences would not lead to particular migration tendencies, and regional wage and income levels would not adjust to reflect those preferences. It is important, then, to know if there are general locational-preference patterns among the population.

Survey work done in the early 1970s investigated just this question. Households across the country were questioned about the preferences they had for the different types of living environments available in different regions. The strength of these preferences was judged by whether those preferences were strong enough to lead the households to want to move (Morgan, 1978, p.22; Weinstein and Firestine, 1978, p. 28.).

The survey results indicated strong, common preference patterns for living environments rich in nonexportable, location-specific qualities. It was the Pacific, Mountain, and sunbelt states that appeared to Americans to offer these qualities. These preferences have not changed significantly since at least 1948. In this survey between one-fifth and one-quarter of the population indicated that they would prefer to live in another region. In the Mid-Atlantic and North Central regions, an above-average percentage indicated that their current locations were sufficiently inferior to what they preferred and judged to be available elsewhere, and that they would like to relocate. In the South Atlantic, Mountain, Pacific, and South Central regions, the percentage of households making this judgment was below average.

The preferred region, according to the preferences expressed in this survey, was the Mountain states. If the population had acted on these expressed preferences in 1970, the Mountain states would have seen their population increase 124 percent, while the Pacific states would have grown 41 percent and the South Atlantic 11 percent. The Mid-Atlantic states would have lost 27 percent of their population and the North Central states about 25 percent (Morgan, 1978, p. 68). The responses were not just idle wishes or vague opinions. As we know, migration trends since 1970 have conformed closely to these expressed preferences, just as they have conformed in earlier periods to the prevailing preferences. The Mountain states have gained the most population in relative terms. The Atlantic states have lost population. People do have preferences for where they live. There are observable patterns to these preferences and these preferences are relatively stable. And people's actions are guided by these preferences.

This is true not only on a broad regional scale. The same questions can be studied at the neighborhood level. Neighborhoods vary considerably in ambient air pollution, ambient noise levels, congestion, cleanliness of streets and parks, crime, etc. The question being raised here is whether there is a general pattern in attitudes toward these characteristics that would influence choice of residence.

Data from the annual housing survey of the U.S. Bureau of the Census confirm the existence of general patterns in people's preferences for living conditions. The survey has asked people since 1973 to indicate their reaction to various aspects of neighborhood deterioration such as abandoned or boarded-up buildings, crime, trash and litter, air pollution, traffic noise, etc. Respondents were asked whether that condition existed where they lived, whether, if it did, it "bothered" them; and whether it bothered them so much they would "like to move from the neighborhood." This provided a general indication of the strength of the preference or aversion. Finally, the respondents were asked for an overall evaluation of "the neighborhood as a place to live" (U.S. Bureau of Census, 1978).

The neighborhood conditions judged most bothersome were street crime, trash, air pollution, and run-down housing. Large percentages of the respondents in neighborhoods with these characteristics indicated similar aversions, aversions strong enough to make them wish to move (Dahmann, 1983).

The empirical analysis reported in Chapter Six indicates that people do act on these preferences. They move. They offer to pay more for property in neighborhoods that do not have these negative characteristics. Property values document the existence and importance of these general preferences for environmental qualities.

Analysis of regional differences in location-specific qualities of the natural and social environments confirm that individuals act on the same set of general preferences. In fact, migration patterns are irrational or inexplicable if regional differences in these qualities are ignored. Recent migration has not been from low-wage areas to high-wage areas or from high unemployment areas to low-unemployment areas, but the reverse (Graves, 1980; Henderson, 1982; Ballard and Clark, 1981; Krumm, 1983). The areas with the most rapid increases in nominal wages have also had the most significant loss of population. The apparent irrationality in this disappears once people's preferences for certain types of living conditions are recognized. People move in pursuit of the location-specific qualities they prefer and they voluntarily sacrifice earnings to obtain them. Employers adjust the wages they offer to the labor-supply conditions, and the net result is lower wages in preferred areas and high wages in areas where people would rather not live. When this is viewed after the fact, it appears that people are moving away from high wages and low unemployment. In fact, they are simply moving to areas they and many others prefer because of those locations' specific qualities. The net result of that movement is lower wages in preferred locations.

6. Differences in Location-Specific Qualities Are the Dominant Explanation for Regional Differences in Wages

An area's "quality" can be gauged in several ways. The natural environment may provide a better or worse climate, more or less attractive vistas, greater or lesser opportunities for outdoor recreation, more or less polluted air or water. Likewise the social environment may be qualitatively superior or inferior depending upon crime rates, congestion problems, the quality of local schools, the stability of neighborhoods, and the degree of local control over the political process. Commercial environment certainly matters, too: the cost of living, the range of economic opportunities, the availability of goods and services. Finally, cultural quality may vary depending upon entertainment opportunities, the quality of the local performing arts, general educational levels, the diversity of arts and crafts available, and educational opportunities for adults.

This list, of course, is incomplete. But it does indicate the broad range of location-specific qualities that matter to people. Some, may argue, Scrooge-like, that such things really do not matter very much to people. But the empirical evidence is all to the contrary. Such qualitative differences explain both where our population is located and what the relative wage levels are in various locations.

Consider a national economy with a well-developed transportation system, competitive national corporations marketing a broad range of goods and services, and a mobile population willing to move to wherever overall conditions are best. The contemporary American economy certainly could be described in that manner.

In such an economy, why would one area draw a larger population than another? Locally specific marketable natural resources are certainly one explanation. If certain valuable resources are available only in particular locations, the economic value of developing them will draw businesses and population to those areas. But extractable commercial natural resources of this sort are of decreasing importance for most communities and regions. Most areas' economies are not resource-based in this sense any more.

Absent such location-specific, marketable resources, what can explain why businesses and population are drawn to one area as opposed to another? The major location-specific characteristics remaining are simply these non-marketed qualities associated with the area that make it an attractive place in which to live and work.

If one introduces those qualitative characteristics into the analysis of location choices, one can make sense out of the choices people have actually been making. No longer do areas such as the Northeast, which have been losing population, appear to offer the highest level of economic well-being simply because wages are highest there. When climate, crime rates, pollution, cost of living, etc. are taken into account, that area appears to be the most inferior in terms of its total contribution to well-being. This, of course, matches the actual migration patterns of those who have been voting with their feet (Henderson, 1982; Graves and Regulska, 1982; Porell, 1982).

The same is true in explaining the wage differentials one finds among regions. Some of those differences are tied to temporary disequilibrium in labor supply and demand. If an area finds itself with an excess supply of labor because of the unexpected decline in a traditional industry, or a shortage in the supply of labor because of rapid expansion in certain industries, wages will obviously be affected, at least for a while, until supply and demand adjust.

But even after workers migrate and businesses adjust to the local situation, wage differences will remain if areas differ in their attractiveness to families as living environments. In fact, after such temporary disequilibrium in labor markets is taken into account, environmental-quality variables emerge as the greatest contributor to differences in wages among areas. People are quite sensitive to the availability of nonmarketed environmental goods, and geographic differences in their availability explain most of the variation in wage rates and local cost of living (Israeli, 1979; Cropper, 1981; Rosen, 1979).

This turns the conventional wisdom on its head. People migrate not just to where wages are highest but to places with attractive living conditions. In contrast to what the economic-base model suggests, people do not just go to where the jobs are, they go to where the mix of local qualities and economic opportunities is most attractive. They may go to where wages are low or employment opportunities are limited. That in turn may attract businesses either because of the new markets or because of the availability of an attractive labor force at relatively low cost.

Local environmental quality may be a driving force in economic development or a retardant to such development. This is not a new idea. Thirty years ago, in an article entitled "A New Force in Regional Growth," Edward Ullman sought to explain growth in the western United States. The new force was not natural resources in the ground or transportation links. It was location-specific "pleasant" living conditions, which he labeled "amenities" (Ullman, 1955). Without reference to those amenities, he could not explain the development taking place in Southern California, Arizona, Florida, and the Mountain West.

The label "amenities" has hung on and has been broadened to refer to any location-specific, nonmarketed qualities that people find attractive. Those qualities were and continue to be a force in regional growth.

7. In a Mobile Economy, No Region Can Be Significantly Better or Worse Off

The fact that local wages adjust to compensate the population for unusually good or bad living conditions renders per-capita income or local wage levels a misleading guide to local economic health. Per-capita income is also a variable largely beyond local control and influence. In a national economy where workers, capital, and businesses migrate to where their total returns are highest, one area cannot long remain superior to others in terms of total economic well-being. If it is superior, workers will migrate there. The labor supply will increase relative to demand, forcing wages downward. In addition, the increasing population will cause at least some local environmental qualities to deteriorate as congestion, pollution, crime, and the rest increase. As a result, both wages and nonmarketed qualities will deteriorate. In the areas judged inferior, the opposite will take place. Such areas will lose population, there will be labor shortages, and wages will rise to attract and hold a quality work force.

Given these adjustment mechanisms, local policies aimed at raising local per-capita income cannot possibly work. If wage levels are boosted so that the area, overall, becomes more attractive, the population will rise, job seekers will flood in, competition for jobs will increase, and wages will be driven back down.

Per-capita income and wage levels must be looked upon as just part of what determines local economic well-being. Total economic well-being is determined by the combination of those money wages, the local cost of living, and the locally available nonmarketed qualities of the living environment.

$$\begin{array}{l}\text{Total real} \\ \text{income to} \\ \text{individual}\end{array} = \frac{\text{Locally available wage levels}}{\text{Local cost of living}} + \begin{array}{l}\text{Value of non-} \\ \text{marketed locally} \\ \text{available qualities} \\ \text{of living environment}\end{array}$$

These three interact to determine the local level of economic well-being. But the migration of workers and capital forces them to move together in such a way that no one area ever is significantly better or worse off overall. Wage levels may be higher in one area, but that will be offset by higher costs of living or inferior living conditions. In other areas, wages may be lower, but total real income and economic well-being will be maintained at national levels by lower costs of living and/or a more valuable flow of nonmarketed goods and services from the natural and social environments.

Overall, there cannot be significant differences in economic well-being between areas without triggering significant migration, which would eliminate the differences by causing all three determinants of total real income to adjust: they will automatically deteriorate in the superior area and improve in the inferior area.

All this suggests that the local level of wages or per-capita income may not be a very productive target for local economic development policies. National economic forces will overwhelm any such efforts. What may be gained temporarily in one of the determinants of total real income will ultimately be lost in the others as shifting economic resources force a downward adjustment that eliminates the initial gain.

This dominance of national economic forces can be seen in the historical statistics on regional per capita income. Figures 8.1 and 8.2 below show how per-capita income and wages stated in dollars of constant purchasing power, have changed over the last thirty years in various regions of the United States. The overwhelming feature of these statistics is the way per-capita income has moved in a very similar manner in all regions. All regions have followed national trends very closely. The main determinant of improvements in per-capita income has not been where a person lived (or the local economic development policies there), but the overall national trends. The vast majority of improvements in local per-capita income have come from the nationwide spread of national trends in productivity and labor force participation.

The other feature of these statistics is the lack of any substantial, systematic narrowing in the differences that do exist between regions despite decades of national economic adjustments. Despite the migration of millions of people from the South to the North, from the North back to the South, and from the East to the West, substantial differences in wages and per-capita incomes remain. At times, as in the 1960s, some convergence in relative wages and incomes appeared to be taking place. But then, as in the 1970s, regional differences reasserted themselves (Clark and Ballard, 1980). The "North-South wage differential" has been the most dramatic and most studied regional wage differential. Recent analysis of the way this differential influences migration and, in turn, is affected by migration indicates that migration of whites between the regions tends to increase the differential, not decrease it. White workers are moving from high-wage to low-wage areas. Nonwage considerations seem to dominate North-South migration and to maintain the wage differentials (Dunlevy and Bellante, 1983). This particular wage differential has existed for a century. The persistence of these regional differences in per-capita money income suggests they are not just temporary phenomena caused by imbalances in the supply and demand for labor. They are a reasonably long-term feature of the economic landscape that may simply be reflecting people's judgments about the relative attractiveness of various areas as living environments (Power, 1980; Henderson, 1982; Graves and Linneman, 1974; Graves, 1980; Diamond and Tolley, 1982; Cropper, 1981; Rosen, 1979; Porell, 1982; Fogarty and Garofalo, 1980).

This suggests, again, that migration of people, capital, and businesses will overwhelm local economic-development policies aimed at simply boosting aver-

Figure 8.1
Correlation between Growth in State and National Real Per-capita Income

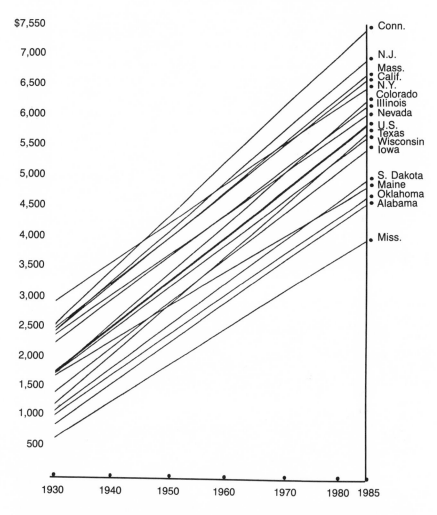

Sources: *State Personal Income, 1929–82*, U.S. Department of Commerce, Bureau of Economic Analysis, *Statistical Abstract, 1985*; *Survey of Current Business*, Aug. 1985.

age wages or per-capita income. Such policies can succeed only to the extent that other aspects of the area deteriorate and make it a less attractive place.

This assertion—that in a mobile economy no area can be significantly worse or better off—should not be interpreted to mean that nothing matters because everything will adjust to the same general level. Local policies can make the local population better or worse off.

Figure 8.2
Long-run Differences in State Per-capita Incomes

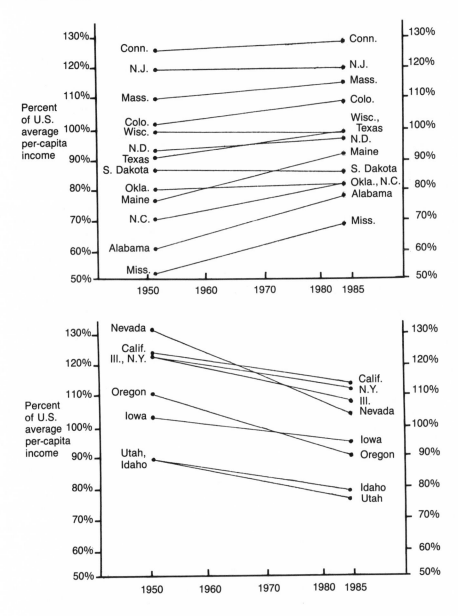

Sources: State Personal Income, 1929–82, U.S. Department of Commerce, Bureau of Economic Analysis; *Statistical Abstract*, 1985; *Survey of Current Business*, Aug. 1985

Over time local wages adjust to the level needed to obtain and hold the work force sought by local businesses. Given the local cost of living and the availability of nonmarketed qualities, local wages will increase or decrease until they are just sufficient to attract or hold the last workers needed. Some people, those who more strongly prefer the qualities specific to that particular area, will be attracted there and be willing to remain there for lower money wages than others. In addition, once a commitment is made to a particular area, residents invest time, energy, and money learning to make use of the opportunities and characteristics specific to that area.

This means that for a good part of the population, the combination of the local living environment, the cost of living, and the money wages does leave them better off than they could be elsewhere. It is only those last workers attracted to or held by local businesses who will be neutral or indifferent about the local level of well-being compared to what is available in other areas. In the jargon, it is the "marginal" workers whose preferences will dictate the necessary money-wage level. The other, "inframarginal" workers can be expected to prefer, not be indifferent to, the combined character of that local area relative to other areas.

Deterioration in locally specific qualities, even if somewhat offset by increased money wages, can leave the committed residents worse off; they will lose something they strongly prefer. The marginal migrants who influence the wage level are losing something about which they did not particularly care.

This may explain some of the conservatism one finds in most areas. Often, a large part of the population will oppose economic and environmental changes that appear to be obviously beneficial in narrow quantitative economic terms. Their objections focus on the perceived changes in the quality of the living environment. The value of the loss to them is not compensated for by the gains in money wages or employment opportunities. The discussion above should make clear that this is not due merely to confusion, lack of accurate information, or economic irrationality. It is eminently rational from an economic point of view. It is quite possible that such changes, despite the high incomes and greater job opportunities, would leave a significant part of the population, even the majority, worse off. There are powerful economic reasons for the observed resistance to environmental and social change.

8. More High-Paying Jobs Are Unlikely to Boost Local Per-Capita Income

One of the more widely accepted local economic-development objectives is to attract more high-paying jobs. This, it is assumed, will raise total earnings per person and boost per-capita income, leaving the population, on average, better off. As intuitively attractive as this strategy may appear, there is no reason to believe it will succeed in the context of the national economy with its highly mobile labor force.

The economic-base model itself points out the problem with this approach to boosting per-capita income. The model assumes that people migrate to where jobs are, and that new high-paying jobs trigger multiple expansions of low paying, derivative jobs.

In this context, consider a local economy whose population size has adjusted over time to the level of economic opportunity available there. If a large factory now locates in the area, offering many relatively high-paying new jobs, the new economic opportunities will, according to the economic-base theory, cause the area's population to increase. There will be new jobs not only in the new high-paying industry but also in derivative industries. As the new high-paid employees spend their income, they will stimulate the expansion of many locally oriented businesses, which will hire additional workers. Those new workers, as they spend their income, will stimulate yet another wave of expansion. The multiplier expansion will be under way.

One thing to keep in mind is that as the new highly paid workers spend their incomes, they will be doing so at locally oriented businesses that traditionally pay low wages: retail trade, restaurants, entertainment, other services, and so on. Each new high-paid employee, according to the multiplier theory, will put several low-paid people to work. Thus the average wage paid in the new jobs—the average of the new high-paying jobs and the more numerous new low-paying jobs—will not be very high. It may not be high enough to raise the area's average wage level at all.

The availability of these new jobs will lead the population to increase. In fact, according to the economic-base model, the population will increase to provide all of the new workers. The existing population may fill some of the new high-paying jobs by leaving low-paying derivative jobs, which would then be filled by the migrants. But if the population had previously adjusted to the existing availability of jobs, it will now have to increase to accommodate the new demand for employees.

The new situation, then, will be as follows: each high-paying job will have brought into existence several low-paying jobs, and the population will have increased. There will be more money income earned locally in both high-paying and low-paying jobs, but there will be more people sharing that total income. What will be the impact of these changes on per capita income? It is impossible to say. There is no reason to believe that per-capita income will rise: low-paying jobs are being generated faster than high-paying ones, and there are more people seeking to fill both sets of jobs. If the local economy adjusts in the mechanical way described by the economic-base theory, there is likely to be no impact at all on per-capita income. If the current shift in employment toward lower-paying service jobs continues, the more than proportional expansion in these jobs may lower per-capita income. Whatever the new high paying jobs do, there is no reason to believe they will boost that particular measure of local economic well-being.

This is not just speculation. Detailed and careful economic-base modeling of regional economies documents the likely ineffectiveness of this approach to improving local economic well-being.

The economic-base approach, for instance, has been used to model in considerable detail the likely impact on the Alaskan economy of various industrial developments there (Kresge et al., 1984). In this projection, a $100-million expansion of Alaksa's "basic" industries, an expansion that increased employment in those industries by 44 percent and boosted total personal income by 30 percent, had almost no positive impact on real per-capita income. It rose by only 2.6 percent. The reason for this was that the population increased by 26 percent and the derivative jobs that were stimulated by the expansion in the economic base were in the trade and services sector, where wages were 30 percent below the state average.

The projected impact of the North Slope gas pipeline was even less positive. This project would create 9,000 high-paying temporary construction jobs. Total employment including derivative jobs would increase by 22,000. But after the construction was over, there would be very few permanent jobs. Thus the construction would provide a sizable but temporary injection of income. The projected results were a temporary increase in population, a boom, and then a drawn-out downward adjustment—a bust. Within six years of the end of construction, employment, income, and population figures would be similar to what they would have been if the pipeline were not built. For the period following construction, per-capita income would fall below what it otherwise would have been. The population would not adjust immediately to the reduced number of jobs. The construction work force, it was projected, would hang on for a time, looking for different jobs. The result would be increased unemployment and lower per-capita income than if there had been no pipeline construction.

The economic-base model has also been used to model the impact on the New Mexico economy of extensive industrial development associated with the Four Corners coalfields. Included in the projected development were 15,000 MW of electric generating facilities, 40 million tons of coal-mining capacity, eight coal-gasification plants, and 30,000 tons of uranium oxide production. This was projected to add 100,000 high-paying jobs to the New Mexico economy. Over twenty-five years, the state's population would double; that of the Four Corners area would increase over threefold.

The projected impact of this extensive industrial development on per-capita income in the Four Corners area was extremely modest. That area in 1975 had a per-capita income only 66 percent of the national average. After the development, the per-capita income was projected to be 73 percent of the national average. Northwest New Mexico would still lag far behind the nation in this quantitative measure of well-being. Relative to the rest of New Mexico, the Four Corners area was projected to make even less progress. Its per-capita income was projected to rise from 81 percent of New Mexico's average in 1975 to 82 percent in the year 2000.

The industrial development would bring very high-paying jobs to an area with very low per-capita incomes. But it would bring a very large influx of migrants, all seeking to share those jobs with the existing local population. In the projection, the influx dramatically diluted the income available per person seeking to be supported. Judged by relative levels of per-capita income, the extensive industrial development was projected to leave the area almost as poor as it was before the development (Spofford, 1980, pp. 201–243).

But one does not have to focus on what the economic-base model projects; one can look at various regions' actual experiences. During the 1960s and 1970s, there was a significant westward shift in the location of economic activities. Employment opportunities grew extremely rapidly in such places as the Los Angeles, Denver, Phoenix, and Salt Lake City areas. In fact, these urban areas led the nation in employment growth. One can study the impact of this employment expansion on average family income to get a feeling for how reliable the connection is between the increase in the number of jobs and an increase in income available to the average family. Table 8.1 compares the growth rates of employment and family income for some of these fast-growing metropolitan areas. The local economy in which manufacturing and overall job growth was the fastest during the 1960s—Anaheim, California, where employment growth was six and a half times the national average—saw family income grow only about as fast as it did nationwide. Several other fast-growing areas—such as Phoenix, Denver, and San Diego, where jobs in general and manufacturing jobs in particular expanded two or three times as fast as the national average—actually saw family income grow significantly less than the national average.

Clearly, job growth does not assure that per-capita or family incomes will grow proportionately. The metropolitan areas listed in Table 8.1 were chosen because of their large divergence between growth in employment and growth in family income. In other areas where jobs grew rapidly, family incomes did too. There is a positive correlation between job growth and family-income growth, but it is very weak (Greenwood, 1981, p. 76). Most of the variation in the growth of family income cannot be explained by variations in employment growth.

One finds the same disconnection between job growth and growth in per-capita income at the state level. The states with the fastest growth in employment—Arizona, Florida, Colorado, etc.—saw their per-capita incomes grow at only about the same rate as elsewhere in the nation. Table 8.2 shows that despite employment growth rates two to five times faster than the national average, these states' per-capita incomes more or less tracked the national trend, varying by only a few percentage points from the national average while employment varied by hundreds of percentage points.

Statistical analysis of the relationship between employment growth and changes in relative wages also casts doubt on any strategy that aims at boosting wages by creating more jobs. Often, relative growth in employment leads to

Table 8.1

Divergence between Employment Growth and Family-Income Growth, 1960–1970

Metropolitan area	Employment growth (rank in U.S.)	Family-income growth (rank in U.S.)	Employment growth relative to U.S. average	Family-income growth relative to U.S. average	Additional family-income growth relative to U.S. average
Anaheim	1st	25th	647%	100%	0%
San Jose	3rd	34th	412%	98%	−2%
Phoenix	4th	37th	286%	97%	−3%
Denver	11th	48th	209%	93%	−7%
San Bernadino	12th	59th	206%	83%	−17%
San Diego	13th	61st	201%	79%	−21%
Salt Lake City	19th	57th	159%	83%	−17%
Sacramento	22nd	62nd	138%	71%	−29%

Source: *Migration and Economic Growth in the United States*, Michael J. Greenwood (Academic Press, 1981), pp. 58–59, 74–75.

Table 8.2

Divergence between Employment Growth and Per-Capita Income Growth in Fast-Growing States, 1950–1977

State	Employment growth rate relative to U.S. average	Per-capita income growth rate relative to U.S. average	Additional per-capita income growth relative to U.S. average
Arizona	5.5 × U.S. avg.	1.02 × U.S. avg.	+2%
Florida	4.4 × U.S. avg.	1.14 × U.S. avg.	+14%
Colorado	2.5 × U.S. avg.	1.02 × U.S. avg.	+2%
New Mexico	2.4 × U.S. avg.	1.04 × U.S. avg.	+4%
California	2.3 × U.S. avg.	0.87 × U.S. avg.	−13%
Utah	2.1 × U.S. avg.	0.96 × U.S. avg.	−4%
Texas	2.1 × U.S. avg.	1.10 × U.S. avg.	+10%

Source: Weinstein and Firestine, 1978, p.19.

lower relative wages, not higher. This has been the case, for instance, in California (Clark and Ballard, 1980a). This same result can be seen in Table 8.1: the rapid growth in employment in the California cities was accompanied by slower than average growth in family income. The migration of people to jobs can put substantial downward pressure on wages.

Case studies of the impact of large new industrial facilities in largely rural areas also show the lack of any necessary connection with more high paying jobs and increases in family or per-capita income. In 1967, the Jones and Laughlin Steel Co. built a mill employing over a thousand workers in rural western Illinois. During the following five years, average family income in the surrounding area actually declined slightly, while in a similar rural area that faced no industrialization and was used as an experimental control, it rose by 10 percent. The work force at the mill was largely male, yet the average income of male heads of household increased by one-third less in the area around the steel mill than in the control area (Beck et al., 1973; Scott and Summers, 1974).

Seyler (1974) analyzed 242 nonmetropolitan counties in the Midwest that had net gains in manufacturing employment between 1965 and 1973 to see what the impact of that industrialization had been on household income. The growth in manufacturing in these counties had been significant. It had boosted aggregated income by almost $2 billion. Thirty to 80 percent of the growth in aggregate personal income in these counties was attributable to growth in manufacturing employment.

But Seyler's analysis showed that this aggregate growth had no reliable impact on family incomes. He sought to answer the question: Has industrial growth in nonmetropolitan areas been accompanied by a significant improvement in levels of household income? The empirical evidence led him to answer no. There was no statistically significant relationship between growth in manufacturing and growth in family income (Seyler, 1974, p. 141).

During the 1970s, the states of Utah and Idaho faced economic growth rates much faster than the national average. In southern Idaho, for instance, jobs grew by 69 percent between 1970 and 1980, almost three times faster than in the nation as a whole. Yet southern Idaho's per-capita income grew somewhat more slowly than the national average, causing the area to fall further behind national levels. For anyone who believes that per-capita income is a measure of economic welfare, this was particularly distressing, since the region's per-capita income was already almost 25 percent below national averages (Idaho Power Company, 1984). Rapid job growth did not succeed in helping southern Idaho catch up.

Job growth was also rapid in Utah during the 1970s. Jobs increased by 51 percent, almost twice as fast as the national average. During that same period, Utah's national rank in terms of per-capita income fell from 38 to 45, giving Utah the lowest per-capita income outside the South. Despite the unusually rapid job growth, per-capita income rose less rapidly than in the nation as a whole, and Utah saw its relative position decline from 82 percent of the national average to

80 percent (U.S. Department of Commerce, 1983).

Utah's low per-capita income despite rapid growth in employment and income underlines another problem with the use of per-capita income to measure economic well-being. The families of Utah have chosen to have more children and to depend more heavily upon one wage-earner. Married women are more likely to work primarily within the home in Utah. This has two effects. First, because the number of children per family is higher, there are more dependents per working adult. Second, because women do not get monetary payment for work in the home, their work does not add to measured aggregate personal income. This means that the total money income generated is lower and the population to be supported by that money income is higher. This assures lower per-capita income. That, however, does not explain the slower growth in per-capita income.

Does that mean that the Utah economy is in trouble or is failing in some sense despite the rapid economic growth it has experienced? Does it mean that the people of Utah are being economically deprived? Neither of these assertions seems reasonable. The people of Utah choose to have additional children and a higher-quality home environment rather than more commercially purchased commodities. They did not do this by mistake or out of ignorance as to what was available in the commercial economy. Nor did they do it because there were not enough jobs available in the state. They clearly felt that their choice left them better off than the more commercial and consumption-oriented alternative. This is similar to the choices families have made to live where job opportunities and wage levels are lower but community and environmental quality is higher. There is no economic basis for insisting that they are worse off. In fact, economics would take their very choices as evidence that they are better off with the alternative they choose, despite the lower per-capita income it produces. Yet our standard measure of economic well-being, per capita income, would contradict that. Measurements of economic well-being that focus only on commercial economic activities are likely to be significantly in error. They will misstate current economic conditions and changes in well-being. The contribution to economic well-being that comes from noncommercial activity within the home and from noncommercial social and natural resources in the region around the home will be ignored. Shifts of economic activity from within the home to the commercial economy—as more meals are purchased outside the home, commercial day-care centers are used, and home maintenance and repairs are provided by people outside the family—will be counted as completely new economic activity that boosts per-capita income. The offsetting decline in household production will be ignored. Economic growth and improvements in well-being will be significantly exaggerated (Ross and Usher, 1986).

It is not only during periods of economic expansion during which per-capita income can give misleading indications of economic health. The same thing can happen during periods of near-collapse. Consider the example of the mining and smelting communities of Butte and Anaconda, Montana. These cities have been dominated by copper production since the turn of the century. In the early 1970s, economic-base analysis identified almost three-quarters of this area's economic base as associated with the activities of the Anaconda Copper Company. In the late 1970s, Anaconda began to shut down its entire operation in the area. In steps, the underground mines, the smelter, and finally the open-pit mines were closed and the work force permanently laid off. By 1982, 60 percent of the 1972 economic base had been eliminated. There were 4,300 basic jobs lost in this relatively small and isolated local economy.

But as the "basic" sector of this local economy was gutted, per-capita income rose as fast or faster than in the state's other urban areas, and faster than the state average. If judged by what happened to per-capita income, the economy of the Butte-Anaconda area improved significantly during this period of economic collapse!

The explanation for this is very simple. As the dominant industry shut down, a significant part of the population moved out of the area. Income fell drastically, but so did the number of people who had to be supported by that income. The rapid decline in population allowed the income available per remaining resident to rise. This rise in per-capita income was not a sign of economic health; it was due to the forced migration of thousands of people, a process that tore many families, and the community, apart. Yet the preferred measure of economic health would suggest that the economy was improving and people were getting better and better off.

To sum up, then, the fact of the matter is that there is not a reliable connection between changes in job availability and changes in per-capita income or wage levels. Economic policies built around the assumption that there is such a reliable connection are likely to be frustrated.

9. Expanding Local Employment Opportunities Will Not Necessarily Put the Unemployed There to Work

The inability to find a job is a personal and social trauma. Work is not only the way we obtain income with which to support ourselves and our families, it is also the primary way in which adults integrate themselves into society. Our social identities and sense of self-worth are closely tied to our employment. Joblessness threatens both and weakens our community.

It is not surprising, then, that there is broad social concern about job loss and high unemployment rates. Joblessness is a major target of most economic-development programs. One major objective is to boost employment growth so that those currently unemployed in the community can be drawn back into the active work force and unemployment can be reduced.

This is another one of those seemingly obvious elements of our economic folk wisdom: if local employment grows, unemployment will fall, and the unemployed in the community will be put to work. This intuitive conclusion follows from both word play and an analogy with the national economy. The wordplay sees in "employment" an opposite or antidote to "unemployment"; the conclusion follows almost by definition. The analogy with the national economy carries the national commitment to full employment through job creation to the local community. At the national level, because immigration is more or less restricted, the size of the labor force is, at least in the short run, relatively fixed. If more jobs are created and filled, it must be currently unemployed people who fill them. But a quite different set of circumstances confronts the local economy.

What this folk wisdom fails to take into account is the mobility of our population. Our citizens can move to anywhere in the country they wish in pursuit of jobs. Our local economies are open to any and all who wish to participate in them. This means that the jobs created in a particular area need not go to people already living there. They can go to new migrants. To make matters worse, more people can come seeking the new jobs than there are new jobs to be had. As a result, unemployment rates can actually rise.

The mobility of our national work force *is* crucial in determining whether local job creation can put unemployed residents to work. The national workforce is very mobile. Over the last several decades the total of in-migrants and out-migrants per decade between our metropolitan areas has totaled between 35 and 40 percent of the metropolitan population (Greenwood, 1981, p. 170). In many areas, over any five-year period, the number of people who have either moved in or out of the area adds up to one-fifth or one-third of the population. For young people, mobility is even higher.

Job opportunities are the one "narrow" economic variable that analysts have had some success in using to explain population movements into particular areas. The national population does shift toward areas rich in employment opportunities and the movement can be quite rapid (Ballard and Clark, 1981).

In this context of a work force ready to shift to wherever there might be better jobs, the success of a local job-creation effort in providing work for unemployed local residents will depend on two things. First, the growth in jobs will have to be faster than the increase in job-seeking migrants. That is, the growth in jobs will have to actually lower the unemployment rate. The competition for jobs from newcomers will have to be relatively minor. Second, the decline in the unemployment rate will have to be due to existing unemployed local residents getting many of the jobs. If the same number of people remain unemployed but the total number of jobs and the size of the work force grow, the unemployment *rate* will fall. But that could leave the previously unemployed local residents still unemployed. It should be clear that a local job-creation program may not accomplish its primary objective.

There is no shortage of local areas where rapid job growth was accompanied by rapid growth in unemployment. When the oil-shale boom hit the West Slopes of Colorado, workers flocked to the area seeking high-paying jobs. One result was a tent city of unemployed workers outside Parachute, Colorado. More people came seeking jobs than there were jobs to be had. As the boom has faded, unemployment rates have continued high (Marston, 1984).

The construction of the Trans-Alaskan Pipeline created thousands of jobs in Alaska, but it also attracted thousands of would-be workers. Unemployment in Fairbanks and other towns got so bad that the Alaska government took to advertising in the lower forty-eight states to discourage further migration of workers. And recall the 22,000 new jobs projected for Alaska from construction of the proposed North Slope gas pipeline. According to that model, no fewer than 35,000 people would move into the state during the construction boom, looking for work—and these migrants would obtain at least 75 to 80 percent of the new jobs. After the construction peak, the number of jobs would decline, unemployment would rise, and the migration would reverse itself. But during this whole period, local residents would face increased job competition, unstable employment, and then rising unemployment.

But one does not have to look at boomtown conditions to see this same problem. It exists in much more normal job-growth situations. The metropolitan areas of the western United States have led the nation in job creation, yet they have had unemployment rates consistently above the national average. Population growth and job-seekers have more than kept up with job creation. Statistical analysis indicates that across all the nation's metropolitan areas, such increased in-migration tends to boost unemployment rates (Greenwood, 1981, 174).

Of the urban areas where jobs grew 50 percent faster than the national average between 1975 and 1979, almost half had unemployment rates above the national average in 1979, and over half saw their unemployment rates fall less than the national average during that period. Obviously, rapid job creation does not assure lower unemployment rates.

The reverse is true, too. One can have low and falling unemployment rates without rapid job creation. The Little Rock area had an unemployment rate in 1979 that was half of the national average, yet its job creation lagged behind the national average by 16 percent. In Milwaukee, employment growth lagged 30 percent behind the nation's, yet the nation's unemployment rate was 50 percent higher than Milwaukee's. Springfield, Mass., saw its unemployment rate fall between 1975 and 1979 over 80 percent faster than the national average, yet its job creation was almost 40 percent slower. Tables 8.3 and 8.4 present these and other examples of dramatic divergence between relative unemployment rates and employment growth.

The fact of the matter is that there is almost no correlation between growth in employment on the one hand and unemployment rates, or changes in unemployment rates, in our large urban areas on the other. The correlation coefficient between these two, when all major U.S. metropolitan areas are studied, is almost zero. It fluctuated between 0.12 and −0.14 during 1975-79. A close connection between growth in employment and unemployment rates would have led to a

Table 8.3

Areas of Unusually Low Unemployment and Slow Job Growth, 1975–1979

Area	Unemployment rate relative to the national average	Percent change in employment relative to the national average
Abilene, TX	48% below	1% faster
Richmond, VA	43% below	8% slower
Salisbury, NC	41% below	3% slower
San Angelo, CA	47% below	22% slower
Sheboygan, WI	41% below	6% slower
Odessa, TX	40% below	2% faster
Joplin, MO	33% below	9% slower
Little Rock, AR	50% below	14% slower
Milwaukee, WI	33% below	30% slower
Cedar Rapids, IA	36% below	14% slower
Charlottesville, VA	34% below	same
Columbia, SC	34% below	3% faster
Enid, OK	55% below	1% faster

Source: *State and Metropolitan Area Data Book, 1982*, U.S. Bureau of the Census.

correlation coefficient close to 1.00. If no relationship exists between the two of them, the coefficient would be close to zero. That this is, in fact, the result certainly suggests that it will be difficult for local areas to do much about their unemployment rates simply by increasing employment opportunities.

The case-study information underlines the way in which industrial development is likely to increase unemployment in local areas. Studies in the Ozarks, for instance, where there was rapid industrialization from 1950 to 1965, showed significantly greater increases in the number of unemployed compared to both Arkansas and the nation as a whole (Jordan, 1967; Scott and Summers, 1974; Peterson, 1974; Lonsdale and Seyler, 1979).

But to accomplish its main objective, job creation has to do more than just reduce unemployment rates. It has to see that the new jobs go to existing residents who are currently unemployed. This may be even harder. The currently unemployed may be disadvantaged in the labor market in any one of several ways. They may have limited job skills, work histories, and job-seeking skills. Migrants, on the other hand, by their very act of moving may be more aggressive and skilled at job-hunting. Migrants tend to be young and more educated. They may also have a better crack at obtaining the new jobs than the existing unemployed if those jobs call for experience or skills not traditionally found in the area. Again, case studies document the fact that new industrial jobs are not usually filled by the

Table 8.4

Areas with Large Reductions in Unemployment but Slow Growth in Jobs, 1975–1979

Area	Percentage decline in unemployment rate relative to the national average	Percentage increase in jobs relative to the national average
Tulsa, OK	64% faster	4% faster
Worchester, MA	86% faster	26% slower
Salisbury, NC	74% faster	3% slower
Springfield, MA	81% faster	37% slower
Parkersburg, WV	61% faster	16% slower
Pascagoula, MO	79% faster	88% slower
Hamilton, OH	56% faster	13% slower
Miami, FL	65% faster	16% slower
Columbus, GA	81% faster	23% slower
Cumberland, MD	62% faster	64% slower
Florence, SC	54% faster	26% slower

Source: State and Metropolitan Area Data Book, 1982, U.S. Bureau of the Census.

previously unemployed in an area. Instead, they are filled by new migrants and new entrants to the labor force (Peterson, 1974; Summers et al., 1976; Lonsdale and Seyler, 1979).

It takes more than simply job creation to draw the currently unemployed back into jobs. It is likely to take local efforts that target the unemployed for specific assistance in developing job and job-seeking skills. Such assistance may be far more important than a simple increase in the quantity of jobs available locally.

Before leaving the topic of local unemployment, it is worth mentioning some of the rather perversely positive aspects of relatively high local unemployment rates. Statistical analysis indicates that manufacturing firms, which in economic-development circles are usually assumed to provide the high-paying jobs, are drawn to areas with relatively high unemployment rates. That unemployment apparently indicates the ready availability of a labor force (Plaut and Pluta, 1983, p. 112). As pointed out earlier, jobs do follow people, just as people follow jobs.

There is evidence that areas that regularly have high unemployment rates also pay somewhat higher wages. This is consistent with the compensating wage differences discussed earlier. If because of the type of industries located in a particular area, job security is lower and employment and income are regularly interrupted, firms will have to pay workers somewhat higher wages to compensate them for these negative characteristics. If they do not, the work force will move on (Rosen, 1979, p. 96).

10. Creating More Jobs Will Not Keep the Kids at Home

One of the most emotionally powerful arguments for quantitative growth, especially growth in jobs, is that it will allow young people to find jobs in their hometowns. If jobs are plentiful, our kids will not be forced to migrate to find decent employment. Our communities and families will be strengthened if this forced migration can be avoided. Migration data document the substantial loss of young people from many communities. With those young people goes the local investment in education. It is easy to see in the data a brain drain of sorts. Implicit in this argument is the assumption that young people move away from their hometowns because of lack of jobs, low pay, or both. If there were more jobs or higher-paying jobs, the young would stay where they were raised. Parents may wish this were the case, but the empirical evidence does not suggest that it is. Young people, in general, do not leave their hometowns because of lack of jobs or low wages. They leave because they are young, well educated, curious, and adventuresome. As they leave, similar young people, having left their own hometowns, migrate into our communities.

One of the most striking things about out-migration is the difficulty in providing any economic explanation for it. For over twenty years, economists have struggled massaging the data, trying more sophisticated models, and gathering more detailed data. But the results are almost always the same: an area's economic characteristics have very little impact on the rate at which people leave. This led one frustrated economist to comment:

> It almost seems as if a metropolitan area emits emigrants like some radioactive rock, proportional to its size (adjusted for age and proportion of habitual movers), but essentially unaffected by environmental conditions such as its economic well-being. (Alonso, 1972, p. 6)

This is not to say that we do not know what it is that determines the rate at which people migrate out of an area. We know a lot. We know that out-migration is strongly associated with various demographic characteristics of the population. Young, well-educated people who come from families who have migrated in the past and who do not yet have substantial work histories in particular industries or occupations are very likely to migrate. Such people are said to have a propensity to migrate: they tend to migrate no matter what the economic conditions where they currently live (Mueller, 1982). Most out-migration is explained after this propensity is taken into account, but then one can begin to see at least some effect of local economic conditions on migration.

But note that young people who have just finished school are the people with the highest propensity to migrate. They are precisely the people who pay least attention to the availability of jobs and the level of wages locally. They are ready to move and do so, from both rapidly growing communities and slowly growing ones. The migration rate for young males is very high, about 50 percent (Mueller, 1982, p. 117). This should not be surprising. We are an increasingly mobile society. Over a decade's time, the percentage of the population moving in and out of a state or city is likely to be between 35 to 40 percent (Greenwood, 1981, p. 170; Clark and Ballard, 1980a, p. 102). Our young people, directly or indirectly, have significant experience with moving. They are not hesitant to do so when they set out on their own.

Some detailed case studies indicate that industrialization of rural areas, by changing cultural attitudes and ways of life, can actually cause out-migration of young people to increase. Andrews and Bauder (1968), for instance, compared two rural Ohio counties, one undergoing rapid industrialization and the other not. They found that after industrialization, a larger percentage of young adults left, while in the control county the proportion of young out-migrants fell. Interviews confirmed a shift in attitudes among the young adults. In the industrializing county, a smaller percentage indicated they intended to stay after the plants went in. In the control county, the proportion intending to stay near home remained constant. Industrialization, by broadening the set of occupational possibilities and ambitions and bringing in large numbers of outsiders, encouraged more young people to explore the economic potentials away from home.

It is not just young people whose migration seems to be influenced by factors other than job availability and wage levels. Migration is not always or usually from low-wage, high-unemployment areas to high-wage, low-unemployment areas (Clark and Ballard, 1980a; Ballard and Clark, 1981; Greenwood, 1981; Mueller, 1982; Graves, 1980; Liu, 1975; Lowry, 1966; Gallaway, 1967). Texas and Colorado, for instance, two of the fastest-growing states, have been receiving migrants from states with greater employment opportunities (Ballard and Clark, 1981). White migration between North and South has increased the North-South wage differential, because it involves movement from high-wage to low-wage areas (Dunlevy and Bellante, 1983). The same is true of the movement of population from metropolitan to nonmetropolitan regions.

As noble as the impulse is to try to provide job opportunities near home for our young people, the evidence is that it will not have much impact on their tendency to explore the possibilities out there in the rest of the world. What those efforts, if successful, will do is to create job opportunities for the children of other distant communities who, in their own trips of exploration happen to migrate through our communities. Job creation to assist our young will not create jobs for our own kids. It will create jobs for someone else's kids. Although that might be nice, it would not appear to have a high priority in any particular community.

11. Economic Growth Is Unlikely to
Reduce Tax Burdens

During the past decade of slow growth and recession, most local and state governments have found it very difficult to make ends meet. The demand for increased services has not abated, but the reduced flow of federal aid combined with the effects of the recessions in reducing state and local tax revenues have led to almost annual fiscal crises.

In the frustration associated with the hard decisions about cutting back on public services and/or raising taxes, it is regularly suggested that if only the local or state economy were growing faster, there would be more people and businesses to help pay for public services, and the tax burden on individual households and businesses could be reduced. The theory behind this hope is that population and employment growth can take place with a less than proportionate increase in government spending. Existing public facilities and services would be better utilized by a larger population, and total tax revenues would increase without tax rates increasing simply because there would be more people around to help pay taxes.

Unfortunately, that is not what usually happens. Instead, as the population in a particular area increases, government spending per person also rises. The cost per resident of providing various public services increases with population (Gardner, 1979; Weinstein and Firestine, 1978, p. 126). If one looks at the experience of some of the states that saw employment grow the fastest over the last three decades, one sees that rapid job growth is no assurance of lower tax burdens. Arizona, California, and Utah, for instance, had employment growth rates two to six times the national average. Yet taxes as a percent of personal income grew faster than the national average in those states. Other states where employment grew especially rapidly, such as Texas and New Mexico, saw tax revenues as a percentage of personal income grow almost as fast as the national average. In some states, especially in the Southeast, rapid job growth was accompanied by tax burdens that grew less rapidly than the national average. But clearly job growth by itself assures no tax relief (Weinstein and Firestine, 1978, Table 5.4).

Not only do national cross-sectional studies show this, but the same pattern appears when individual states are studied. Consider Maryland: During the 1960s, the population of the counties adjacent to the District of Columbia and Baltimore grew rapidly. They became part of the Boston-to-Washington metropolitan corridor. Other Maryland counties grew hardly at all. An analysis of the impact of these differential economic growth rates on tax burdens contradicts the hypothesis that growth will reduce tax burdens. The fast-growing counties, which during the decade saw their population increase 56 percent, saw their per-capita property taxes increase 50 percent faster than those of the slower-growing counties (Foster and Bailey, 1974). In addition, tax rates rose in the rapidly growing areas while they fell in the slower-growing areas. And local public debt per capita, a measure of residents' future tax responsibility, rose twice as fast in the rapidly growing counties. Statistical analysis of the impact of population growth on residential property taxes in Oregon showed the same positive relationship (Buchanan and Weber, 1982).

It should not be surprising that total government spending rises with increased population. The new population needs roads, parks, playgrounds, schools, police and fire protection, water and sewage facilities, hospitals, libraries, etc. In fact, the larger a local economy becomes, the more sophisticated the range of local public services that the local population demands. Small urban, suburban, and exurban communities can get by without sidewalks and with some unpaved roads, individual water wells and septic systems, almost no police, and relatively simple school systems. As a community grows larger, a much broader range of services ends up being needed. Crime problems grow; the community has to take more formal responsibility for welfare; school systems expand to include vocation-technical schools, community colleges, libraries, and museums. Air and water pollution have to be dealt with centrally. Some form of mass transit may be funded. This tends to boost the level of taxes needed per capita since a greater variety of services is called for.

In addition to growth in the level of services the government is expected to provide, economic growth may bring diseconomies of scale. The cost of providing the same level of public service per capita may rise, not fall. This may be true because with population growth and industrialization, some problems increase more than proportionately—crime, welfare, poverty, pollution. That may also be true simply because the cost of providing some services rises rapidly with population. The provision of roads and highways is one of these. The number of square feet of roadway required *per person* is twelve times as great for a city of 1,000,000 as for a city of 10,000. A hundred-fold increase in population requires a 1,200-fold increase in road construction (Foster and Bailey, 1974, p. 3). Again, government expenditures per person may have to rise.

Economic growth in general, then, will not reduce tax rates. Other changes accompanying the growth in population and economic activity will increase the demand for public services more than proportionately. The result will be higher taxes. The result is also likely to be a higher level of public services. This may mean that the local population is better off: its taxes are up, but so is the level and quality of public services received. But this result is not the one usually heralded by the proponents of economic growth as a solution to high tax burdens.

12. Taxes and Local Economic Growth: Competing Away the Benefits of Growth

Local and state governments usually come under considerable pressure to do something to spur the growth of any local economy that is not booming. Average, slow, or no growth in one of the quantitative measures of economic growth is taken as a sign of a poor economic health.

Unfortunately, in a private-enterprise, market economy, state and local governments have very little influence over the level and character of commercial economic activity. Local government has almost no handles with which to manipulate the commercial economy. But political pressure is often such that local governments cannot simply admit that and focus upon things they can control. Instead, local governments grasp at any policy they believe might allow them to stimulate local commercial activity.

The list of suggestions is usually drawn up by the local business community, and includes easing all those local-government policies that the drafters consider a burden upon business. Taxes, zoning, planning restrictions, environmental standards, labor rights, and the like are usually on the list. Although some might see this as blatantly self-serving, the business community's public logic is that if these measures burden them, they must also burden and discourage new and expanding businesses and thus limit economic growth.

Also likely to be included on the list are positive steps the local government can take to subsidize business expansion: providing access to capital at reduced interest rates, pre-building industrial parks, providing sewer, water, and utilities at reduced cost, etc.

Rarely is any analysis provided to indicate that any of these steps will have a significant impact on local economic development. Instead, the logic is that (a) the government must do *something*, and (b) these proposals are "the only parade in town." To this rather weak justification is added the fact that other cities and states are taking similar steps to attract business. If this particular area does not do the same it will lose out. This adds an implicit threat of actual loss of existing business to other areas if the local government does not act.

This political situation almost forces local governments to engage in a vigorous competition among themselves to cut taxes, reduce restrictions on business, reduce the rights of labor, and increase various subsidies to businesses. Local economic-development policy becomes one of giving away as much as possible to local businesses, or at least to new local businesses. This has the serious potential of competing away the claimed benefits of new business firms. New businesses were supposed to add to the tax base, yet cutting their taxes and funding business subsidies out of other taxpayers' funds can keep them from doing that. If new businesses were supposed to bring high-paying jobs, reducing labor rights and encouraging primarily nonunion, footloose operations to move into the area may do no such thing. New economic activity is supposed to invigorate the community, but the abandonment of zoning, local planning, and environmental protection may simply degrade the community.

At the very least, given that the community is being asked to make some significant sacrifices in order to attract new firms, one would want some evidence that the steps suggested are likely to accomplish their stated goals. It does not seem to be too much to ask for more than wishful thinking and self-serving proposals. It is usually hard-nosed business people who make these proposals. It is reasonable for the local population and government to be equally hard-nosed and demand evidence that a costly measure is likely to work. It would be unbusinesslike to do less.

Economists have been studying the effectiveness of incentives on businesses' location decisions for over three decades now. There is substantial literature on the subject. In general, it lends very little support to economic development built around such giveaway programs. We will review this literature by focusing on the impact that state and local taxes have on business location and economic development.

Local tax burdens do vary significantly between regions. In 1970, for instance, the Mid-Atlantic region had relative tax rates that were 2.3 times those found in some of the Southern states (Newman, 1983). If one were to compare counties or cities in different regions, the disparity would be even greater. Suffolk County, New York, for instance, had a per-capita property-tax rate of $688 in 1976–77. Chattahoochee County, Georgia, on the other hand, had a per-capita property-tax rate of $12. If one judges overall local tax burden by direct local government spending per capita, similar disparities stand out. Randall, Texas, near Amarillo, spends only $126 per capita while Hoppewell City, Virginia spends $1,757. (U.S. Department of Commerce, 1983). If local tax burdens are a significant factor in business location decisions, there seems to be more than enough variation in those taxes for their impact to be clearly observed.

But thirty years of economic and statistical analysis has almost always found little significant connection between local taxes and local economic development. Sometimes it has found the opposite of what local boosters suggest—high taxes are associated with higher rates of economic development. Those few studies that have found some relationship between economic growth and local tax rates have found the impact of local taxes on business location decisions to be generally quite small. This is rather startling given the consensus in the business community that this is an effective economic-development tool.

In 1984–85, New York state undertook a comprehensive study of the effect of its business-tax structure on its own economic development. That study not only reviewed thirty years of economic analysis on the role of taxes in economic development, but also involved a modeling of the impact the state's specific taxes had on various types of industries. The conclusion of that study was:

> The combination of three decades of research and analysis and the microsimulations conducted specifically for New York suggest that changes in business taxes cannot be viewed as an effective means of influencing business locational decisions. Interstate differences in corporate, sales, and property taxes among the states do not seem to have a large impact on after-tax rates of return (Pomp, 1985, p. 2).

Earlier, Schmenner (1982) had used Dun and Bradstreet data on all new branch-plant locations to study the impact of a variety of factors on the location decisions. He, too, found that local and state taxes played no major role. Carlton (1983) has used the same extensive data base on all new plant locations. He focused on narrowly defined industries and individual cities to see if, for specific plant-location decisions, the impact of local taxes and other business incentives could be determined. He purposely studied industries that were footloose in the sense of not tied to particular locations by raw-material supplies or transportation costs. He found that neither corporate- nor property-tax rates were significant determinants of these firms' locations. In addition, state business-incentive programs were not significant.

Newman (1983) studied the change in employment in various broadly defined industries to see if they were related to changes in state tax rates relative to national averages. In nine of the thirteen industries he studied, he found no significant impact of changes in states' relative tax burden on growth in employment. In the other four, relatively capital-intensive industries where he did observe some impact of tax changes on employment, the impact was quite small.

Bartik (1985) studied specific location decisions using the Dun and Bradstreet data on new branch plants, looking separately at business property-tax rates and the effective corporation income tax rate. He found that the local property-tax rate did not have a significant impact on the likelihood of a branch plant locating in a particular area. The corporate tax rate did appear to have a measurable impact, but it was quite small: a 10 percent cut in corporate taxes was associated with a 2 percent increase in the likelihood of a branch plant locating.

These studies found that differences in local taxes did not have a major influence on businesses' location decisions. This is reason enough to question the efficacy of tax incentives to boost local economies. But there is empirical evidence that is even more problematic for such incentives. Steinnes (1984) studied the impact of taxes and the availability of industrial-development bonds on manufacturing employment in various states. He considered taxes that fell specifically on manufacturing firms rather than some general measure of local tax burden. The issuance of industrial-development bonds, he found, never was a statistically significant factor in determining increases in manufacturing employment. Often, the issuance of more bonds was actually associated with a decrease in manufacturing employment. High and increasing local taxes on manufacturing were also often associated with increases in manufacturing employment—the opposite of the relationship assumed by tax-incentive programs. This "perverse" relationship was statistically significant.

Plaut and Pluta (1983) analyzed the impact of various components of a state's "business climate" on industrial growth. They found that higher corporate, personal-income, and sales taxes were associated with higher levels of industrial development, although the coefficients were not statistically significant. However, they also found that the greater the extent to which states tax the wealth and economic activity available for taxation (i.e., the higher the "tax effort"), the slower the rate of industrial development.

Although most studies have not found local taxes to have a significant negative impact on economic development, or have found evidence of a positive impact, several studies have found some evidence of a small but measurable negative impact. Carlino and Mills (1985) found that per-capita tax rates did appear to have a retarding effect on population growth. Their analysis indicated that people did not follow jobs, but that jobs followed people. That was their reason for focusing on the impact of taxes on population growth. Newman (1983) had little luck explaining expansion of individual industries using changes in state's relative tax rates, but when he pooled the data on all industries, he was able to see a negative impact of relative tax increases on employment growth in manufacturing. In both of these studies, the impact of taxes was relatively small—a 50 percent cut in taxes would result in about a 7 percent increase in employment or population.

The lack of any significant connection between local taxes and local economic development calls for some explanation. Taxes are, after all, a real cost to businesses, and they do vary significantly between taxing jurisdictions. Why, then, do they seem to have little or no impact on local economic development? Several important explanations can be offered:

• Local taxes are small relative to other major business costs such as wages, transportation, and raw materials. A small change in any of these other costs can easily swamp any tax differences between one location and another. In New York, for instance, it was calculated that a 2 percent change in wages was the equivalent to a 106 percent change in state corporate income taxes. Clearly, in that situation, a business firm will worry much more about wage levels than tax levels or differences in tax levels.

• Local taxes are not just a cost. They are also the way in which businesses, and other citizens, purchase necessary public services. Business does need adequate roads, sewage treatment, water supply, police protection, etc. In addition, many businesses seek a well-educated work force. Those who run the businesses want an attractive community in which to live and good-quality schools and other public services for their families. Businesses do not look only at taxes any more than they look only at the price they have to pay for a particular input. They also look at the quality of what they get in return if they choose to pay that price. It is the balance of the tax cost and the value of the public services provided that matters to a business firm. Higher taxes balanced by higher quality services may be attractive to businesses.

• Under the pre-1986 federal tax code, payment of state and local taxes was partly offset by reduced federal taxes. With a marginal federal tax rate approaching 50 percent, this meant that almost half of any differences in local taxes was eliminated by the federal tax deduction. This reduced the impact of local tax changes on business firms.

• Local and state property taxes are likely to affect the value of industrial sites and buildings. They get capitalized into that value. High local property taxes reduce the value of industrial sites. This means that a significant part of the taxes are shifted away from businesses to the owners of the land and buildings. A business firm in a high-tax area will pay less for the land it purchases. The property tax will be paid by someone other than that business. This, too, offsets the effective impact of local taxes on businesses' location decisions.

• Business-tax breaks are not necessarily permanent. Local and state governments can, and do, change their tax codes regularly. A business firm making a long-run investment in a particular location may well pay little attention to the relatively small tax cost, given the regular changes in that cost it expects over the life of its facility.

• The nominal tax rates often used in describing the differences in taxes between jurisdictions are rarely the taxes actually paid by any new business. States are busily competing to see who can forgive the most taxes on new businesses. The result is that the real differences in the effective tax rates applied to a new business may be much smaller than the nominal rates suggest.

Whatever the explanation, this lack of a strong and reliable relationship between local tax levels and almost any measure of economic growth suggests that economic-development strategies built around this particular way of improving the "business climate" are likely to fail. In addition, to the extent that low taxes come at the expense of poorer public services, inferior schools, and a run-down infrastructure, they may harm local development prospects.

13. Conclusion: Attaining the Objectives of Quantitative Growth

The point of this chapter has been to examine the connection between the quantitative growth in various local economic indicators (such as income, employment, and population) and improvements in local economic well-being. In most discussions of economic development, the appeal of such growth is taken for granted. In our economic folk wisdom, both the appropriateness of these growth objectives and the policies that pursue them are presented as intuitively obvious. In that context, it appears that anyone but a pathological naysayer would have to support them.

We have tried to make two points. First, conceptually, mere growth in these quantities is only distantly related to improvements in local economic well-being. They are inappropriate measures of economic well-being to start with, and it is not clear why communities would wish to pursue them. In addition, local economic-development policies are unlikely to be able to manipulate them in the manner recommended by advocates of quantitative growth. National economic forces, especially migration, are likely to frustrate such manipulation. Finally, even if local policies could boost these measures, the results are unlikely to be the positive ones intended. We may get something quite different than what was sought. We could even get the opposite of what we were pursuing.

This is not offered as a blanket condemnation of local economic growth. In certain circumstances, given community objectives, local economic growth may accompany and assist improvements in local economic well-being. Our point is that one cannot begin by assuming that mere growth in various quantities associated with the local commercial economy defines improvement in well-being and dictates appropriate local economic policy. It emphatically does not. Quality and noncommercial economic resources and activities are crucial to local economic well-being. If these are systematically ignored at the expense of growth in the commercial sector, the community is unlikely to move in a positive direction. It will not even know the economic direction in which it is moving. It will be without any measure of just how far it has moved. Such blindness is a dangerous condition for any public policy. It invites catastrophe, large and small.

Abandoning the almost exclusive emphasis on growth in the commercial sector does not leave local economic-development policy without any guidance. Realizing the importance of the pursuit of quality and of noncommercial economic resources and activities gives new focus to community efforts to improve local economic well-being. It is to this more encompassing vision that we now turn.

CHAPTER NINE

The Local Pursuit of Quality: A "Can't-Lose" Economic-Development Strategy

1. Introduction

The previous chapters have sought to broaden the meaning of "economic" and "the economy" to escape the commercial and quantitative bias that distorts most discussions of the local economy. Those chapters have been highly critical of the way in which the local economy is conceived, in our folk economics and in the theoretical models of professional economists alike. Both lead to policies being urged that are either ineffective or actually damaging. This chapter seeks to draw on our analysis in a positive way, to develop an alternative approach to local economic development.

First, we explicitly face just what it is we are seeking when we pursue economic development. We offer a short list of primary economic goals, stated in such a way that they are free of a commercial or quantitative bias and do not prejudge or prespecify strategies in a way that prematurely narrows the alternatives open to a community.

We then discuss the larger economic context in which any local economy operates. The forces of the national and international economies severely constrain the local economy. Local policy must acknowledge those forces and constraints, or it is unlikely to achieve its objectives. Modesty is an economic virtue when it comes to local economic-development policy.

Finally, we turn to the analysis of economic development strategies based on local objectives that directly benefit residents and improve their economic well-being, even when they do not succeed in drawing new economic activity and new economic actors into the area from the outside. We argue that that sort of "can't-lose" strategy is superior to the risks and costs of the "business-climate" and industrial-recruitment approach that dominates local economic-development strategy.

2. Goals: What Is It We Want from the Economy?

There is no point in talking about how to encourage economic development until we know just what we are trying to achieve. What is it that we are not getting from the local economy that we wish we were getting and that the local economy can provide? Those goals should be stated in noneconomic terms without reference to how they are to be achieved. They should focus on what it is that people want rather than on some abstract description of the economic process.

In drawing up a brief list of priority economic objectives, we have been guided by two of the conclusions from earlier chapters: first, the economy does not consist only of commercial businesses and market-oriented activities. Second, the pursuit of attractive, but discretionary, qualities is the driving force behind economic activity.

With that broadened definition of what is "economic," we suggest the following primary objectives of local economic development efforts:

a. The availability of useful and satisfying work for members of the community.

b. Security for members of the community in access to biological and social necessities.

c. Stability in the community.

d. Access to the qualities that make life varied, stimulating, and satisfying.

e. A thriving, vital community.

Some will see this list as simply a more elaborate but much vaguer restatement of the "jobs and income" objectives that now guide, implicitly or explicitly, most local development efforts. It might be suggested that local growth in employment and income would satisfy all of these objectives. As the discussion below will indicate, this would be both a serious misinterpretation of the stated goals and factually incorrect. This list of objectives is much more specific than simply more jobs and higher incomes.

These goals have been purposely stated in nonmonetary, nonmarket terms. We are pursuing the direct usevalue, not some market-related intermediary. Thus, we mention the necessities and the discretionary qualities that people seek rather than the income that might (or might not) be used in their pursuit. We mention satisfying work rather than the narrower, market-oriented concept of a job. We do not specify a quantitative objective like growth but a qualitative one, "thriving."

In addition, the intended beneficiaries of the economic-development efforts are specified: current local residents who are committed to staying in the community. We assume that the purpose of local economic-development policy is not to provide jobs and support for people no matter where they happen to be living currently or no matter what their commitment to the local area is. Local economic-development policy does not seek to solve the nation's unemployment or poverty problems.

That is the reason for the third objective. We know that most people can move to other areas and find jobs and obtain the income to take care of the necessities. Migration is one way to pursue the first two objectives. But that is not usually considered a good solution by local residents, which suggests that community stability is a high-priority objective by itself. We do not want to force families who are a part of the community to leave. There is, for many residents, a very high emotional cost associated with having to abandon a community where they have put down roots. Such forced migration destroys the emotional glue that holds a community together. It can be very costly both to migrants and remaining residents. It is because of these serious social costs that we seek to solve the problem of access to work and basic necessities locally.

a. The Availability of Useful Work for Existing Residents

A job is not the same thing as "satisfying work." A job involves working for someone else in return for monetary compensation. Its character and quality are unspecified. "Useful work" makes clear that the quality of the work matters to people. It is also a broader category that covers more than simply working for someone else for a wage. It also includes work in the informal sector of the economy, work within the household, and self-employment in a commercial setting.

Work is important not only or primarily because it generates income. Very rich people usually work; poor people regularly do voluntary work for no pay. It is through work that adults define themselves and relate to the larger community. It has a personal and social value beyond the money income it generates. In that sense, it is an economic objective separate and apart from money income, and with a higher priority. Lack of work opportunities is usually seen as a more serious problem than low wages or low family income.

More jobs in the local economy is not the objective. The objective is good work for a particular class of people: current, committed residents who do not have such work. More jobs that do not go to these people do not meet the objective.

b. Security in Access to Necessities for Local Residents

Local economic growth does not assure that currently disadvantaged local residents will solve their problems in providing their families with the necessities. The growth may benefit migrants or the already prosperous. In addition, growth that is part of an unstable cycle does not provide security.

The objective here is very specific: protection and assistance for community members during hard times. At least part of the response ought to be equally specific: a network of government and nongovernment "safety nets" that provide solutions as well as temporary relief. This suggests that our public unemployment and welfare programs, as well as the activities of private, not-for-profit organizations providing services and support to the disadvantaged, should be looked upon not simply as an exercise in charity but as part of the community's economic-development program.

If we are concerned about low-income households or households that are having difficulty finding and holding jobs, we should focus our local economic policy on those problems directly rather than grandly assume that mere growth in the overall commercial economy will solve them. This moves us away from simplistic boosterism and forces us to craft more focused local economic policies. It also forces us to face the question of who the priority targets of our assistance programs are. It suggests that local economic policy ought to be trying to knit together public and private assistance programs with retraining, work counseling, financial management, and development of household self-sufficiency skills and then aiming these programs at committed existing residents who are in difficulty. The focus here on helping committed local residents is not meant to suggest that local areas have no responsibility for indigent transients. All of our communities must make some efforts at assisting these people. But that responsibility is largely unrelated to local economic development. Local development, presumably, concentrates on improving an existing community, not assisting transients.

c. Community Stability

If the ready availability of jobs and high pay were the major objectives of economic-development policy, then the mining and construction camps of the West would be our models. But those boomtowns are hardly anyone's idea of what a community should be. A concentration of footloose strangers in a particular place is not a community at all, and does not make for very attractive living conditions. Most people, at least after becoming adults, prefer the ties that create a sense of community. High in- and out-migration can threaten this. The forced out-migration of committed residents tears the fabric of the community and demoralizes it. Some degree of community stability should definitely be an objective of local economic policy.

One implication of this focus on stabilizing the community and reaching the intended beneficiaries of that policy, the existing residents, is that we should not try to reduce or eliminate the out-migration of the footloose segment of the population. Those who come and go depending on the temporary availability of jobs and differences in wages have little commitment to any particular place, and there is little social cost to a particular community when they move on. Such out-migration is a relatively costless adjustment, a safety valve for the community that allows it to protect its ''core'' while making necessary adjustments to shifting economic conditions.

This targeting of local economic policies on existing, committed residents may not be easily achieved. There are constitutional limits that prevent certain types of discrimination between these residents and new arrivals, but it is still important to make this distinction.

If local-government policy cannot legally discriminate in this way, it may be that an important part of the economic-development policy will have to be carried out by private organizations that can use their knowledge of the community to see that assistance gets to those for whom it is intended. Local private organizations could, for instance, supply job training, job counseling, leads on new jobs, support for new small businesses, connections with banks, supplemental subsistence support, and the like for committed residents.

d. The Local Availability of Diverse, Satisfying Qualities

As repeatedly emphasized in previous chapters, the qualities that are of economic importance to people are not all generated by the commercial economy. Many of them come from the not-for-profit sector, government activities, household production, and the social and natural environments. That is the reason for stating this objective in terms of the real objectives, the various attractive qualities we seek, rather than simply listing increased real money income per capita as the goal. Some qualities can be pursued privately by spending money in commercial markets, and some cannot. Local economic policy should seek to increase the range and availability of preferred qualities the local residents can enjoy regardless of whether those qualities are the product of commercial or noncommercial activities.

If scenery, high-quality outdoor recreational opportunities, or clean air are qualities preferred by local residents, the environmentalist working to protect air quality, beautiful landscapes, or natural areas is engaged in economic development, just as an entrepreneur is who opens a business providing a good or service not previously readily available to local residents. Similar things can be said about cultural efforts, government services, etc. There is no intent here to minimize the importance of the commercial market. A rich and diverse set of private businesses is fundamental to a thriving local economy. Part of what gives a community its vitality is the interchange that comes from a lively commerce. The emphasis here is intended to correct a tendency to ignore the economic importance of qualities that flow from noncommercial sources. Local economic policy may find that it has little control or influence over the character of the commercial sector. That would not mean that it can do little to protect and enhance the range of qualities available to residents. It may be that the qualities flowing from the noncommercial sector are more easily controlled by local policy. In that situation, an efficient and effective local development policy might emphasize the noncommercial sectors not because they are dominant in some sense or have higher priority, but

simply because they offer the most effective handle available to local government
to improve local economic well-being.

e. A Thriving, Vital Local Economy

There is power in words. One of the reasons the concept of economic growth has
dominated local and national economic policy is that it carries with it connota-
tions of a dynamic, invigorating set of social changes. The contrast is with
stagnation where the range of economic opportunities is steadily narrowing—
where the community loses its people and with them its confidence and pride in
place and ends up demoralized, drifting into social and cultural backwaters.
Those are powerful images.

But "growth" is too narrow and single-dimensional for what we seek. The
economy we really seek grows in certain stages of its development but in general
is not growing. New economic activities replace old. Change is constantly occur-
ring within limits. A broad range of economic activities, increasingly diverse as
the economy matures, is stimulated. The economy is alive in the way a stable
natural system is alive: sometimes going through successions, other times stable
in its diversity. Some firms and industries are always dying. That is part of the
natural economic process. It is not a reason for concern or a call for public
intervention. The key to overall economic health is whether new economic
activities are taking their place. Those new activities start small and often go
unnoticed, while the deaths of well-established firms are headline news. But such
new ventures are also very fragile, and it is difficult for public agencies to be
directly involved in supporting them. That again underlines the difficulties of an
effective, well-focused local economic-development policy.

A vital, thriving economy is richer than a merely growing one and less
disruptive, too. A thriving organism is one that is in balance with its environment, developing its potential in a productive way, not systematically eroding
that environment. Although it is usually not growing in the quantitative sense, it
is anything but stagnant.

Change that does not threaten the core values of a community introduces a vital
quality most people appreciate and seek. But that type of vitality can be obtained
without pursuing purely quantitative growth. Besides, that kind of growth may
actually undermine community vitality by creating conflict and threatening the
connections between people, their social organizations, and the land that are the
life of the community.

The growth-versus-stagnation dualism leaves communities to choose between
a disruptive explosion of commercial activity, which primarily benefits outsiders
while degrading values very important to residents, and being left in the dust and
decay of economic decline. That sort of choice only generates unproductive
conflict or demoralization. The concept of a thriving economy is one that both the
advocates of growth and those who seek to preserve community quality should be
able to support.

3. Modesty as an Economic Virtue:
The Importance of Respecting the Limits to
Local Economic Policy

One of the chief weaknesses of most local economic policy is that it lacks modesty. It seeks to do too much, to do what it cannot possibly accomplish. As a result, it appears to be more of a political, public-relations ploy, a public charade, or a modern economic rain dance than effective policy. The focus seems to be on heading off any negative political fallout from economic downturns, or on exploiting those hard times in the pursuit of a private political agenda rather than doing something effective to protect or enhance the local economy. Such policies mislead residents instead of enriching the local economic dialogue. This leads to frustration, cynicism, and an even deeper sense of helplessness on the part of the citizenry. Hopes are raised through the political process and then dashed. This reduces feelings of well-being even further than the objective economic conditions themselves would have.

Before formulating local economic-development policy, it is important to understand the context in which that policy will have to be implemented. That context severely constrains local policy; we have to understand what we will not be able to accomplish locally even under the best of circumstances. Facing reality in this way is not intended to discourage economic and social imagination. It simply ensures that local policy is grounded in the harsh reality of the forces that the national and international market economies bring to bear.

a. Local Policy Cannot Eliminate the Business Cycle

National recessions will continue to plague local economies. There is no practical way for a local economy to insulate itself completely from national business cycles. The more connected a local area is with the national economy through the exports of its goods and services, the more it will feel national economic downturns. This is important to realize because it is usually during national hard times that the cry goes up for local government to do something about the local economy now that it suddenly appears to be falling apart. Local policy has to distinguish between economic problems that are being imported and those that are of local origin.

This is not to say that there is nothing local policy can do to minimize the damage from national recessions. It may try to confront that imported instability and counteract it in some way. But that would require very particular countercyclical, stabilizing policies. General growth and business-expansion policies will not do. They might only make matters worse by increasing the connections with the unstable national economy.

Since the local economy and local economic policy are not the source of the national recession, it should not be surprising if local policy can do little to counter its effects.

b. Local Economic Policy Cannot Control
International Markets

The United States' economy is increasingly enmeshed in a highly competitive worldwide economy. The value and level of American production are increasingly determined by international market forces. This is especially true for raw materials and basic products such as steel, aluminum, copper, timber, oil, and agricultural products. But it is also increasingly true of manufactured goods.

When there is a glut of a particular good on the international market or when the value of the dollar makes American products increasingly expensive abroad, the demand for that product will fall. Production facilities will cut back operations and lay off workers. It is very unlikely that any local economic policy can override the economic forces causing this problem. When world oil prices plummeted in 1986, production and exploration across the United States fell drastically. Local policy in oil producing states could not possibly have stopped that.

This is not to say that nothing can be done locally to minimize the impact of international economic forces. Local policy can play a role in reducing the loss and possibly avoiding as painful an adjustment the next time around. But that would call for policies that dealt with something other than the industry that is in trouble or industries similarly vulnerable. Again, it would call for very specific policies aimed at the particular problem or impact. Generalized commercial expansion or subsidies for the affected industry, cannot be offered as reasonable policies or as solutions.

c. Local Policy Cannot Reverse Long-run Trends
in the National Economy or in Particular Industries

Industries have life cycles of their own. They begin as innovative and fragile enterprises, struggle to survive and, if successful, enter a phase of dynamic growth. They mature into stable businesses serving fairly well-defined markets. But over time, they face increasing competition from new products and new technologies. Even what were once the most crucial industries then enter periods of decline and even death. The production of horses, steam engines, oil and gas for lighting, coal and wood for heating, wool for clothing, and copper for communication all once were dominant industries that became relatively minor ones.

Local tax breaks, wage concessions, subsidies, or other policies cannot reverse such cycles. Local economic policies or conditions do not cause the declines, and there is no use pretending that they do. The economic forces at work have to be faced, realistically analyzed, and soberly adapted to. Local policy has to promote that adaptation, not try to hold off the inevitable at significant cost to the local economy. Smoothing the transition is a major undertaking by itself. That is more than enough for local policy to bite off.

d. Local Economic Policy Cannot Prevent the Regular Failure of Local Businesses

Business failure is not an extraordinary event in a market economy. It is not a sign that there is something wrong with the local economic environment. Business failure is part of the normal functioning of a market system and it can be eliminated only at the cost of growing inefficiency and falling productivity. Local policy is unlikely to be able to prevent it at all.

All areas, those that are thriving as well as those that are in decline, have similar, high rates of business failure. Those high rates are not signs of an unhealthy economic environment. The difference between areas with thriving commercial economies and those in decline is in the rate of new business formation. Areas in decline have far fewer new businesses being formed or existing businesses expanding.

That suggests that if local policy is going to enhance the commercial sector of the economy, it should not concentrate on failing businesses but on supporting new businesses. Business failure we will always have with us, but thriving new businesses we may not.

e. Local Policy is Unlikely to Stop the Migration of People Into and Out of the Community

As the previous chapters have made clear, migration is one of the more powerful economic forces over which the local community is likely to exercise little direct control. American citizens have a constitutional right to move anywhere they wish. Migration can have a significant effect on the net results of local economic policy. If it is ignored, policies that were aimed at providing benefits for local residents may do little for them, or may do the opposite of what was intended.

Similarly, much out-migration, especially among the young and mobile segments of the population, is beyond local control. Demographic forces, not local economic conditions, tend to dominate. It is not differences in outmigration that mainly determine whether an area's population is growing or shrinking, but differences in in-migration. In setting the objectives of local policy, this fact must be squarely faced.

f. Local Economic Policy will Not be the Primary Determinant of the General Level of Local Economic Well-Being

Because of the mobility of people and resources, all areas of the nation tend to have similar levels of economic well-being. As productivity rises nationally, the level of well-being in all areas rises at a similar rate. The primary determinant of changes in per-capita real income in any area is national trends, not what happens to be going on in the local economy. Areas do not drift significantly out of line with national levels of economic well-being, because population flows tend to eliminate such differences.

This suggests that the level of per-capita money income is not a reasonable target of local economic policy. Local policy will have little impact on that compared to the impact of national forces. Local policy ought to deal with much more specific objectives, such as the availability of good work or the relief of particularly painful economic adjustments or the enhancement of local qualities of particular importance to residents.

Flows, cycles, trends, and changes will generally go on regardless of local economic policy. Local policy must begin with a realization that it will not stop them. The community will simply have to adjust to these overwhelming forces. The adjustment process may be an important focus of local economic policy, although local policy does not have to be merely reactive. But even with the best-designed local policies for smoothing the adjustment, an area is still likely to suffer significant economic pain imported from the external economy. In a private-enterprise economy dominated by markets, that is a fact of life.

This has to be clearly understood by both local policymakers and the general public. If it is not, local economic policy will become a political football, the source of much empty rhetoric but few productive results. The national trends that are beyond local control will become the focal point of local economic-policy discussions as hard times are used to advance the political agendas of various special-interest groups. The insecurity and fears of the local population will be exploited in unproductive ways. Local economic discussions will degenerate into the worst sort of demagoguery. This will add conflict and tension to the community, but will not lead to any improvement in economic well-being. One of the main things local economic policy has to accomplish is to make sure that the residents understand the character of the local economy and the forces that constrain local policy. If that understanding is not there, the political forces that develop during periods of economic stress are likely to render local policy ineffective just when it is needed most.

4. A "Can't-Lose" Economic-Development Strategy: Supporting Local Enterprise

We begin our discussion of an effective local economic development strategy where most discussions of economic development begin: with the commercial economy.

As pointed out above, this is not the only place to begin, and it may not be the most effective place. The noncommercial sectors may be more reliably influenced by public policy than can any part of the commercial economy. But it is usually the commercial sector that is most on peoples' minds when they think about the problems in the local economy. So we start there.

a. The "Sweepstakes" Approach to Development

The usual approach to improving the commercial economy is to go outside of the local area for help. Recruiting of new industry has become the dominant "economic-development" activity. The recruiting begins by attempting to change the local "business climate" in a way that will make it more attractive to outside firms. This involves asking local residents to make certain sacrifices. They are asked to lower taxes, especially business taxes, but not to reduce the services provided to businesses. They are asked to give up their rights to bargain collectively for wages and working conditions and/or to accept significantly lower wages. They are asked to weaken the regulations protecting the quality of their air, water, and neighborhoods. All of these are supposed to make their community more attractive to outside business firms.

Residents are asked to make these sacrifices ahead of time as a prelude to active recruiting on a national scale. The sacrifices are the asserted cost of a ticket to enter the national smokestack- and silicon chip-chasing sweepstakes. The number of players in this sweepstakes is very large. Almost every town with a population of more than a few thousand has an economic-development group. Most cities are represented in multiple ways in the recruiting game: cities within regions band together, states act for all of their cities, and groups of states combine to recruit. There are tens of thousands of economic-development groups, each seeking to land that big firm that will bring prosperity to the community.

At the same time, there are very few firms at any given moment that could actually move to where the package of giveaways is most attractive. Most firms are tied to markets, suppliers, and raw materials in a way that makes them anything but footloose.

As a result, at any given time, we have tens of thousands of organizations recruiting a few hundred companies. The odds of success for any community are quite low. Those low odds, combined with the very real costs local residents are asked to bear ahead of time, ensure that the value of the payoff is negative. The community is almost certain to be left worse off by these particular economic "improvement" efforts.

b. Focusing Locally

There is an alternative to this narrowly defined, "business-climate," industrial-recruiting approach to improving the local commercial economy: namely, supporting the expansion of existing local firms and the creation of new small businesses. This approach would concentrate on what the local commercial sector already has and its potential to expand. It would also draw on local entrepreneur-ial skills to further diversify and expand the local economy.

There are several advantages to this approach. First, because it focuses local development efforts on existing small businesses, it is within the resources of most local economic-development organizations. It does not involve entering a national competition with a set of giveaways worth millions or hundreds of millions of dollars. It is a much more modest enterprise whose scope can be expanded to whatever scale the local organization feels comfortable with.

c. Focusing Where the Jobs Are

The second advantage is that such an approach would target the type and size of business that in fact has been the source of most of the new jobs in the nation. One exhaustive study of the job-creation process concluded that almost two-thirds of all jobs were created by commercial establishments with fewer than twenty employees. The large, nationally prominent Fortune 1000 firms were responsible for only about 1 percent of new jobs (Birch, 1979). More recent analysis suggests that these figures understate the role that larger businesses play in the job creation process (Armington and Odle, 1982; Maier, 1985). But it seems safe to conclude that at least half of all new jobs are being created by very small businesses. That is a powerful enough reason for local economic policy to turn its efforts to these firms rather than trying to lure some (perhaps imaginary) large new industry into the community. The familiar recruiting approach to development is, in that sense, based largely on a misunderstanding of how jobs are created.

d. Plugging the Leaks

This strategy receives support from the export-base model of the local economy too. The stimulation that export-oriented economic activity can give the local economy is limited by the rate at which local income "leaks out." The more dependent the local area is on importing goods and services, the smaller will be the job and income multiplier associated with export activity. It is the leakage of income out of the local economy that finally brings the multiple expansion of the economy to an end. Economies that are more self-sufficient have higher multipliers.

Because of this, an alternative to expanding the export sector of the local economy is to focus on import substitution. Replacing goods that used to be imported with locally produced goods reduces the leakage of income out of the community. That reduction in leakage has the same sort of multiple, stimulating impact as an expansion of exports. Although the multiplier is somewhat smaller because there is no initial injection of income into the local economy, the effect is similar.

Thus, even in the limited terms of the export-base model, an expansion of the export-oriented sector is not necessary for economic development. The growth of locally oriented enterprises that reduce a community's dependence on imports will stimulate development, too.

The impact of improvements in the economic self-sufficiency can be dramatized by considering household energy consumption. Most communities obtain their electricity, natural gas, and petroleum products from outside the local area. The counterflow to the importation of these resources is a major flow of income out of the community to pay for them. Those are dollars that could have been spent locally, creating work opportunities for residents. That dollar flow is usually very large, as much as several thousand dollars per household each year (King, 1977, p. 55).

If conservation or local energy-resource development could stem that flow, it would be like those several thousand dollars flowing back to each household. It would be the equivalent of a very large industry locating in the community. Local jobs would be stimulated as a result of both the conservation and energy development and the additional discretionary income being spent in local businesses.

The import substitution can be direct, as in the case of energy or of a local bakery replacing imported bread, or it can be indirect. As the variety of goods and services produced locally expands, the richer commercial economy attracts and holds more of the residents' dollars. Local dollars that would have otherwise flowed out of the community, to purchase things that would add variety and quality to residents' lives, stay in the community to purchase local services. Live theater and music, instruction in personal skills, recreational facilities, etc. attract and hold dollars that otherwise would have flowed out to finance imports.

e. Weaving a Web of Local Economic Relationships

Local economic development does not consist of "importing" ready-made factories to expand the export-oriented sector. Nor is becoming more dependent on the existing export-oriented industries a progressive economic development. Heavily export-oriented economies are primitive, distorted, and unstable. Colonial economies provide an extreme example of how distorted and underdeveloped such economies actually are. Poverty, dependency, and instability characterize such places. Developed economies, in contrast, do not have an obvious export base. They are so diverse that particular sectors do not stand out as dominant. That diversity develops as an area begins to replace more and more of its imports with locally produced goods. Those locally oriented firms create a complex web of local dependencies that are characteristic of a dynamic, developed economy. Promoting the relocation of firms and the expansion of existing exports does little to enhance this type of development, and may well retard it (Jacobs, 1984).

Local import-substitution firms, at the start, are small and unimpressive. They are likely to appear peripheral or even trivial to the overall economy. But it is in these firms that the seeds of real economic-development are found. That is what makes them difficult targets for local economic-development strategies: they are almost invisible, and when visible appear hopelessly outclassed by the national firms currently servicing the local market with imports. There is nothing "sexy" or glamorous about them. This makes them unattractive targets for an economic-development agency oriented toward public relations.

Supporting the establishment and expansion of locally oriented enterprises that make the local economy more diverse and self-sufficient creates the more sophisticated economic and social fabric we seek, integrating each of us into a richer and richer social organization. Such an economy is likely to be more stable in the face of shocks coming from the external economy and better able to provide the variety of work and purchased qualities that we seek.

f. Supporting Local Enterprises: The Supply of Capital

It is usually suggested that one of the chief problems new and expanding local firms face is lack of access to adequate capital. They have difficulty finding the money they need to make the necessary investments. Describing the problem in that way also suggests a solution: public intervention to make the capital available. This can be done by lending money directly to firms, by guaranteeing loans, and by subsidizing the interest rates firms pay to obtain investment capital. Local and state governments have gotten involved in all of these types of programs.

The usual suggestion is that there is a capital shortage of sorts that restricts local business expansion. On its face, this seems quite unlikely. Capital is one of the most mobile resources in the national and international economies. It flows readily to profitable opportunities. Before local development programs consider capital-subsidy programs, they should carefully explore the character of the alleged capital shortage. Such an analysis is likely to indicate that most forms of investment capital are in fact available locally. The problems local firms have gaining access to the investment capital have more to do with those firms' business skills, the risks associated with their businesses, and the impact that risk has on the cost of the capital.

If local and state governments simply assume that there is a local shortage of capital and that public programs making capital more readily available to local businesses will solve the problem, they will find no shortage of firms seeking that capital. The demand will appear to prove the relevance of the strategy. But most, if not all, of that publicly supported capital will flow to firms that would have been established or expanded anyway using private capital. Other firms, whose risk and potential profits did not really justify them receiving any additional capital, may also get funding but fail anyway. Any business will seek out capital at the lowest rate available. If the government is providing cheap capital, local firms will not pass it by. But that is not evidence that publicly supported capital was necessary. When you give something valuable away, a line almost always forms. If the capital goes to those who would have expanded regardless, the program cannot claim any credit for the expansion. The public support simply represents a waste of public resources. Similarly, it is a waste when the capital goes to firms whose potentials do not justify investment at all. Given the limited resources a local community is likely to have available to support local development, such waste is a serious matter. The community's limited means can easily be swallowed up without having any impact at all on local development.

Capital is not usually the limiting resource for a well-planned, profitable business expansion. Inadequate business and financial-management skills are more likely to limit firms and their access to capital. That aspect of the problem will be discussed later in this chapter.

It is possible that an area, especially a relatively small, isolated area, may have a capital shortage of a particular sort. New and expanding small businesses may have difficulty gaining access to the sort of high-risk venture capital that is needed. Conventional bank loans and bond issues cannot provide the equity investment necessary to establish or expand a new business. Communities some distance from major urban areas may find the local sources of supply for this type of capital very limited and unorganized. Venture-capital investors like to know in detail the businesses in which they consider investing and be involved in overseeing management. That makes tapping distant sources of equity capital difficult.

But this is not an easy place for local and state governments to intervene. Small businesses, especially new small businesses, are very risky to start with. Their failure rate is very high. The type of capital needed would be last in line for recovery if the businesses failed, which makes such investments doubly risky. Private investors undertake investments of this sort only if the potential return is very high. If public agencies get involved in providing this type of capital, they will either face substantial losses or will have to insist on a high return. Neither of these is likely to be politically feasible. If there are losses, it will appear that public money is being poured down a rat hole. Even if there are not losses, the necessary high return will appear to defeat the original intent of making cheap capital more available.

This is not to say that local and state governments cannot participate in providing venture capital. Some have done so successfully. But the public agency must take a very hard-nosed, businesslike attitude and demand a return proportional to the risk being undertaken. But given these difficulties, it may be that local economic-development agencies ought to be taking a different route to support local businesses.

One indirect role that local development agencies can play in dealing with a shortage of high-risk capital is to try to locate venture capital for local firms and package the investments so as to reduce the risk to the investors. There may well be a serious information gap about just what the potential for profitable investment is in the local economy. The local development agency can help prepare detailed descriptions of the local investment potentials and work to find nonlocal investors who might be interested. This is a matter of knowing both the local capital needs and the regional or national capital markets.

One of the things that contributes to the impression of a serious local capital shortage is the apparent reluctance of local financial institutions to invest in new and expanding businesses. Local banks, for instance, are notoriously conservative when it comes to new, small businesses. This is understandable. The local bank has to limit the way it extends credit to local firms because it knows that if the local economy turns down, many local firms are likely to be in trouble at the same time. It has to protect itself against that by being very careful in its lending. Development agencies can help solve this problem by packaging local investment needs appropriately and by helping tap outside sources of private capital. This helps investors diversify their risks and increases the capital sources available locally.

Local banks in relatively small towns may also face little competition and exercise considerable monopoly power. Restricting the supply of capital may be part of a classic monopolist strategy. In any case, in such situations the bank can discriminate and block access to capital markets for some businesses. Government intervention may well be called for to improve local access to capital.

Clearly, development agencies can play an important role in making capital available to local firms without getting directly into the capital-investment business. They can help coordinate investors and investment opportunities. This is likely to be a far more productive and less costly role for a public agency to play than actually undertaking high risk investments with public funds or subsidizing capital costs.

Sometimes the argument for direct government involvement in local investment is not simply that there is a shortage of capital. The argument instead is that the private investor only takes into account part of the returns on the investment, those the investor will receive. But, in addition, the entire community may gain because of the increased work opportunities and income flows. This suggests that the total return on the local investment is higher than it appears to the investor. In that situation, the level of private investment is likely to be below the socially rational level. This, it is argued, justifies public intervention to subsidize additional capital investment.

It is certainly possible for investment to have such positive ''external'' benefits, and it is true that in that circumstance, underinvestment is the likely result. But it is hard to imagine how a public agency could seek to correct this situation and not become the provider of subsidized capital to every business seeking additional capital. All local investments have such external benefits. Should we subsidize all local investment? Such an effort would quickly swamp any local development agency and would become very, very costly; and, in any event, most of that aid would go to firms that did not need the subsidy. This would make such an effort a very inefficient development strategy.

The point is that, except in cases of local monopoly, direct public involvement in capital markets can be costly and difficult and result in few development gains. If it is undertaken at all, it should be as narrowly defined and focused as possible and should involve the public agency in a coordinating role rather than the role of capital supplier. As important, local businesses have other, noncapital needs that can be more easily serviced by development groups.

g. Supporting Local Enterprises: Technical Business Skills

Often new and expanding businesses have difficulty gaining access to capital not because there is some sort of capital shortage but because they appear to be too risky an investment. Lack of basic business skill can add to the apparent and real risk failure.

Many small businesses do not know how to put together a good loan or investment package. They do not keep adequate books. They do not plan sufficiently for taxes. They do little formal analysis of their market or their costs. The result is that they are less in control of their economic environment than they need to be, and their risks are accordingly much higher. Investors see this and choose not to invest, or offer to invest only on terms that make the venture nonviable.

Lack of adequate business skill is often both the chief threat to the survival of a new business and the primary reason the business has difficulty obtaining capital. It is possible that the local economic-development agency can make a valuable contribution in supporting local businesses by focusing on this problem.

Years ago the nation and almost every state made a commitment to help millions of small businesses of a particular sort survive hard times. Federal and state agencies were set up to develop programs that would transfer to those businesses the management skills, bookkeeping skills, and knowledge of technology that would allow them to survive stiff competition. Extension-agency offices were set up in most counties. State universities ran research programs that developed the methods and technologies that were then distributed through the extension offices. It was an extensive program that helped transform the family farm.

We are no longer a nation of farmers, and the farm sector is professional enough now that it no longer depends upon these public agencies for support. But the agricultural extension-agency model may be a useful one for local economic development. An urban-oriented small-business extension program could seek to provide fledgling businesses with the same sort of technical support. With help in improving financial planning, marketing, bookkeeping, tax planning, cost control, and technology assessment, the survival rate of small local businesses could be improved and their access to capital markets increased.

Such an approach to supporting local enterprise is also more likely to be within the abilities of the economic-development agency. Its scale of operations can be adjusted to the level of resources available. Large sums of public money do not have to be put at risk. The public agency limits itself to offering training rather than getting involved in investment and management.

This type of approach, both the focus on small local businesses and the improvement of their business skills, assure a benefit to the local economy whether or not the effort stimulates quantitative growth. The money gets spent locally, rather than on chasing footloose businesses around the country or on transferring local incomes and revenues to national corporations. Local residents and their enterprises get the benefits. Local people with business experience are likely to be hired to do the training. The community works together to improve the quality of the local economic environment, to create and sustain new work opportunities, and to expand the range of goods and services produced locally. Such an approach directly pursues the objectives discussed above in a manner and on a scale appropriate to almost any community.

h. Entrepreneurial Spirit, Economic Imagination, and the Local Business Climate

This discussion should make clear that a vital, thriving local economy is not built around the hoopla of industrial recruiting or the selective austerity of "improving the business climate." Vitality does not come from importing factories or purchasing machines or simply investing capital. Economic development is a local process, built around enterprising individuals and groups seeing a local opportunity and improvising, adapting, and substituting. Initially, these efforts start on a small scale and usually aim to serve a local market (Jacobs, 1984, p. 39).

One of the primary resources this type of local development process needs is a social environment that supports this sort of economic imagination and innovation. The community has to be flexible, to respect and reward the type of creativity and energy that leads residents to see opportunities locally and risk trying to develop them.

There is a potential for serious conflict here. Those who seek to protect community values and ways of life are fundamentally conservative: they want to preserve what they believe is right and good in the community. That conservatism can degenerate into a resistance to any change. It can become a traditionalism that rejects innovation. That type of social environment can make it very difficult for the spirit of enterprise to blossom and for small local firms to play the creative, vital role they should. The irony of this sort of traditionalism is that by discouraging a local process of development built around new and expanding local firms, the commercial economy is made to depend upon larger, export oriented firms and national corporations. This breeds both instability and dependence, neither of which allows local control or protects local ways of life. The resistance to a locally oriented economic development process condemns the community to depend on forces it cannot possibly control, or to accept stagnation and drift.

In an important way, the community attitude toward local enterprise and innovation is the crucial business climate, not that suggested by zoning and pollution regulations or local tax levels. A community can vigorously protect and enhance its social and natural environmentals against degradation and still support an enterprising spirit among its residents.

There need be no conflict here, but there may be. What the community needs to do is to establish clear standards and regulations for business firms to meet, establish a fair and nondiscriminatory tax structure that will support the services a thriving economy requires, and then encourage and support a broad-ranging spirit of enterprise. The regulations and taxes, taken by themselves, may be seen as discouraging enterprise, but in combination with the community qualities they provide and protect, they are part of what allows the community to attract and hold residents. Those taxes and regulations become part of the economic background against which innovation takes place. The community, if it finds that its business regulations and taxes have gotten so complicated or contradictory that they are confusing or discouraging new or expanding local businesses, should take steps to correct the problem. However, this does not mean dismantling effective regulations. It may mean simplifying. It may mean streamlining. It may mean providing businesses with a clear "road map" of the regulations and an advocate within local government to help them comply.

The community support for enterprise has to be cultural in the sense of the community truly respecting this frame of mind and these efforts, but it also can take the form of active policy. The small-business extension service discussed above is one kind of active support. The support given to public and private educational and research organizations is another. The character and design of the educational and research programs also will influence the prevalence and intensity of the spirit of enterprise. Here there is a need for both public and not-for-profit entrepreneurs who seek ways for their own institutions, and perhaps for others to contribute to the vitality of the local economy.

This is quite definitely not a call for merely vocational education and research. Enterprise and innovation are not built on rote mastery of existing ways of doing things. It is creativity and improvisation that need to be encouraged in our educational institutions. An exclusive focus on the practical adaptation to reality encourages neither of these. In that sense, they are economically impractical and ineffective.

Jane Jacobs has emphasized the fact that the roots of invention are to be found in motives like curiosity, especially an aesthetic curiosity, and incorporate at the very beginning an element of play. Most metallurgy, hydraulics, rocket propulsion, railroads, new materials, computers, etc. were developed first for play and then were adapted to industry (Jacobs, 1984, p. 222). This says something about the character of a local culture that supports a spirit of enterprise. It is not crude, practical commercialism that needs to dominate; quite the opposite. Again, at the very beginning of economic activity, it is a set of aesthetic and even playful qualities, that is crucial. The practical, quantitative logic of the accountant and business manager are crucial to keeping a business alive. But the spirit of enterprise that allows a local economy to thrive is built upon something quite different.

This discussion paints an unusual picture of what a "supportive business climate" is and how a community can help create it. A rich and diverse culture, liberal-arts-oriented schools, and a critical but open-minded citizenry are crucial. A passive population focused narrowly on the "bottom line," willing to give away almost anything to outsiders who promise to develop their economy for them, does not create a productive business climate in the sense of supporting a local spirit of enterprise. These characteristics are a sign that such a spirit is absent, and signal an acceptance of dependence and, ultimately, decline.

5. A Can't-Lose Economic-Development Strategy: Improving the Quality of Public Goods and Services

An economic-development strategy need not focus on the commercial sector of the economy. In fact, that may be a very difficult part of the economy to influence. The export sector is oriented toward national and international markets, and usually dominated by large corporations that have little commitment to or involvement in the local community. The locally oriented small businesses tend to be fragile and volatile; they come and go with disturbing frequency. National recruiting of existing, relocating firms can be expensive, and holds little likelihood of success.

This is not to suggest that it is always useless to focus local development efforts on the commercial sector. But it is difficult for local public agencies with limited resources to make a positive difference in local economic well-being by doing so. Any such programs must be specific and target particular changes in the commercial economy. Broad, general programs aimed simply at "stimulating" business are unlikely to have much of a positive impact and can be quite costly.

But the boundaries of the local economy lie far beyond just commercial business. There are other, noncommercial aspects of the economy that can be the focus of local economic-development efforts. Figure 10.1 in the next chapter provides a schematic diagram of the "total" economy, including these noncommercial sectors. It is to these that we now turn.

a. Education, Training, and Knowledge: The Sources of Productivity and Growth

Economists have long been fascinated with the sources of the expansion in material productivity that has characterized the last two centuries in Western Europe, North America, and Japan. That growth, although fitful and erratic, has been sustained enough to make it an unusual historical phenomenon.

The sources of the growth in the economy over the last fifty years have been

the subject of a series of statistical analyses sponsored by the Brookings Institution (Denison, 1962, 1967, 1974, 1985). If one measures growth in terms of
increases in output per worker, the increased use of capital per worker accounted
for only about 10 percent of our economic growth during this century. Nuts and
bolts, concrete and steel contributed little to that growth. Over 50 percent of the
growth was associated with "advances in knowledge." Another 25 percent was
tied to the increased education of the work force—that is, to a higher-quality work
force (Denison, 1974, p. 13; 1985, p. 38). Fully three-quarters of that material
advance was related to education and knowledge primarily developed by public
and not-for-profit institutions.

These studies focused on the national economy as a whole, not on local
economic development. But they do underline the economic importance of
schools and research institutions. These results are mirrored in studies of business location decisions. One of the considerations almost every such study sees as
important to commercial businesses is the quality of the local labor force and the
local educational system.

Education is a good public and private investment. It pays off for the individual, for the community, and for the commercial businesses located there. It is also
a relatively reliable focus for local efforts to improve economic well-being. If the
improved quality of schools and labor force do not attract new businesses or
facilitate the birth and expansion of new local businesses, they improve the skills
of the individuals who have attended the schools. Educational investments are, in
that sense, part of a can't-lose local development strategy. If the investments do
not stimulate change in the local commercial sector, they directly benefit local
residents and improve their access to work and income elsewhere. If one of our
objectives is to increase the access of local residents to work and to both the
necessities and the qualities obtainable with money income, local spending on
education is a relatively safe long-run investment.

Technology development is very important in the national economy—in fact, it
is the primary source of the growth we have experienced over the last half-
century. It is the diffusion of technology to all areas of the nation that leads
productivity to rise in a similar fashion in almost every local economy. But this
very mobility makes technology an unlikely target for local economic development policy.

Technology does not "stay put." It is readily brought to wherever it can be
productively used. This means that a local area does not have to generate new
technology itself in order to be productive. It simply has to be flexible and
innovative in adapting its production processes to using the technology developed
elsewhere. Similarly, a new technology developed by a local firm or research
institution may have little impact on the local economy. The more productive uses
of that technology may well lie elsewhere. If that is the case, the technology will
be adopted elsewhere while causing almost no changes in the area of its origin.

This is not to say that technology should be ignored in local economic-development strategies. The adoption and adaptation of new technology may well be important in the competitive survival of local firms and in determining their productivity and local income generation. It is possible that local policy and educational institutions can assist in this. A business-oriented extension program, such as that discussed earlier, could have this as part of its job.

In addition, some industries need the active support of research institutions. Some of those industries that have come to be labeled ''high-tech'' operate in a symbiotic relationship with institutions of higher education and labs doing basic research. Those local economies that already have such institutions certainly may find it productive to encourage the development of such a relationship between the not-for-profit institutions and the commercial economy.

b. Fighting Isolation: Improving Transporation and Communications Infrastructure

The dominant cause of the limited commercial development in small local economies is isolation from markets, inputs, and raw materials due to high transportation costs. The dramatic impact of the railroads on the economic geography of the nation in the last century and the equally dramatic impact of the highway system in the second half of this century underline how important transportation costs can be in determining the location of economic activity.

During the second half of this century, there has been a significant decentralization of economic activity. Manufacturing has ceased to be concentrated solely in urban areas and in certain states. Manufacturing as well as population has shifted to previously rural areas and states. Facilitating this shift was a major improvement in transportation and communication systems. Good highways, airports, and telecommunication systems linked previously remote areas to the rest of the nation. This provided firms with ready access to markets and necessary inputs and reduced the feeling of isolation and cultural deprivation associated with living in these areas. Small cities in rural areas became linked with other population centers. The cost of living and doing business in those areas fell dramatically. This gave the population the opportunity to act on its preferences for high-quality natural and social environments at a reduced cost, and gave business firms access to a relatively high-quality and low-cost work force. Economic activity shifted geographically as a result.

This suggests that the character and quality of the local transportation and communications infrastructure is very important to the economic development of an area. Since this is heavily controlled or influenced by public agencies, it may well be a productive target for local development efforts. Improved highways, airports capable of handling modern air traffic, sophisticated telecommunications links, etc. all enhance the attractiveness of the area for people and business activities.

Primitive road and highway systems and road networks in disrepair raise the cost of doing business in an area and reduce the quality of living there. They increase the amount of time spent simply moving about the area, increase fuel costs, and increase the wear and tear on vehicles. At the same time, an inadequate road system increases congestion, air pollution from traffic, and the general inconvenience of living in the area. Even if public improvements in transportation do not draw new firms, local residents and businesses enjoy the benefits of those investments directly. In that sense, some economic benefit is assured.

Telephones and other private means of communication—including express delivery services, and broad television and cable access—are also important, although not as easily influenced by public efforts. All of these link the area to the larger economy and allow more decentralized economic activity.

c. Protecting and Enhancing the Natural Environment

Air and water pollution are economic problems. They harm people directly. People recognize this harm and make major expenditures and location decisions to avoid pollution. In addition, air and water pollution discourage additional commercial activity. Most areas have limits on the overall degradation of air and water quality allowed. If an area is at or approaching those limits, additional commercial activity may be possible only to the extent that existing sources of pollution are reduced or eliminated. Pollution, then, is not simply an aesthetic problem. Community efforts to reduce it should be considered a part of the overall economic development efforts.

Scenic beauty and recreational opportunities are also important economic resources. These are goods and services that local residents enjoy directly. They add measurably to their overall economic well-being. As manufactured goods dominate our expenditure patterns less and less and as incomes rise, we will place a greater emphasis on natural amenities and recreational opportunities. Their economic value to us for the direct benefits they provide will increase. In addition, their importance to a variety of businesses will rise. Recreationally oriented businesses are booming, and are becoming one of the dominant industries in many areas. For all of these reasons, efforts to protect and enhance the natural features of an area can also be an important part of an economic-development strategy.

d. The Human-made Environment

The human-made or social environment of a local area is the one in which local residents live and conduct their business. It is the one that dominates on an hour-to-hour and day-by-day basis. It affects business potentials.

Crime is a good example. It seriously harms both those who are victims and everyone else who fears they may become victims. In addition, it raises the cost of doing business and discourages business from being carried out in certain areas. Crime is not just a social problem. Improvements in the security of people and property directly improve economic well-being. Effective crime-reduction programs are economic-development programs, too.

The quality of the human-built environment matters too. Run-down neighborhoods, public buildings, and commercial districts are not attractive to people or businesses. Urban blight has a spreading and cumulative impact. It is not something that individual action by itself can control. As some residents let their property become run-down, the value of other residents' property falls and the incentive to invest in maintaining it declines. The blight can spread despite the intentions of the individuals involved. Cooperative action is usually needed to stop this type of economic decline.

Public agencies can play an important role here. They can encourage neighborhood associations to take the initiative to protect and improve the physical characteristics of their neighborhoods. Zoning regulations and their enforcement may be a necessary context for cooperative, voluntary efforts at neighborhood improvement. Business districts can be encouraged to control and reverse physical deterioration in similar ways. Public revenues and expenditures can be coordinated with business expenditures to improve the community's commercial districts.

The local government can contribute to this directly by the way in which public buildings and property are maintained. Public parks, squares, the landscaping and cleaning of streets, etc. have a significant impact on the "feel" of a community. They say something to both residents and potential residents about the community's confidence and pride. Both of these are crucial to a vital, thriving economy. This physical character is not just window dressing. It is an integral part of a community's spirit and character and, therefore, of its economy.

e. The Cultural Life of the Community

Our major metropolitan areas realize that cultural activities and institutions play a major economic role. A rich cultural life draws well-educated and creative people to those areas, provides extensive choice in entertainment for residents, and is a major tourist attraction. Orchestras, museums, dance and theatrical companies, galleries, festivals, and the like enliven the community and enrich its commerce.

Smaller urban areas cannot hope to reproduce such an atmosphere, but it is still important to realize that cultural institutions and undertakings contribute to the economic life of the community. Among the most rapidly growing nonmetropolitan cities during the 1960s and 1970s were university and college towns. Their growth was not simply tied to a rising student population. Those towns became attractive places for adults as well as businesses because of the atmosphere those educational institutions created.

Local governments tend to play a relatively small role in the cultural development of a city. It is private, not-for-profit organizations that typically take the lead in this field. Commercial enterprises contribute significantly, too. This, however, does not prevent an economic development group from recognizing the importance of cultural development in improving the quality of life for existing residents, stimulating local employment opportunities, and attracting people and businesses to the community.

f. Protecting Access to Basic Necessities

Economic expansion by itself cannot be counted upon to assure that all committed residents have access to the necessities. Shifts in the economy, changes in the family, injury or disability, lack of education, training, or experience or a variety of other situations can leave some local residents at a disadvantage in seeking work. Deprivation or forced migration may be the only solutions if there is no community intervention.

As noted earlier, the migration of people who are indifferent about the area in which they are currently located does not do much damage to the community. It is a relatively costless adjustment mechanism. For committed residents, this is not the case. This suggests that some way needs to be found to identify those for whom migration would be damaging. It is on these people that the community ought to concentrate its assistance.

That assistance ought to concentrate on solving the problems that put job-seekers at a disadvantage while providing temporary subsistence support. Retraining, additional education, job-search skills, etc. ought to be integral parts of the program. Contacts with local employers should also be used to place these individuals in jobs rather than having most of those jobs taken by new in-migrants. The relief and assistance programs should be looked at as part of the community-development efforts, not as simply charitable exercises.

6. "Can't-Lose" Versus "No Free Lunch"

In the discussion above , we have suggested that there are economic-development strategies that have far more likelihood of success than "improving the business climate" and industrial recruiting. We have suggested that these alternative strategies are "can't-lose" strategies in that they will make local residents better off even if they fail to stimulate an expansion in the local commercial economy.

To some, that may sound too good to be true: a costless economic activity. That is not what is being suggested. Economists do not believe in the economic equivalent of the frictionless plane or perpetual motion machine. There are few costless economic activities except the elimination of pure waste. By calling these development no-lose strategies, we were not suggesting that we had found an unclaimed free lunch.

These development strategies are no-lose in the sense that they primarily involve shifting local resources within the local economy rather than sending these resources out in hopes of getting something back. The proposed strategies are redistributive in the sense that they use tax or other revenues collected from one set of residents to provide benefits to what may be another set of residents. There is a community gain, but it may be offset by the loss associated with raising the revenues in the first place, especially if no new commercial activity is stimulated.

We have not attempted to weigh the losses associated with raising the revenues through taxes, contributions from organizations, or other fund-raising efforts. Nor have we attempted to calculate the expected net benefits from development activities. Our reference point has been an assumed existing development effort that is focusing on industrial recruiting and improving the local "business climate" through giveaways. We propose instead to shift those development resources to other activities that, even if they failed to promote "growth," would benefit the local population. They cannot lose in the sense that they will provide at least some benefits locally. The industrial-recruiting approach cannot assure that.

This leaves unaddressed the question of the appropriate level of resources to commit to economic development. That is a much more complicated issue and is rarely dealt with. All we are suggesting is that shifting the targets of the existing programs away from industrial-recruiting sweepstakes and "business-climate" enhancement cannot help but improve things.

Finally, this no-lose strategy does not circumvent the limitations imposed on any local economic policy by the free flow of capital and people and by fluctuations in national and international markets. This strategy seeks to acknowledge those limits and forces and adapt to them. But much of the local economy will remain effectively out of the control of any local economic-development program.

CHAPTER TEN

Grander Visions, Grander Problems

1. Introduction

This book has sought to broaden the meaning of "economic" and "the economy" to include all of those resources, goods, and activities that contribute to our economic well-being whether or not they are associated with commercial markets. In that expanded context, the book has recast local economic-development efforts. It has shown why growth-oriented efforts are likely to fail to improve local economic well-being. It has also suggested that despite the limits imposed upon such efforts by national and international market forces, there are alternative ways in which communities can improve the economic well-being of their residents.

In doing this, the book has glossed over some very serious problems with the way a capitalist market economy limits, diverts, or distorts efforts to improve well-being. We now turn to this darker side of our economy. We then return to our analysis of appropriate economic-development strategies to seek the seeds of an alternative vision of an economy free of the limits our economic system now imposes upon us.

2. The Dominance of Markets and the
Prevalence of Market Failure

Our dominant economic institution is the commercial market. Most coordination of economic activities, distribution of economic goods, and motivation of productive behavior is left to the market. The market is the centerpiece of our system of economic organization, and we have made strong political, social, and cultural commitments to it.

For most of the last several centuries, we have experimented with extending the range of the individual and social activities that can be disciplined and coordinated by the market. Today, for instance, we are increasingly turning to commercial organizations to take over much of what has been noncommercial "housework" or "homemaking": child care, the preparation of meals, the care and cleaning of our homes, etc. We are farming out the operation of our prisons, parks, schools, and hospitals to private firms. The ultimate range we will allow to the market is yet to be determined. The political thrust of the 1970s and 1980s in both Britain and the United States has been to extend the domain of commercial markets significantly.

Yet, as this book has repeatedly emphasized, commercial markets regularly fail to handle adequately a broad range of very important economic resources and goods. Not everything that is important to us economically can be provided adequately through the commercial sector. In fact, many of the things most important to us are not adequately handled through commercial activities: education and the pursuit of knowledge, the distribution of necessities, the richness of our culture, and the quality of our communities and the natural environment are some of these.

When markets cannot be relied upon completely to provide goods and services that are important to us, we tend to find ourselves in a social and intellectual limbo. We either have to suffer from the loss of these goods and services or take remedial action outside of commercial markets. That noncommercial action tends to be limited by and suffer from a serious political ambivalence. Noncommercial activities, especially government activities, seem to have violated the spirit of our economic system and social order. They are always vulnerable to the charge of being somehow illegitimate or foreign, "socialist" elements that are in conflict with our basic way of doing things. That certainly has been the charge, for instance, against environmental protection, zoning, welfare and most government intervention in the commercial economy.

This imposes a serious political limit on efforts to protect and improve local economic well-being. Almost any efforts at such collective action, especially those that go beyond subsidization of private commercial activities, can and will be undermined by our commitment to a private-enterprise ethic. If initial steps are successfully taken, those efforts will still be seen as of secondary priority, subordinate to the needs to commercial economy. In conflicts between commercial and noncommercial activities, the commercial needs are likely to dominate; the noncommercial values we seek will suffer. This will leave us deprived. We will be given some things we do not particularly want, and will be kept from pursuing what is more important to us, all because some are well-handled by commercial markets and others are not.

3. Economic Instability:
Cycles of Boom and Depression

Our economic system is inherently unstable. It swings through a variety of cycles, some short like our regular recessions and recoveries, some long like the Great Depression, the postwar expansion of the 1950s and 1960s, and the relative stagnation of the 1970s and 1980s. As discussed above, these cycles are certain to buffet the local community no matter what it does to protect itself.

Over the long run, successful capitalist economies expand. It is hard to think of a capitalist economy not growing in the quantitative sense this book has argued is only distantly related to improvements in economic well-being. That impulse to quantitative growth is tied to the logic of capital accumulation and investment. It cannot simply be turned down or off. It is endogenous to the system, part of the basic mechanics of a capitalist economy. This, too, leaves local communities in a rather powerless position. When industry and economic activity began to shift south to the Sunbelt, individual communities in North Carolina or Texas or southern California had little say over what would happen to them. The growth in population and industry simply proceeded beyond their control and changed dramatically the character and quality of their communities. For many of those communities, the change, at least initially, may well have been largely positive. But positive or negative, the change was beyond residents' control.

Growth can be expected to continue, unevenly, across the country. Community doubts about whether there are real benefits from growth simply in the number of people and dollar volume of business are unlikely to influence its course. There is a dynamic built into the incentives and distribution of power within capitalism that drives that growth onward. Quantitative growth may smother local efforts to pursue something else.

The economic downturns and periods of stagnation have another impact. They discipline the participants in the economic process. By threatening the security of individuals through the loss of work and income, recessions and depressions modify aspirations and behavior. By dramatizing the vulnerability of each of us, they force us to respect and heed those who provide us with jobs and income, namely commercial firms. Communities are disciplined in this way just as individuals are: if communities are not careful in their treatment of local businesses, they are threatened with the loss of a major source of jobs and income, with having to watch helplessly as part of their population is forced into migrating away. This obviously narrows the range of actions in which both individuals and communities can safely engage.

4. The Consequences of Powerlessness: The
Emphasis on Commercial Goods

The threat of job and income loss disciplines and restricts the activities of both individuals and communities. Individuals do not simply pick and choose among jobs that are available. They often have to desperately take whatever job is available and learn to live with it. With the threat of unemployment regularly kept vivid, there is limited opportunity for most workers to modify the quality of their jobs.

The same thing is true of communities. They cannot afford to seriously offend existing businesses. Given the regular hard times imposed on the local economy, a community also cannot look very critically at new firms that would like to locate in their area. Communities have to greet these new firms with enthusiasm or actually compete to get them to come. Otherwise, the community faces no replacement for the jobs lost during downturns and general decline.

In general, the community has almost no control over itself. It cannot easily pursue local-improvement programs. Its character and quality are largely determined by forces over which it has no control. In that situation, it should not be surprising to find that most residents do not think there is much that can be done to protect or improve community life.

Two of the more important determinants of individuals' well-being are the quality of their work and the quality of the community in which they live. The discipline the instability of a capitalist economy imposes on individuals and communities assures that neither of these can be easily enhanced. Rational individuals do not waste time and effort pursuing likely dead ends. Instead, they refocus their efforts where those efforts are more likely to bear fruit.

Most individuals have done exactly that in their pursuit of the various qualities this book has discussed. Instead of pursuing community quality through political or social means, they pursue it individually through commercial markets, for example, by seeking to purchase a home in the "right neighborhood" or by moving to some other area entirely.

The commercial sector of the economy offers a dazzling array of qualities that can easily be pursued individually, if one has the money income.

We tend to read the net results of these rational adjustments to limited opportunity as evidence that Americans are obsessively materialistic. Their desires for more income and more commercial goods and services appear to have no bounds. But that is likely to be a misinterpretation. It is true that individuals are spending more and more on their homes, but a good deal of that has nothing to do with "material" pursuits. What is really being purchased is access to high-quality social and natural environments. Private efforts through commercial markets are the easiest way to pursue these given the way the economy is organized. Similar things can be said about most of the other major consumer durable goods purchased. We are still pursuing satisfying qualities. It is the economy that channels us into pursuing them individually, through commercial purchases, rather than through social efforts.

5. The Treadmill of Competitive Consumption

The primary assumption around which a market economy is built is that economic welfare can be and should be individually pursued. We individually are the best judges of what it is we want, and, if we are allowed to pursue those things privately through commercial markets, we are most likely to get them.

Earlier, we discussed the fact that some things just cannot be practically pursued through markets. We have collectively decided we do not want some other things pursued through commercial markets at all. In those situations, we either go without or we find ways of acting cooperatively rather than individually to obtain them.

But it is not just in those particular areas where welfare cannot be successfully pursued individually. Welfare is socially determined whenever the satisfaction obtained from a good or service depends not just on our direct enjoyment of it but also on the satisfaction we get from knowing that others either do or do not enjoy the good. For some goods, there is satisfaction in the fact that other people also enjoy them. It is hard to play tennis by oneself. Many of us also care deeply about whether others are deprived of access to social or biological necessities. That deprivation reduces our enjoyment of what we have.

For other goods, the satisfaction derives from knowing that we have something others lack. The good gives us status, and that is one of the reasons we pursue it. Early in this century, Thorstein Veblen popularized the notion of the pursuit of status in consumption decisions, and coined the phrase "conspicuous consumption" to describe this behavior. The "keeping up with the Joneses" syndrome is familiar to all of us. It, too, reminds us that much consumption is carried out in competition for relative position or status.

With such "positional goods" the satisfaction obtained is partially determined by how many others also obtain them. The social setting determines the level of welfare attained. Consider one function of a college education. Going to college was seen by most of our parents as a ticket to a better job and greater economic security. For that reason, they sought such an education for themselves and/or their children. But the value of a college education in attaining the desired relative economic status depended entirely on others not getting the same education. If all high-school graduates go to college, going to college will not improve the average status of anyone. It provides a differential advantage and privileged access to jobs and income only if someone does not go. Of course, if most others go and you do not, you are in trouble. You have to go just to maintain average access to jobs and income.

But that points out the net loss in welfare that competition for positional goods causes. It is very much like an arms race. We all struggle to obtain those goods to protect our relative status, but in the end, almost none of us improves our status. The effort and expenditure do not improve the average level of well-being, but simply maintain the status quo at an enormous mutual cost. In that sense, many of our consumption expenditures are maintenance costs from which no collective benefit is derived. In this situation, what is needed, as in an arms race, is an agreement among all the parties to scale down the competition so that the costs are contained. Without that sort of social agreement, we are all on a treadmill pursuing goods and services, wasting our energy and destroying our communities and the natural environment but not improving our well-being.

The general point is that, to a large extent, our feelings of well-being are not determined just by what we have but by what we have relative to others. The individual pursuit of goods and services cannot, for the vast majority, improve well-being because all of us cannot improve in relative status. This raises serious questions about just what is gained from much of our private economic activity. But a capitalist economy is built around such competitive behavior and the pursuit of inequality. It encourages it and then provides the goods to feed it. The economic insecurity that our economy generates also feeds this competitive behavior. Those are two of the engines that drive it to expand (Power, 1982).

6. The Undirected Economy: The Antirationality of Conventional Economics

A good part of this book has focused upon what it is that we want and how we can go about getting it. It assumes that rational social behavior is both possible and desirable. Not everyone would agree. The ideology of capitalism as well as the philosophy behind much of conventional economics would suggest that any form of social or economic planning is neither possible nor desirable. Individuals can and should seek to act rationally within the context of commercial markets, but similar behavior on the part of governments, we are told, will undermine the economic system. A market economy is not supposed to be consciously directed. It moves in directions and ways no one controls. We do not know just where it is headed. All we are alleged to know is that wherever it heads, it will satisfy desires as well as can be done, and it will do so efficiently.

This view is as old as Adam Smith's attack on mercantile regulation and his glorification of the "invisible hand." It is as new as Jane Jacobs' attack on any attempt to regulate economic development. She describes economic development as:

> an improvisational drift into unprecedented kinds of work that carry unprecedented problems, then drifting into improvised solutions which carry further unprecedented work carrying unprecedented problems . . . (1984, pp. 221–222)

Public planning for economic development is neither possible nor desirable in this context of intentional "drift." All that can be done to assist in development is to maintain a social context that encourages the spirit of enterprise and innovation.

The assumption in this is that the economy is far too complicated for anyone or any group to comprehend, understand, and control. No organization, no matter what its computer capabilities, could amass the necessary information and issue the detailed directions to make economic planning work.

Most of us accept this point of view and look with at least healthy skepticism at proposals to involve government agencies in economic planning. But the large private corporations that dominate many parts of our national economy do not have any such skepticism about their own ability to engage in economic planning. They regularly exert the economic and political power they have to control their economic environments. They do not sit by, accepting whatever the buffeting forces of the market may bring. They try to exercise what control they can over that market and to insulate themselves from those forces they cannot control.

This leaves communities and individuals in a vulnerable position. They are not supposed to act collectively to control the impact market forces have on them. But the other economic actors, many of whom have more political and economic power than any local government, are free to do so. The result is a very unequal distribution of economic power and the reinforcement of the feeling that local political and social activity are hopeless.

7. The Amorality of Economic Analysis and the Market Economy

Not only do economics and the market economy resist conscious rational direction, they also provide little room for moral direction or control. This can be seen both in the way they treat limits and in the motivational schemes they advocate.

Although economic analysis begins with the premise of scarce resources, modern resource economics treats limits as a short-run constraint that a dynamic economy will find a way around. From a long-term point of view, there is no limit but that of our imagination. Neither resources nor anything else is seen as constraining what the economy can ultimately do (Simon, 1982).

Yet most moral analysis focuses on setting limits, declaring that certain things that we could do we will not do because it would not be proper or right. These limits, at least in the abstract, are not established on the basis of some self-centered benefit-cost analysis. Those moral principles seek to constrain what it is we do or try to do. The Ten Commandments begin, ''thou shalt not . . .'' Moralists have always viewed unbridled ambition and covetousness with suspicion.

Capitalism and economics make a virtue out of covetousness and ambition, both in individuals and for the society as a whole. They embrace a world and society without limits. In this sense, they can be said to be amoral, without moral direction or control.

Economists would object that economics is a science and is supposed to be value free. It is intentionally not built around any particular set of values. They would add that an economic system does not have morals of its own; it gets them from the participants. Neither of these responses is very convincing. Conventional economics is not value-free. It quite clearly espouses the virtues of individualism, of competition, of the pursuit of self-interest, and of unlimited material expansion. It reacts against the imposition of moral limits in public policy. Economists, for instance, have been very critical of both the Clean Air Act and food and drug regulations that establish human health as the paramount objective. Under these regulations, if certain actions are harmful to health, those actions are illegal. The commercial costs of that ban are to be legally ignored. To economists, this is irrational, and they say so. They want to weigh the value of health against the value of other goods and choose the course of action with the highest net value. Setting moral priorities among objectives apparently is objectionable to economists because it is inefficient.

Similarly, economists have difficulty with the Endangered Species Act and with some wilderness classifications. They see the limits imposed by these laws as possibly carrying very high economic costs. Yet the laws allow no weighing of the costs and benefits of protection and preservation against those of economic development. Again, the restrictions appear to the economist to be irrational, imposing arbitrary limits rather than weighing the advantages and disadvantages of following all alternative courses of action. In that sense, it can be said that economics resists moral principles and limits and may be dangerous.

In this, economics is only mimicking the market economy. The market respects only the bottom line, the net commercial value that can be obtained. If the commercial benefits of an activity outweigh commercial costs, there will be strong, almost irresistible pressure for someone to engage in it. Whatever the activity, it will be seen as a manifestation of the spirit of enterprise, the spirit that is the mainspring of motivation throughout a market economy. Even if the product of that activity is distasteful or objectionable, the motivation for its production will be seen as understandable and acceptable. Thus, environmental catastrophes that kill hundreds or thousands are not seen as crimes or signs of moral failure; they are simply part of the costs of doing business for which, at best, compensation must be offered. Moral principles and limits have little role to play in this context. That certainly may have serious long-run consequences for the larger society.

8. Grander Visions

This brief exploration of some of the darker aspects of our economic system and the way they are likely to limit local economic-development initiatives is not offered to discourage such efforts to improve the local economy. On the contrary, it is offered to protect against naive optimism and quick frustration.

The alternative approach to local economic development sketched in the previous chapter not only laid out a practical focus for local policy, it also suggests a vision of what our economy could be as the limits discussed above are weakened and circumvented. We want to conclude this book by underlining some of those aspects of that grander vision.

a. A Better Balance Between the Commercial and Noncommercial Aspects of Our Communities' Lives

By focusing a significant part of local economic-development efforts on the noncommercial aspects of our economic well-being, we will underline the limited role the commercial market plays even in our capitalist market economy. By acting to protect and enhance those noncommercial aspects, we will also be delimiting the market and encouraging alternative centers of economic well-being and activity to develop.

This is not offered as an antimarket or anticommercial program. The commercial market allows and encourages individual initiative and enterprise. It promotes a particular and valuable type of economic freedom. It maintains a discipline that encourages efficiency and discourages waste. It is an ingenious information-collector and -distributor. The commercial market is a vital aspect to any workable economic system.

Nor is the point to draw a rigid line around the current commercial sector and insist that it not expand. We have not exhausted private enterprise yet. New areas will constantly be developing where the commercial sector is best suited to providing the qualities we seek. But we will also be running regularly into the limits of pursuing vital qualities through commercial markets alone. We should not be afraid to experiment with extending the commercial sector into new areas of economic activity or withdrawing it from other areas.

The point is that we have to understand the limited role the commercial sector now plays and the importance of the goods, services, and resources developed outside of the world of commerce. Only then can we look in a balanced way at the total economy and pragmatically choose where to draw the line that limits commercial activity. Currently, the ideology of the market obscures a large part of the economy or relegates it to secondary importance. That ideological bias damages our economic well-being by limiting and frustrating our pursuit of quality. The intent here is to work on removing that bias by directing economic-development efforts toward important noncommercial, but quite economic, areas. That is not easily done, even intellectually, given the ideological fog. But it is a crucial first step, if we are to move in the right direction.

Figure 10.1 schematically outlines the "total economy." It follows the conventional definition of the economy as that part of our social organization that develops scarce resources and transforms them into useful goods and services. It is clear that it is not only or even primarily the commercial sector that does this. It is even clearer that the corporate, export-oriented sector that is the focus of the export-base model represents a tiny minority of the total economy. Local economic-development policy cannot afford to accept the limited view of the economy offered by that popular model.

The noncommercial sectors have always been depended on to provide the basic context in which private commercial activity could productively and profitably take place. As our urban society becomes more complex and interdependent, as once-plentiful resources in the "commons" become more scarce, and as our shifting preferences turn more to noncommercial qualities, the importance of the noncommercial economy can do nothing but increase. As we collectively recognize that and shift resources in our pursuit of well-being, the dominance of the commercial sector may weaken.

b. Enriching the Range of Cooperative Activities

The recognition that the commercial market often fails to provide the qualities we seek in an acceptable way points to the inadequacy of depending entirely on individual action to improve economic well-being. As important as individual initiative is, cooperative social and political action is often the only way that important qualities can be pursued. This calls for a different kind of entrepreneur, one who can organize and motivate people outside of commercial business organizations, one with a different set of political and social skills.

Such cooperative political and social efforts also help to undermine the ideological dominance of the commercial market as well as the competitive individualism that goes with it. Those efforts give us direct experience with the limits of individual efforts to obtain what is important to us. They underline the personal importance of social and political efforts and give us experience with the satisfaction that goes with such noncommercial activity. That, too, weakens the tendency to focus economic activity almost exclusively on individual actions within the commercial economy.

c. Constraining Coercive, Bureaucratic Government

Cooperative, noncommercial efforts need not be public or governmental efforts. They certainly do not have to center on the federal or even state government. Outside of the commercial sector, there is a broad range of private, nongovernmental alternatives. That is why noncommercial "entrepreneurs" are needed. A vital and thriving community is built around a diverse mix of commercial and noncommercial organization. The familiar dichotomy between business and government in American political dialogue is the product of a strangled social imagination. There are lots of alternatives in between; what we need to do to escape this dichotomy, which paralyzes many local economic-development efforts, is to concentrate on that broad area in between government and commercial

Figure 10.1
The Total Economy

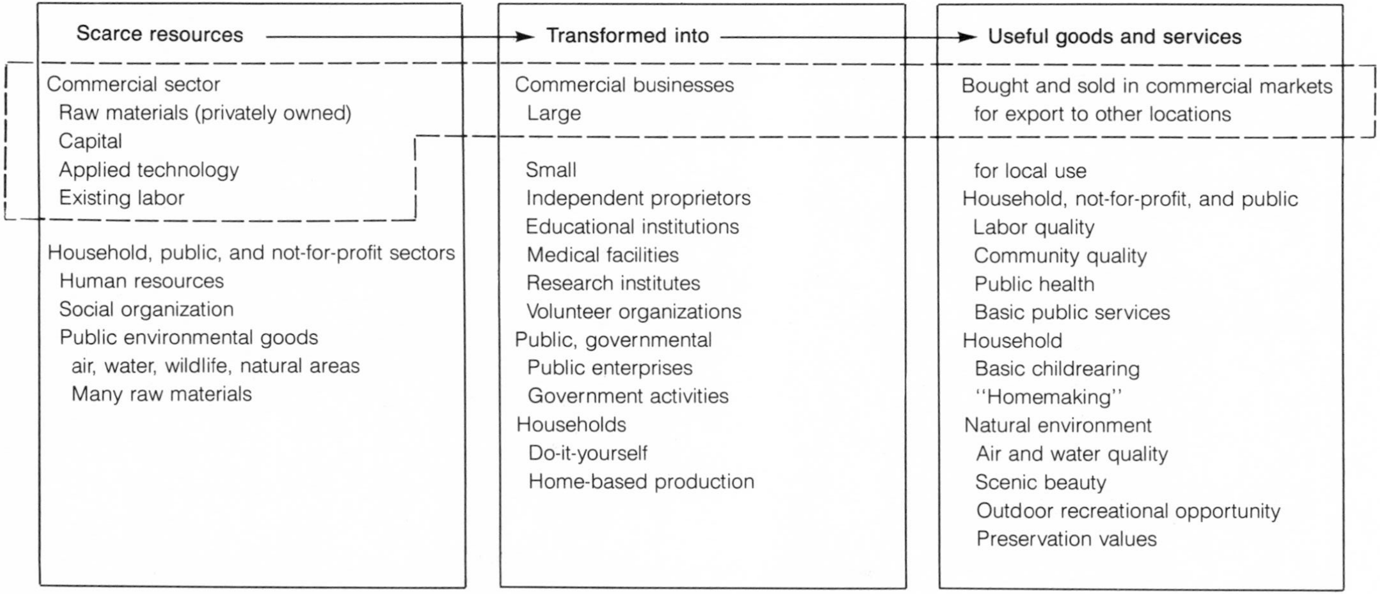

Scarce resources →	Transformed into →	Useful goods and services →
		Bought and sold in commercial markets for export to other locations
Commercial sector	Commercial businesses	
Raw materials (privately owned)	Large	
Capital		for local use
Applied technology	Small	Household, not-for-profit, and public
Existing labor	Independent proprietors	Labor quality
	Educational institutions	Community quality
	Medical facilities	Public health
	Research institutes	Basic public services
Household, public, and not-for-profit sectors	Volunteer organizations	Household
Human resources	Public, governmental	Basic childrearing
Social organization	Public enterprises	"Homemaking"
Public environmental goods	Government activities	Natural environment
air, water, wildlife, natural areas	Households	Air and water quality
Many raw materials	Do-it-yourself	Scenic beauty
	Home-based production	Outdoor recreational opportunity
		Preservation values

[_] The "economy" as seen in the export-base, corporate vision.

business. If we stop for a minute and think about the range of organizations pursuing improvements in our well-being, we will see how silly and narrow that dichotomy actually is. Since the early days of this nation, Americans have been ingenious about creating a broad range of not-for-profit, nongovernmental institutions.

This is not meant as an attack on government or the legitimacy of government action. Often, not-for-profit organizations can successfully pursue their objectives only because governments have created the necessary legal and financial environment. The emphasis here is simply on jogging our social imagination so that we can get out of the government-versus-business dichotomy that forces an unenthusiastic choice between two unattractive or incomplete alternatives. A move away from this demoralizing antagonism that frees other collective social action of the prevailing antigoverment burden can only strengthen noncommercial centers of economic activity.

The strengthening of local government, the focus on local solutions, and the emphasis on renewing community also reduce the need to rely on a distant government bureaucracy to solve local problems. This should involve a significant decentralization of political and government action. This, too, reduces the perceived coercive power of government.

d. Supporting the Individual and Household within a Social Context

The emphasis on the need for collective action to achieve our economic objectives does not in the least threaten the autonomy of the individual or household. The emphasis on the "total economy" sketched in Figure 10.1 underlines the importance of the household as an economic unit producing some of the qualities that are most important to us. The emphasis on the spirit of enterprise in maintaining our communities as thriving social organisms underlines the importance of individual initiative and responsibility. But that enterprising spirit is not only needed in the commercial sector; in fact, it may be threatened there by the dominance of large corporate bureaucracies. That enterprising spirit is also needed in government and the not-for-profit sector. In that sense, collective action and the spirit of enterprise are not in conflict at all. In both the commercial and noncommercial realms, it takes individuals with imagination and skill to organize people to produce a new product or service or to maintain the availability and quality of old ones efficiently. Increasing the range of available, satisfying economic activities beyond the commercial realm automatically reduces our dependence on commercial activities. That helps reduce the distortion in activities now forced on most individuals. The individual will face a broader range of real choices.

e. Replacing "Growth" with "Vitality"

Abandoning the concept of economic growth allows us to escape the narrow, one-dimensional, quantitative orientation of the commercial market when we design community-development programs. That single intellectual step opens up a broad range of qualitative objectives for such programs and allows us to tailor the programs for specific objectives.

The choice of the words "thriving" and "vital" makes clear that the objective is not a no-growth traditionalism that seeks to keep things the way they are or once were. Instead, we recognize change and welcome it as long as it does not threaten core community values. We seek stimulating changes and the development of diversity within a stable, if evolving, social context. We can have the vitality that is usually associated with economic growth while we abandon the mindless pursuit of quantitative expansion for qualitative improvement. This automatically calls into question the quantitative growth that is so much a part of capitalism. It raises questions about just how beneficial its primary thrust still is. At the very least, it keeps local governments from subsidizing growth that serves only a minority's economic interests.

f. Pursuing Directly the Qualities We Want

Once the convenient summary statistics of the shopkeeper are abandoned as inadequate and inappropriate in designing and evaluating economic development programs, we are forced to define just what we want from the local economy. More jobs, income, people, and business activity will not do. We have to go behind these quantities and think about what it was we thought they could help us with.

This, too, helps move us away from the ideology of the market. We cease to state our economic objectives solely in commercial terms. The dominance of the commercial mentality that has confined our social imaginations is weakened in a productive way. We go back to understanding exactly what it is we want, and then ask whether it can be best pursued through commercial or noncommercial means, individually or collectively, through government or private, not-for-profit organizations, etc.

This approach ensures that the diversity of what we seek will be apparent as well as the diversity of routes to obtaining it. Just as important, it will force us to conceive development programs with specific goals in mind, rather than pursue vaguely defined quantitative objectives and engage in wishful thinking about what has been actually accomplished for local residents. The result will be less frustration for citizens and less distortion in their activites. Satisfaction in a broad range of activities is likelier; in the process, the dominance of commercial activities will recede.

g. Shifting the Scale: Local and Small

The approach to local economic development we have outlined shifts our focus to what is actually happening within our local communities. It abandons the chase after national corporations with a fistful of bribes in preference for small existing local businesses. Or else it abandons efforts to influence the commercial sector with subsidies altogether, and concentrates instead on the noncommercial sectors of the local economy and the way they affect local quality. The residents of the community and their needs are the point, not some abstract economic quantity. In addition, the approach clearly recognizes the forces of the national economy over which it can exercise little control and does not waste scarce local resources trying to do what cannot be done.

This local scale, dealing with the needs of real people and actual small businesses, makes economic policy less abstract and mysterious. It encourages local participation. It opens up the possibility that at least local economic policy can be reasonably popular and democratic.

h. More Self-Sufficient Local Communities

One part of the local economic-development approach sketched in the previous chapter was import substitution. Real economic development takes place as the community becomes increasingly able to take care of its own needs, and that involves a certain degree of local self-sufficiency.

Increased local diversity and self-sufficiency helps limit the local impact of fluctuations in the national and international economies. That, in turn, increases the economic security of the community and gives it the breathing room to react with something other than panic to declines in export-oriented firms. This economic security is important. Without it, a community is always under the gun, forced to accept the dictates of outside forces. In that situation, there is little likelihood that productive local economic policies that pursue local objectives can be developed. Insecurity undermines the community and demoralizes the political system. Anything that helps to stabilize the local economy against external shocks strengthens the community and its institutions.

i. Qualities and Activities in Place of Material Goods

An economic policy that focuses on the pursuit of quality, and that emphasizes noncommercial economic activities in that pursuit, clearly indicates that "things" are not the primary economic objectives. "Things" may be the means by which we develop and enjoy various qualities and activities, but they are means, not ends. When, in addition, the primary inputs to the production process are seen to be knowledge and labor quality, both developed mainly outside of the commercial economy, the production process itself is seen as something other than just a set of privately-owned productive "things."

In the context developed throughout this book, a stable, vital community, security against crime, natural beauty, recreational opportunities, reduced congestion and noise, attractive neighborhoods and shopping centers, good schools, a healthy population, and the like are all valuable economic resources, goods, or services. They are of increasing importance to all of us. But their pursuit would not usually be labeled materialistic. An economic-development policy that underlined the importance of all of these to our well-being would remind us that what we seek from our economy is not only or even primarily an increasing flow of material goods. We seek something quite different and more sophisticated.

The focus on the pursuit of quality rather than on the accumulation of material goods (which are sometimes the necessary means or tools for pursuing certain qualities) significantly broadens the range of economic objectives. The qualities sought can be those associated with social restraint, just as they can be associated with the excitement and energy of new and uncertain pursuits. Civilization and culture have always been built around social restraint. The restatement of our economic objectives in qualitative terms allows the reintroduction of moral considerations directly into economics. Economics need not remain amoral, nor do commercial values have to justify immoral activities or results. Economics started as a branch of moral philosophy. It can be reconstructed on a moral basis.

j. Good Work, Not More Jobs

The emphasis on quality rather than quantity extends to work opportunities just as it does to consumption, community, and the surrounding environment. Work is adult "play." It is the way adults develop and demonstrate their skills and become productive members of the community. There is no shortage of work that needs to be done, although there is often a shortage of paying jobs in our economy.

The shifts taking place in our economy create at least the potential for more high-quality work. The shift from manufacturing to services can reduce the assembly-line aspect of work and replace it with much greater human contact and interaction. The shift from muscular effort to information, knowledge, and human service allows a greater range of abilities. The increasing range of government and not-for-profit enterprises expands the range of work beyond that driven solely by the bottom line and allows the expression at work of a broader range of human objectives. The strengthening of our communities increases the range of community-oriented activities into which residents can be drawn. The increased emphasis on supporting new and existing small, local businesses extends the opportunities for self-employment. A greater recognition of the importance of our homes as the source of quality in our lives and our community's lives, and as the locus of important economic activity, will increase the status of the women and men who focus a significant part of their work effort there.

"Jobs" can be dull, repetitive, tedious exercises carried out in an impersonal and authoritarian environment with little reward other than a paycheck. More of that does not improve our welfare. Such use of our energies is a tragic waste, for it taps little of the creative potential of the individual and denies the worker a primary source of satisfaction—pride in productive work well done. Real economic development must emphasize a broad range of quality work opportunities, commercial and noncommercial, not just more nondescript jobs in the commercial sector.

k. A Community Approach to Poverty

Inequality in income has not been emphasized in our analysis because it too centers on a quantitative measure of well-being. Some inequality in money income has nothing to do with differences in economic well-being, but is tied to different combinations of commercial and noncommercial goods and services that people have chosen. Still, this does not deny the reality of serious deprivation for a significant minority of our population. Income equality is not the objective; rather, it is the elimination of the sense of exclusion and deprivation that goes with relatively low incomes.

Our emphasis has been on identifying both those who need assistance where they are (as opposed to solving the problem through migration) and the specific assistance they need. That assistance should be provided by the community through a variety of institutions in a way that solves the problem rather than perpetuates it. The community needs to take care of its own in a sympathetic, creative way that removes the obstacles to those individuals' becoming full participants in the local economy. The mere distribution of money through a bureaucratic apparatus that degrades people further is not a solution. Something more personal and involving a greater degree of community participation is called for. To the extent that local development efforts have succeeded in creating a sense of community, this approach to dealing with the problems of disadvantaged citizens will be practical and effective. As noncommercial "public" goods, services, and qualities increase in importance, the importance of money income and private expenditures falls: individuals take more of their income in kind, directly enjoying certain qualities associated with their communities and their natural environment. Since those qualities are available for all residents to enjoy, the community automatically becomes more egalitarian.

As "good work" outside the commercial economy increases in importance as a source of satisfaction, as people choose quality work rather than simply high-paying jobs, the size and importance of income differentials will again decline. Money income and expenditures in the commercial sector will be sacrificed for qualities available elsewhere. This emphasis on good work, some of it outside the commercial economy or outside the formal economy altogether, offers more routes to social participation than the current emphasis on the purchase and display of material goods. Income is no longer necessarily the main way of participating in or gaining satisfaction from these activities. Lack of income does not exclude people from participation or enjoyment. In that sense, the more serious problems associated with poverty, exclusion from social activities and lack of status, are reduced. Status becomes associated not only with earning and spending income. It becomes more associated with a broad variety of social contributions tied to the activities in which people participate and the contribution of those activities to the quality of the community.

9. Putting the Pieces Together

These are all bits and pieces of an alternative economy that can be worked on now, as we go about the task of developing local economic policies. Those local efforts by themselves will not transform our economy, but they may be part of a long transformation. They allow us to work practically to change things now guided by a vision of what we want.

Approaching economic development in this way changes the way we see and understand and experience the local economy. By re-establishing the importance of community, by emphasizing the actual use values we seek, by understanding the limited contribution the commercial economy can make to our economic well-being, and by seeing the importance of a broad range of cooperative, noncommercial economic ventures, we place ourselves in a much better position to pursue real improvements in our local economies. The social context in which we must pursue our dreams becomes obvious. Our values become clearer, and we develop a confidence in what we seek. The ''economy'' is no longer lost in the arcane language and theories of economists and corporate business leaders who are really ideologues pursuing their own agendas. With clear vision and purpose goes an ability to make changes and cope with the naysayers who try to explain why things have to be the way they are. This approach to the local economy allows us to see clearly and experience the social life of the community. At the same time, with its emphasis on creativity and enterprise, it challenges the individual to search for ways to improve that community and to organize people and resources to make those improvements a reality. Creative individual activity in the context of a supportive and challenging community is the basis for a truly vital, thriving economy. There is no single leap that will get a community there. The problems are too immense. There is no formula for success. The problems are too complex for that. It will be a long, drawn-out process that nibbles away at the overwhelming problems our local communities face, undermining the barriers to change quietly but systematically. The first step has to be to step away from our current view of the economy as primarily a set of commercial enterprises that provide goods to satisfy our survival needs while generating valuable quantities. This book has sought to provide an alternative vision of the economy, emphasizing the reality of our pursuit of quality, the social character of that effort, and the broad range of noncommercial activities that it encompasses. It is our hope that this will provide a more productive point of departure for communities seeking to protect and improve their economic future.

References

Alonso, William. 1972. "Policy Implications of Inter-Metropolitan Migration Flows." Working paper no. 177. Institute of Urban and Regional Development. Univ. of California, Berkeley.

Andrews, Wade H., and Ward W. Bauder. 1968. "The Effects of Industrialization on a Rural County: Comparison of Social Change in Monroe and Noble Counties of Ohio." Ohio Agricultural Research and Development Center, Dept. Series A.E. 407, Wooster, Ohio.

Armington, Catherine, and Marjorie Odle. 1982. "Small Business—How Many Jobs?" *The Brookings Review*.

Baden, John, and Richard L. Stroup, editors. 1981. *Bureaucracy vs. Environment*. Ann Arbor: University of Michigan Press.

Ballard, K. P., and Gordon L. Clark. 1981. The Short-run Dynamics of Interstate Migration: A Space-Time Economic Adjustment Model of In-migration to Fast Growing States, *Regional Studies* 15(3):213–228.

Bartik, Timothy J. 1985. "Business Location Decisions in the United States: Estimates of the Effects of Unionization, Taxes and Other Characteristics of States." *Journal of Business and Economic Statistics* 3(1):14–22.

Bassi, L. J. 1976. "The Diet Problem Revisited." *The American Economist* 20:35–39.

Bayless, Mark. 1982. "Measuring the Benefits of Air Quality Improvements: A Hedonic Salary Approach." *Journal of Environmental Economics and Management* 9:81–99.

Beck, E. M., et al. 1973. "The Effects of Industrial Development on Heads of Households." *Growth and Change* 4(3):16–19.

Birch, David. 1979. *The Job Generation Process*. MIT Program on Neighborhood Change, Cambridge, Mass.

Bradford, David F., and Harry H. Kelejian. 1973. "An Econometric Model of the Flight to the Suburbs." *Journal of Political Economy* 81(3):566–589.

Brookshire, David S., et al. 1982. "Valuing Public Goods: A Comparison of Survey and Hedonic Approaches." *American Economic Review* 72(1):165–177.

Brown, Gardner, Jr., and Jon H. Goldstein. 1984. "A Model for Valuing Endangered Species." *Journal of Environmental Economics and Management*, 11(4):303–309.

Brown, Gardner M., Jr., and Henry O. Pollakowski. 1977. "The Economic Valuation of Shoreline." *Review of Economics and Statistics* 59(3):272–278.

Buchanan, Shepard C., and Bruce A. Weber. 1982. "Growth and Residential Property Taxes: A Model for Estimating Direct and Indirect Population Impacts." *Land Economics* 58(3):325–370.

Carolino, Gerald A., and Edwin S. Mills. 1985. "The Determinants of County Growth," Working paper no. 85-3, Federal Reserve Bank of Philadelphia.

Carlton, Dennis W. 1983. "The Location and Employment Choices of New Firms: An Econometric Model with Discrete and Continuous Endogenous Variables." *Review of Economics and Statistics* 65(3):440–449.

Cebula, Richard J. 1983. *Geographic Living-Cost Differentials.* Lexington, Mass.: D.C. Heath, Lexington Books.

Chappie, Mike, and Lester Lave. 1982. "The Health Effects of Air Pollution: A Reanalysis." *Journal of Urban Economics* 12:346–376.

Clark, Gordon L., and Kenneth P. Ballard. 1980. "The Demand and Supply of Labor and Interstate Relative Wages: An Empirical Analysis." *Economic Geography* 57(2):95–112.

Connaughton, Kent P., et al. 1984. *Tests of the Economic Base Model of Growth for a Timber Dependent Region.* Forest Sciences Laboratory, U.S. Forest Service, Missoula, Montana.

Cropper, M. L. 1981. "The Value of Urban Amenities." *Journal of Regional Science* 21(3):359–374.

Cropper, M. L., and A. S. Arriaga-Salinas. 1980. "Inter-City Wage Differentials and the Value of Air Quality." *Journal of Urban Economics* 8:236–254.

Dahmann, Donald C. 1983. "Subjective Assessment of Neighborhood Quality by Size of Place." *Urban Studies* 20:31–45.

Dalton, George. 1971. *Economic Anthropology and Development: Essays on Tribal and Peasant Economics.* New York: Basic Books.

Denison, Edward F. 1962. *The Sources of Economic Growth in the United States and the Alternatives Before Us.* Washington, D.C.: Brookings Institution.

———. 1967. *Why Growth Rates Differ: Postwar Experiences in Nine Western Countries.* Washington, D.C.: Brookings Institution.

———. 1974. *Accounting for United States Economic Growth, 1929–1969.* Washington, D.C.: Brookings Institution.

———. 1985. *Trends in American Economic Growth, 1929–1982.* Washington, D.C.: Brookings Institution.

Diamond, Douglas B., Jr. 1980. "Income and Residential Location: Muth Revisited." *Urban Studies* 17:1–12.

Diamond, Douglas B., Jr., and George S. Tolley. 1982. *The Economics of Urban Amenities.* New York: Academic Press.

———. 1982. "The Economic Roles of Urban Amenities." *The Economics of Urban Amenities.* New York: Academic Press.

Dorman, Peter. 1985. "Compensating Differentials for Hazardous Work: Theory and Evidence from an Efficiency Wage Perspective," draft, Guilford College, Greensboro, N.C.

Douglas, Mary Tew. 1979. *The World of Goods: Towards an Anthropology of Consumption.* New York: Basic Books.

———. 1982. *In the Active Voice.* London: Routledge & Kegan Paul.

Dubus, Rene. 1968. *Man, Medicine, and Environment.* New York: Praeger.

Dunlevy, James A., and Don Bellante. 1983. "Net Migration, Endogenous Incomes, and the Speed of Adjustment to the North-South Differential." *Review of Economics and Statistics* 65(1):66–76.

Fogarty, Michael S., Gasper Garofalo. 1980. "Urban Size and the Amenity Structure of Cities." *Journal of Urban Economics* 8:350–361.

Foster, Phillip, and Mark Bailey. 1974. *Population Growth, Property Taxes, and Public Debt in Maryland*. College Park, MD: Cooperative Extension Service, University of Maryland.

Freeman, A. 1979. "The Benefits of Air and Water Pollution Control: A Review and Synthesis of Recent Estimates," for the Council on Environmental Quality.

Freeman, A. Myrick III. 1979. *The Benefits of Environmental Improvement: Theory and Practice, Resources for the Future*. Baltimore: Johns Hopkins University Press.

Gallaway, L. E., et al. 1967. "The Economics of Labor Mobility: An Empirical Analysis." *Western Economic Journal* 5:211-230.

Gardner, John L. 1979. "City Size and Municipal Service Costs," in *Urban Growth Policy in a Market Economy*. George S. Tolly, et al., editors. New York: Academic Press.

Giarratani, Frank, and Paul D. McNelis. 1980. "Time Series Evidence Bearing on Crude Theories of Regional Growth." *Land Economics* 56(2).

Gibson, Lay James, and Marshall A. Worden. 1981. "Economic Base Multiplier: A Test of Alternative Procedures." *Economic Geography* 57(2):147-154.

Ginzberg, Eli, Dale L. Hiestand, and Beatrice B. Reubens. 1965. *The Pluralistic Economy*. New York: McGraw Hill.

Graves, Philip E. 1980. "Migration and Climate." *Journal of Regional Science* 20(2):227-237.

Graves, Philip E., and Peter D. Linneman. 1979. "Household Migration: Theoretical and Empirical Results." *Journal of Urban Economics* 6:383-404.

Graves, Philip E., and Joanna Regulska. 1982. "Amenities and Migration Over the Life-Cycle." *The Economics of Urban Amenities*. Douglas B. Diamond, Jr. and George S. Tolley, editors. New York: Academic Press.

Gray, Charles M., and Mitchell R. Joelson. 1979. "Neighborhood Crime and the Demand for Central Housing," Chapter 2 in *The Cost of Crime*, Charles M. Gray, editor. Sage Criminal Justice System Annuals, Vol. 12. Beverly Hills, Calif.: Sage Publications.

Green, G. 1966. *Community Size and Agglomeration of Trade, Service, and Other Locally Oriented Industries*. Institute of Urban and Regional Studies, No. WP5, Washington University, St. Louis, Mo.

Greenwood, Michael J. 1981. *Migration and Economic Growth in the United States*. New York: Academic Press.

Grimes, Orville F., Jr. 1983. "The Influence of Urban Centers on Recreational Land Use," in *The Economics of Urban Amenities*, Douglas B. Diamond, Jr. and George S. Tolley, editors. New York: Academic Press.

Harrison, David, Jr., and Daniel L. Rubinfeld. 1978. "Hedonic Housing Prices and the Demand for Clean Air." *Journal of Environmental Economics* 5:81-102.

Hayek, Frederick A. 1945. "The Use of Knowledge in Society." *American Economic Review* 35(4): 519-530.

Hellman, Daryl A. and Joel L. Naroff, 1979. The Impactal Crime on Urban Residential Property Valves, *Urban Studios*, February, 16:105-112.

Henderson, J. Vernon 1982. "Evaluating Consumer Amenities and Interregional Welfare Differences." *Journal of Urban Economics* 11:32-59.

Henry, Mark S., and J.C.O. Nyankori. 1981. "The Existence of Short-Run Economic Base Multipliers: Some New England Empirical Evidence." *Land Economics* 57(August):448-458.

Herskovits, Melville. 1965. *Economic Anthropology: The Economic Life of Primitive Peoples*. New York: W.W. Norton.

Hirschman, Albert O. 1982. "Rival Interpretation of Market Society: Civilizing, Destructive, or Feeble?" *Journal of Economic Literature* XX(4).

Horn, Marilyn. 1968. *The Second Skin: An Interdisciplinary Study of Clothing*. New York: Houghton Mifflin, 245.

Idaho Power Company. December 1984. *Economic Forecast*. Boise, Idaho.

Israeli, Odel. 1979. "Externalities and Inter-City Wage and Price Differentials." *Urban Growth Policy in a Market Economy*. George S. Tolley, et al., editors. New York: Academic Press.

Jacobs, Jane. 1984. *Cities and the Wealth of Nations: Principles of Economic Life*. New York: Random House.

Johnson, Allen. 1978. "In Search of the Affluent Society." *Human Nature* 1(9):50–59.

Jordan, Max. 1967. "Rural Industrialization in the Ozarks: A Case Study of a New Shirt Factory in Gassville, Arkansas." U.S. Department of Agriculture, Economic Research Service. *Agricultural Economics Report* 123.

Kakalik, J., and S. Wildhorn. 1977. *The Private Police: Security and Danger*. New York: Crane Russak.

Katzman, Martin T. 1980. "The Contribution of Crime to Urban Decline." *Urban Studies* 17:217–286.

Kelman, Steven. 1981. "What Price Incentives?" *Economists and the Environment*. Boston, Mass.: Auburn House.

King, Jill A. 1977. "The Distributional Impact of Energy Policies." Office of Data Services, Federal Energy Administration, CR–03–60901–00, June 30, 1977.

King, Paul A., editor. 1984. *Building Cost Manual 1984*, 8th edition. Carlsbad, Calif.: Craftsman Book Co.

Knetsch, Jack L. 1984. "Legal Rules and the Basis for Evaluating Economic Losses." *International Review of Law and Economics* 4:5–13.

Knetsch, Jack L., and J. A. Sinden. 1984. "Willingness to Pay and Compensation Demanded: Experimental Evidence of an Unexpected Disparity in Measures of Value." *Quarterly Journal of Economics* XCIX(3):507–521.

Kresge, David T., et al. 1984. *Regions and Resources: Strategies for Development*. Cambridge, Mass.: MIT Press.

Krumm, Ronald J. 1983. "Regional Labor Markets and the Household Migration Decision." *Journal of Regional Science* 23(3):361–376.

Lancaster, Kelvin. 1971. *Consumer Demand: A New Approach*. New York: Columbia University Press.

Lappe, Frances Moore. 1982. *Diet for a Small Planet*, 10th Anniversary Edition. New York: Random House.

Liu, Ben-chieh. 1975. "Differential Net Migration Ratios and the Quality of Life." *Review of Economics and Statistics* 57:329–337.

Lonsdale, Richard E., and H. L. Seyler. 1979. *Nonmetropolitan Industrialization*. New York: John Wiley and Sons.

Lowry, I. S. 1966. *Migration and Metropolitan Growth: Two Analytical Models*. San Francisco: Chandler.

Lutz, Mark A., and Kenneth Lux. 1979. *The Challenge of Humanistic Economics*. Menlo Park, Calif.: Benjamin Cummings.

Mckeown, Thomas. 1976. *The Modern Rise of Population*. London, England: Edward Arnold, Publisher.

McNulty, James E. 1977. "A Test of the Time Dimension in Economic Base Analysis." *Land Economics* 53:360–368.

Maier, Mark. 1985. "Is Small Beautiful? Few Jobs, Poor Conditions in Small Firms." *Dollars and Sense*: 12–14.

Marston, Ed. 1984: "What Happened to the Oil Shale Towns." *Planning*: 25–29.

Mendelsohn, Robert, and Guy Orcutt. 1979. "An Empirical Analysis of Air Pollution." *Journal of Environmental Economics and Management* 6:85–106.

Miernyk, William H. 1984. *Regional Analysis and Regional Policy*. Cambridge, Mass.: Oelgeschlager, Gun and Hain.

Moody, Harold T., and Frank W. Puffer. 1970. "The Empirical Verifications of the Urban Base Multipliers: Traditional and Adjustment Process Models." *Land Economics* 46(February):360–368.

Morgan, David J. 1977. "Patterns of Population Distribution: A Residential Preference Model and Its Dynamics." The University of Chicago Dept. of Geography Research Paper No. 179, Chicago.

Mueller, Charles. 1982. *The Economics of Labor Migration: A Behavior Analysis*. New York: Academic Press.

Naroff, Joel L., Daryl Hellman, and David Skinner. 1980. "Estimates of the Impact of Crime on Property Values: The Boston Experience." *Growth and Change*: 24–30.

Needleman, L. 1976. "Valuing other People's Lives." *Manchester School of Economic and Social Studies*, 44(4):309–342, December 1976.

Newman, Robert J. 1983. "Industry Migration and Growth in the South." *Review of Economics and Statistics* 65(1):78–86.

North, Douglas C. 1955. "Location Theory and Regional Economic Growth." *Journal of Political Economy* 63:243–58.

————. 1956. "Exports and Regional Economic Growth: A Reply." *Journal of Political Economy* 64(2):165–168.

Olson, Craig A. 1981. "An Analysis of Wage Differentials Received by Workers on Dangerous Jobs." *Journal of Human Resources* XVI(2):167–185.

Ostro, Bart D. 1983a. "The Effects of Air Pollution in Work Loss and Morbidity." *Journal of Environmental Economics and Management* 10:371–382.

————.1983b: "Urban Air Pollution and Morbidity: A Retrospective Approach." *Urban Studies* 20:343–351.

Peterson, John M. 1974. "Effects of Rural Industrialization on Labor Demand and Employment," in *Rural Industrialization: Problems and Potentials*. Larry R. Whiting, editor. North Central Regional Center for Rural Development, Iowa State University Press, Ames, Iowa, 1974.

Plaut, Thomas R., and Joseph E. Pluta. 1983. "Business Climate, Taxes and Expenditures and State Industrial Growth in the U.S." *Southern Economic Growth* 50(1):98–119.

Polanyi, Karl. 1968. "Our Obsolete Market Mentality," in *Primitive, Archaic, and Modern Economics: Essays of Karl Polanyi*. George Dalton, editor. Garden City, N.Y.: Doubleday.

Pollard, Robert. 1982. "View Amenities, Building Heights and Housing Supply," in *The Economics of Urban Amenities*, Douglas B. Diamond, Jr. and George S. Tolley, editors. New York: Academic Press.

Pomp, Richard D. 1985. *A New York Perspective on Tax Incentives*. Multistate Tax Commission, Vol. 1985(2).

Porell, Frank W. 1982. "Intermetropolitan Migration and Quality of Life." *Journal of Regional Science* 22(2):137–158.

Power, Thomas M. 1980. *The Economic Value of the Quality of Life*. Boulder, Colorado: Westview Press.

————. 1982. "Social Organization and Environmental Destruction or Capitalism, Socialism, and the Environment." *International Dimensions of the Environmental Crisis*, Richard Barrett, editor. Boulder, Colorado: Westview Press.

Randall, Alan. 1984. "Benefit Estimation for Scenic and Visibility Services," Chapter 10 in Peterson, George L., and Alan Randall, *Valuation of Wildland Resource Benefits*. Boulder, Colorado: Westview Press.

Register, U. D., and L. M. Sonnenberg. 1973. "The Vegetarian Diet." *Journal of the American Dietetic Association* 72(3):253–261.

Richardson, Harry W. 1973. *Regional Growth Theory*. New York & Toronto: John Wiley & Sons.

Richardson, Harry W., 1978. The State of Regional Economics: A Survey Article, *International Regional Science Review* 3(1):1–48.

Riddle, Dorothy I. 1986. *Service-Led Growth: The Role of Service Sector in World Development*. New York: Praeger Publishers.

Rosen, Sherwin. 1979. "Wage-Based Indexes of Urban Quality of Life." *Current Issues in Urban Economics 3*, Peter Mieszkowski and Mahlon Straszheim, editors. Baltimore: Johns Hopkins University Press.

Ross, David P., and Peter J. Usher. 1986. *From the Roots Up: Economic Development as if Community Mattered*. Croton-on-Hudson, N.Y.: Bootstrap Press.

Sagoff, Mark. 1981. "Economic Theory and Environmental Law." *Michigan Law Review* 79:1393–1419.

Sahlins, Marshall. 1972. *Stone Age Economics*. Chicago: Aldine-Atherton.

—————. 1976. *Culture and Practical Reason*. Chicago: Univeristy of Chicago Press.

Sant, Roger W., Dennis W. Bakke, and Roger F. Naill. 1984. *Creating Abundance: America's Least-Cost Energy Stratgegy*. Novato, Calif.: McGraw-Hill.

Sasaki, Kyohei. 1963. "Military Expenditures and the Employment Multiplier in Hawaii," *Review of Economics and Statistics* 45:298–304.

Schmenner, R. 1982. *Making Business Location Decisions*. Englewood Cliffs, N.J.: Prentice Hall.

Schulze, William D., et al. 1981. "Valuing Environmental Commodities: Some Recent Experiments." *Land Economics* 57(2):151–172.

—————. 1983. The Economic Benefit of Preserving Visibility in the National Parklands of the Southwest, *Natural Resources Journal* 23(1):149–173.

Scott, John T., Jr., and Gene F. Summers. 1974: "Problems in Rural Communities after Industry Arrives," in *Rural Industrialization: Problems and Potentials*. Larry R. Whiting, editor. North Central Regional Center for Rural Development. Ames, Iowa: Iowa State University Press.

Shahidsales, Shahin, et al. 1983. "Community Characteristics and Employment Multipliers in Non-Metropolitan Counties, 1950–1970." *Land Economics* 59(1):83–93.

Simon, Julian. 1982. *The Ultimate Resource*. Princeton, NJ: Princeton University Press.

Spofford, W. O. Jr., et al. 1980. *Energy Development in the Southwest*. Resources for the Future. Research paper R–18. Baltimore: Johns Hopkins University Press.

Steinnes, Donald N. 1984. "Business Climate Tax Incentives and Regional Economic Development." *Growth and Change* 15(2):38–47.

Summers, G. F., et al. 1976. *Industrial Invasion of Non-Metropolitan America*. New York: Praeger.

Taylor, Robert B. 1973. *Introduction to Cultural Anthropology*. Boston: Allyn and Bacon.

Tiebout, Charles M. 1956. "Exports and Regional Economic Growth." *Journal of Political Economy* 64(2):160–164.

Tolley, G. S., et al. 1983. "Establishing and Valuing the Effects of Improved Visibility in Eastern U.S." Final Report 807768–01-0, U.S. Environmental Protection Agency.

U.S. Department of Agriculture. 1982. *Food Consumption: Households in the United States*. National Food Consumption Survey, 1977–79, Report No. H–1, Human Nutrition Information.

U.S. Department of Agriculture. 1983. *Family Economic Review*. "Cost of Food at Home." No. 2:28.

U.S. Department of Commerce. 1978. Bureau of the Census, *Survey of Housing*.

U.S. Department of Commerce. 1983. Bureau of the Census, *State and Metropolitan Area Data Book*, 1982.

U.S. Department of Commerce. 1984. Bureau of Economic Analysis, *Survey of Current Businesss*, July.

U.S. Department of Commerce. 1984a. Bureau of Census, *U.S. Statistical Abstract*.

U.S. Department of Defense. 1984. "Unit Supply Update." Headquarters, Department of the Army, Washington, D.C., AR 190-11, September 1, 1984.

Ulmann, Edward. 1955. "A New Force in Regional Growth." *Proceedings of the Western Area Development Conference*. Palo Alto, Calif.: Stanford Research Institute.

Walsh, Richard G., et al. 1982. *Wilderness Resource Economics: Recreational Use and Preservation Values*. Denver: American Wilderness Alliance.

Weinstein, Bernard L., and Robert F.L. Firestine. 1978. *Regional Growth and Decline in the United States: The Rise of the Sunbelt and the Decline of the Northwest*. New York: Praeger.

Wilkinson, Richard G. 1973. *Poverty and Progress: An Ecological Perspective on Economic Development*. New York: Praeger.

Williamson, Robert B. 1975. "Productive Power of the Export Base Theory." *Growth and Change* 6(1):3-10.